Baseball's Complete Players

To my wife,
Betsy,
without whose support and patience
this book would not have been written

Baseball's Complete Players

Ratings of Total-Season
Performance for the Greatest
Players of the 20th Century

by
MICHAEL HOBAN

McFarland & Company, Inc., Publishers
Jefferson, North Carolina, and London

50503610554154

"You have to ... believe that if the answer to the Mays-Mantle-Snider question is found, then the universe will be a simpler and more ordered place."

— David Halberstam

The answer (for Hall of Fame players):

Willie Mays	#2	1101
Mickey Mantle	#16	971
Duke Snider	#26	930

— The Author

Library of Congress Cataloguing-in-Publication Data

Hoban, Michael, 1935–
      Baseball's complete players : ratings of total-season
performance for the greatest players of the 20th century / by
Michael Hoban
          p.   cm.
      Includes index.
      ISBN 0-7864-0633-X (softcover : 50# alkaline paper) ∞
      1. Baseball players — Rating of — United States.
      2. Baseball players — United States — Statistics.   I. Title.
GV865.A1H54   2000
796.357'0973 — dc21   99-54918

British Library Cataloguing-in-Publication data are available

Manufactured in the United States of America

*McFarland & Company, Inc., Publishers
      Box 611, Jefferson, North Carolina 28640
      www.mcfarlandpub.com*

Table of Contents

Introduction

The Need for a Valid Total-Season Statistic

I believe that it is important from the beginning to clarify two points. First, the essential goal of this book is not to create a listing of "baseball's greatest players" in the vein, for example, of the *Sporting News'* publication *Baseball's 100 Greatest Players.* Rather, this book serves as an introduction to a unique rating system that fans can use to compare the offensive and defensive accomplishments of players regardless of the position that each plays. The comparison is based *only* on the numbers that the player has accumulated and can be done for a season or for a career.

Secondly, the HEQ (an acronym for Hoban Effectiveness Quotient, pronounceable as "heck") rating system, which is introduced here, is intended to present the fan with a simpler, yet accurate way to measure, in a quantitative manner, how good a season a player had. It is one mathematician's way of suggesting that over the past two decades some of the attempts to present statistics have tended to *over-quantify* baseball to the extent that relatively few fans can understand where some of the "new statistics" come from or what they mean.

Baseball fans have always been enthusiastic about statistics. Perhaps more than for any other sport statistics form an almost integral part of the game — at least from the fan's point of view. And yet, despite this fact, a very important distinction is sometimes overlooked by even the more knowledgeable followers of the game. Percentage-based statistics such as the batting average, on-base percentage or fielding average have an important role to play as *in-season references.* Once the season ends, however, their importance is greatly diminished. If we wish *to compare the seasons* of two different players after the season is over, then we need a *post-season comparative measure,* which should be a sum of the player's actual accomplishments — *a total-season statistic.*

Once the season ends, we know exactly what each player has accomplished, and therefore it is no longer necessary to use percentages — since the purpose of parentheses is to give us some idea of how a player is doing *relative to that point in the season.* For example, if we are about one-third of the way through the season and I know that John Doe is hitting .315 with 200 at-bats, then I know that if he continues at that pace he is going to have a good offensive season. But once the season is over, I can simply look at his totals in the various categories and put them together in some thoughtful way, and then I know *exactly* what kind of a season he had.

The problem is that this point is often missed. So we have a situation where some fans try to compare the seasons of two players by looking at obsolete percentages instead of examining the players' actual season accomplishments.

Perhaps the best example of this sort of inexact thinking is reflected when we use the batting average (BA) *after the season is over* to judge how good a season a player had. For example, in 1980 George Brett had a BA of .390 and Mike Schmidt had a BA of .286. Both players were named the Most Valuable Player in their league for that season. Many people would make the mistake of thinking that Brett had a better season, when in fact he did not. As we will demonstrate, the BA is an in-season reference and cannot validly be used as a *post-season* comparative measure. One of the main reasons for this is that percentage-based statistics do not and cannot take playing time into consideration.

Perhaps the best example of the limited value of the BA is illustrated by the case of Shoeless Joe Jackson. Jackson was in the majors for thirteen seasons and has the third highest BA in history (.356); only Ty Cobb and Rogers Hornsby have a higher career BA. Does this mean that Jackson was comparable to these players? No way! Using just the numbers in the record book, the HEQ rating system shows that Cobb and Hornsby are the 8th and 10th most effective players in history while Jackson would rank only 93rd among the 105 position players in the Hall of Fame who played in the twentieth century. Jackson does not have "Hall of Fame numbers."

The author is a professor of mathematics who has been a student of the game for more than fifty years and has recently concluded a three-year study aimed at creating a fairer, more simplified way to compare the achievements of baseball players: that is, a single score that measures quickly and accurately both a player's offensive and defensive contributions for a season (while taking playing time into account).

The product of this research is a set of formulas to quantify hitting and fielding data for each season and to produce a single score (called the HEQ — Hoban Effectiveness Quotient) for that season. The data itself defines a score of 600 as representing a great hitting season, a score of 400 a great fielding season, and a combined HEQ score of 1000 an outstanding all-around season.

For example, in 1997 Ken Griffey Jr. had 718 hitting and 424 fielding for a HEQ season total of 1142, the greatest all-around season in thirty-five years —

since Willie Mays in 1962 had a score of 710 + 449 = 1159. And in 1998 Sammy Sosa's offensive score of 763 was the most effective offensive score since Jimmie Foxx had 777 in 1938 — 60 years before!

How good is a HEQ offensive season of 600? To get some idea, imagine that you produced the following numbers in a season: 200 hits, 30 home runs, 20 doubles, 5 triples, 80 walks, 100 runs scored, 120 runs batted in, and 20 stolen bases. Very impressive numbers indeed! A career season for many players. These numbers yield a HEQ offensive score of exactly 600.

The HEQ study has examined every season of every Hall of Fame player who played since 1900 and has calculated a HEQ career score for each player based on the *10 best seasons* in a player's career.

The HEQ score essentially creates a single number score that reflects how *effective* a player was in a season or in his career. The argument is made that it is this effectiveness that should be examined when seasons or careers are compared.

Since the system is based exclusively on the numbers that the players have put into the record books, the study gives a whole new meaning to phrases such as "Hall of Fame numbers," "MVP numbers" and "Gold Glove numbers."

The author suggests that the HEQ score gives a much more accurate idea of how good a season a player had than any other single statistic available, such as the batting average, slugging average or fielding average. These percentage-based in-season references can be misleading once the season is over.

Perhaps the most significant contribution of the study is the quantification of defensive skills in a logical and accurate manner.

Now any fan with access to the numbers can use the formulas easily to find the HEQ season score for any player and compare it to the best players who have ever played the game. And, perhaps best of all, he or she will just need a calculator (and not a degree in statistics) to do this!

One last point. As mentioned above, it is important to note that the lists that appear in this book are not intended to be lists of the "greatest" players — essentially an undefined term. For example, Earl Averill emerges as #15 on our list of the most effective players of the twentieth century while Mickey Mantle is #17. Does this mean that Averill was a better player than Mantle? No. It means that during his 10 best seasons, Averill put better numbers into the record books than Mantle did in his 10 best seasons. Who was the better player depends upon your definition of the term "better."

The Method: What the HEQ Is It?

The HEQ (Hoban Effectiveness Quotient) method produces a score to represent how good a season a player had. This score includes offensive production, defensive production and playing time. It tells us how effective a player was during that season. It does this essentially by adding together in a logical manner the offensive and defensive accomplishments of the season.

Key Features of the Method

1. The HEQ is a comprehensive statistic (hitting, fielding and playing time) that the average fan can easily understand and calculate. It uses only readily available and understandable data.

2. The HEQ deals only with the *sums* of the offensive and defensive numbers produced by the player. It eliminates all use of percentages, conjecture or bias. It may be the first completely objective and comprehensive look at a player's accomplishments.

3. The HEQ score gives a better idea of how good a season a player had than any other single statistic available today that deals with the player's actual numbers.

4. Since the HEQ deals only with numbers, it gives new meaning to the phrases "Hall of Fame numbers," "MVP numbers" or "Gold Glove numbers."

5. It introduces the idea of leveling the playing field, comparing the careers of players by examining the 10 best seasons that each enjoyed.

6. The quantifying of defensive skills may be the most significant contribution of the HEQ.

7. The HEQ method will enable a fan to compare players by using a single comprehensive score. For example, in 1996, in the American League, Ken Griffey Jr. had a HEQ of 1090 while Alex Rodriguez had 1073. Both had absolutely fantastic seasons. Whereas Juan Gonzalez, the MVP, only had a HEQ of 788 because he played so little in the field. Ken Caminiti, the MVP in the National League, had a great season with a HEQ of 984.

How Do We Know That the HEQ Method Works?

Whenever one speaks of "validating" a rating system, there is always an implicit assumption that there is a universally agreed-upon starting point. One of the more common assumptions is that measures developed using team statistics can be used to rate individual players. However, the author rejects this assumption and maintains that the best way to compare players is to do this independently of the team statistics as far as possible. Is it possible to be a great player on a mediocre or even a poor team? Of course it is. Just look at Mark McGwire or Ken Griffey Jr. in 1998.

Consider the results of the HEQ study and see how those results compare to the commonly held beliefs that other research and writings have advocated. The fact that the HEQ results correspond so closely to so many of the things that we already knew or suspected is the best proof that the system actually works. And the surprises that emerge make us go back and re-examine some of our previous beliefs.

Here are a few examples:

• Babe Ruth and Willie Mays emerge as the #1 and #2 players on the list of the most effective players of the twentieth century (see Appendix A).

• Look at the top ten hitters according to the HEQ study: Babe Ruth, Lou Gehrig, Jimmie Foxx, Ted Williams, Willie Mays, Hank Aaron, Stan Musial, Rogers Hornsby, Joe DiMaggio and Ty Cobb. Someone may argue for some adjustment in the rankings, but the fact that the HEQ formulas yield these results based on the raw numbers is significant.

• Brooks Robinson is the best fielding third baseman and Rabbit Maranville is the best fielding shortstop (with Ozzie Smith close behind).

And, perhaps, a few surprises:

• A closer look at the numbers suggests that Willie Mays, Joe DiMaggio and Ty Cobb are the most complete players in history, with Stan Musial close behind.

• Richie Ashburn is the most effective defensive outfielder ever and Ray Schalk is the most effective defensive catcher in the HOF. (Yes, I did say Ray Schalk!)

• Cal Ripken Jr. is one of the top fifteen most effective players of all time.

It is probably accurate to say that no approach is going to satisfy every baseball fan. But the HEQ method does represent a new and accurate and relatively simple way to focus on a player's accomplishments, free from anyone's opinion or bias.

The HEQ study is a significant contribution to the research of the game. Is it perfect? Of course not — what is? Will devoted fans find many points to question and discuss? You bet! But then, isn't that what baseball statistics are all about?

Some Important Definitions

Mathematicians have a tendency to define terms rather carefully in an effort to avoid any possible misunderstandings. Here are some terms that we will be using in this book.

1. *Hitting Effectiveness—Season* (*HEQ offensive score*). The sum of a player's hits, walks, runs scored, runs batted in and stolen bases according to the following formula:

$$S + 2D + 3T + 4HR + .5BB + R + RBI + SB$$

A HEQ offensive score of 600 is considered to be a great offensive season. If player X had a higher score than player Y, then X was a "more effective hitter" than Y for that season.

Most fans would say "X was a better hitter than Y" for that season.

2. *Fielding Effectiveness—Season* (*HEQ defensive score*). The sum of a player's putouts, assists, double plays and errors according to the following formulas:

For outfielders:	PO + 4A - 2E + 4DP	x	1.00
For catchers:	PO + 3A - 2E + 2DP	x	.445
For second basemen:	PO + A - 2E + DP	x	.460
For third basemen:	PO + A - 2E + DP	x	.888
For shortstops:	PO + A - 2E + DP	x	.548
For first basemen:	.25PO + 3A - 2E + DP	x	.510

A HEQ defensive score of 400 is considered to be a great defensive season. If player X had a higher score than player Y, then X was a "more effective fielder" than Y for that season.

Most fans would say "X was a better fielder than Y" for that season.

3. *Player Effectiveness—Season* (*HEQ score*)— the sum of the HEQ offensive and defensive scores for that season. A HEQ score of 1000 is considered to be a great all-around season. If player X had a higher HEQ score than player Y, then X had a "more effective season" than Y.

Most fans would say "X had a better season than Y."

4. *Career Effectiveness*— the 10 most effective seasons that a player enjoyed according to his HEQ scores.

5. *Hitting Effectiveness (Career)*— the average HEQ offensive score for a player's ten most effective seasons. If player X had a higher score than player Y, then X was a "more effective hitter" than Y.

Most fans would say "X was a better hitter than Y."

6. *Fielding Effectiveness (Career)*— the average HEQ defensive score for a player's 10 most effective seasons. If player X had a higher score than player Y, then X was a "more effective fielder" than Y.

Most fans would say "X was a better fielder than Y."

7. *Player Effectiveness (Career)*— the average HEQ score for a player's 10 most effective seasons. If player X had a higher score than player Y, then X was a "more effective player" than Y.

Most fans would say "X was a better player than Y."

Chapter 1

The Dream

I was a kid growing up in New York City during the late forties and early fifties. The neighborhood that I lived in was just a short walk to the Polo Grounds where the New York Giants played ball. Despite this fact, most of the young people were either Yankee or Dodger fans because of the recent success of those two clubs.

Looking back now, of course, there are many details of those years that are but vague memories. However, one memory that is very clear is that during the early fifties, while we played stick-ball or curb-ball in the street, we were constantly debating the relative merits of Mickey Mantle, Willie Mays and Duke Snider.

Everyone believed that all three were great players and assumed that each was a future Hall of Famer, but I remember how frustrated I was by the fact that there was no organized way to really prove who was the best player of the three. We knew that all three were very solid hitters and did not leave a lot to choose among them offensively. But I knew (in my youthful infallibility) that Willie Mays was easily the best fielder of the group, and yet I could not really demonstrate this in a commonly acceptable way to others. If only there was some way to combine offensive and defensive productivity for a season into a number that would establish who was better than whom.

In 1957, when I was twenty-one, the Brooklyn Dodgers and New York Giants deserted New York for greener pastures (as in money) in the far west. Greed had triumphed over tradition. And I, like thousands of other fans, felt completely betrayed by the lords of baseball. I still loved the game itself (and play competitive softball to this day) but the manner in which I followed major league baseball changed dramatically. I had become a "casual fan" with no team of my own.

When the National League returned to New York in the form of the Mets, some of my interest as a fan was re-kindled but my old enthusiasm never really returned. I still saw greed ruling the beautiful game that I loved.

The reason why I am briefly recounting my own experience with the game is to explain the background that I brought to the present study. I believe that my life-long love for the game, my "alienation" from major league baseball for the better part of forty years, my discovery of what had happened to baseball statistics in my "absence," and my background as a mathematician, when taken together form a somewhat unique set of circumstances that made it possible (even necessary) for me to pursue the HEQ study.

In 1995 I visited Cooperstown and the Baseball Hall of Fame. Like so many visitors I was somewhat overwhelmed by the numbers that dance out at you from virtually every exhibit. But I was amazed that after so many years no one had come up with a legitimate score to represent the quality of a player's season. It was at that time that my adolescent dream of developing a *single score* to represent a player's offensive and defensive contributions for a season was rekindled.

I wondered if it would be possible to create a single, understandable score that would be an accurate representation of how good a season a baseball player had at bat and in the field. So that if I say that in 1993 Barry Bonds had a season of 709 offensive + 328 defensive = 1037, a dedicated fan would know exactly how good the season was: a fantastic season at bat, an average season in the outfield and an outstanding season over all.

This is the question that I asked myself in the summer of 1995 and that I have explored for the past three years. I am aware that there are some observers of the game (both past and present) who believe that this cannot be done. Many believe that if it could be done, it would have been done already. And I believe that some researchers may have been discouraged from attempting this task because of this view.

The outcome of this effort is that I have devised a set of relatively simple formulas that can be used by the avid fan to do his/her own computations and comparisons. And, most importantly, the results of these comparisons are accurate.

The basic premise of the study is that the simplest and fairest way to determine how good a season a player had is to add his offensive and defensive accomplishments in a logical manner. This represents quite a departure from most of the previous attempts that have been made along these lines. These have concentrated, for the most part, on expressing everything in percentages and/or in creating such complicated formulas that only relatively few devoted fans could follow them.

We all know that if we want to determine who is the career home run king, we simply add up all the home runs that each player hit. Hank Aaron hit 755, so he is number one. What could be more simple or more fair?

What I have achieved in this three-year study is to design a relatively simple method of finding the sum of a player's accomplishments during a season and representing them by a single number, then finding the player's *10 best seasons* and assigning a "career" score.

So, for example, we can say that Babe Ruth had the best ten years in history with a career score of 1110. Willie Mays was a close second with 1101. (See Appendix A for the HEQ/HOF List—a comparison of all the Hall of Famers who played in this century.)

Because this method is essentially so simple and understandable and fair, it has the potential to replace the batting average or any other statistic as the best description of a player's season or career. When a fan becomes familiar with the HEQ, he or she will know exactly how good a season Bonds had in 1993 with a HEQ of $709 + 328 = 1037$.

As I begin my explanation for what I have done, it is very important to realize that the comparison of accomplishments by baseball players is not an exact science. That is, there is no right way or wrong way to do this. Different writers and statisticians have suggested various approaches to comparing baseball players and these approaches have been embraced or denounced by others depending on their view of baseball "greatness."

Writers such as Bill James and Pete Palmer have made significant contributions to the game through their research into baseball history. The Society for American Baseball Research (SABR) is dedicated to advancing the state of baseball knowledge. The HEQ study lays no claim to being the definitive comparison of players. It is essentially a simpler and more complete approach (because it does more with fielding and playing time) than any existing system.

What we must keep in mind is that these efforts (especially where they are concerned with the comparison of players' years or careers) are simply attempts to shed new light on the existing numbers. That is, the players did what they did — we cannot change that. But we can suggest new ways of looking at what they did in order to make those accomplishments more meaningful to the fans of the game.

In this context I hope (and believe) that the present study will shed some new light on how we look at a baseball player's accomplishments.

Essentially what the study advocates is that the fairest way to compare players' seasons is by computing a sum of their actual offensive and defensive achievements, while taking playing time into account. Any use of averages, percentages or theoretical estimates or projections can be misleading. Some of these artificially contrived concepts such as "park factor" tend to favor (and excuse) those players who did not in fact accomplish as much as others in a given season. They seem to be saying, "He would have accomplished as much if..."

Some baseball people who work with numbers seem almost obsessed with the need to change everything into a percentage (batting average, fielding percentage, slugging percentage, etc.) when a more straightforward, common sense approach sometimes does the job better. In anything dealing with mathematics a simple and elegant solution to a problem is to be preferred to a heavy-handed, number-crunching approach as long as the simpler method does in fact accomplish the objective. The comparison of players' seasons by a system like the HEQ is a good example of where simpler is better.

After that visit to Cooperstown in 1995 I decided to try to create my "dream formulas." Having been a student of the game for more than fifty years, a teacher for forty years and a Ph.D. in mathematics, I figured I was as qualified as anyone to try to put such formulas together. Perhaps my specialty of working with students who have not had much success with math would help in designing an understandable set of formulas.

I felt that it would be desirable for the average fan to have available a relatively simple (and understandable) system so that, armed only with a player's performance numbers and a hand calculator, he or she could determine whether that player had a great year.

For example, was Ted William's MVP season in 1949 a more effective season than Mickey Mantle's in 1956? (Ted's was more effective: a score of 1144 versus 1118.)

During that visit to the Hall of Fame I first heard of SABR and I soon discovered some interesting literature on the subject, such as *Total Baseball* (2d ed.) by John Thorn and Pete Palmer and *Bill James' Historical Baseball Abstracts* — two marvelous achievements. Using these two volumes as a starting point, I read everything that I could get my hands on.

I was intrigued by some of the "new statistics" created by various students of the game over the years. However, I had one problem with some of these new statistics of the game. As a mathematician, I found some of these concepts to be interesting, but I wondered whether some of these complicated mathematical manipulations could have much relevance to the average fan.

I was somewhat disappointed by the fact that some writers appear to have complicated the raw numbers of the game by changing everything into percentages or averages without shedding much new light on the subject. These percentages and averages may have some value in addressing certain questions, but some of the mathematical manipulations are so intimidating that many fans are put off by them.

As I will demonstrate, the numbers themselves (that the players have put into the record book) can be used directly for our purposes.

Well-Defined Terms

Mathematicians are taught never to engage in any discussion unless the terms being used are "well-defined" and understood in the same manner by everyone involved. As even the most casual observer will notice, many discussions about the relative merits of different baseball players are very confusing because the people involved are actually talking about different things.

If someone wishes to argue that Mickey Mantle was a "better player" than Willie Mays, then it will be very important to define what is meant by "better player." And, ideally, the definition will be based on measurable criteria and not on opinions or conjecture. To compare players in an equitable way, some set of clear, understandable and objective criteria must be set down in a well defined manner.

This study will determine who were the "most effective" players to play baseball in the major leagues in this century. I have chosen the word "effective" for a number of reasons. It is a word that is not used extensively in common baseball parlance. Yet most people have a sense of its meaning "to get the job done." And that is the precise thing that the "best players" do, they get the job done (hitting and fielding) in the most effective manner. For example, Cal Ripken may not be as "smooth" a shortstop as Ozzie Smith, but the numbers show that they are in a virtual dead-heat for defensive effectiveness as shortstops.

In the Introduction, I have given seven definitions which use the word "effectiveness." I have done this in order to avoid any confusion in anyone's mind as to what I mean when I say that, for example, Joe DiMaggio is the fifth most effective baseball player of this century or in 1996 Ken Griffey Jr. was a more effective player than either Juan Gonzalez or Alex Rodriquez. It may be that some fans will not like my definitions or will question my methods. But it is my hope that they will know precisely what I mean and where the conclusion came from. Then we have a solid foundation for a discussion.

The Task

What I have done is to develop a new approach to comparing the great players of the game. It is an approach whose value, I hope, will be in its logic, its simplicity, its accuracy and in its usefulness to the fans.

I decided to first examine those players who have been inducted into the Hall of Fame and to determine who were the best of the best, keeping the concepts and procedures as simple as possible.

In order to do this I first established some ground rules which I explain below. I then proceeded to quantify offensive (hitting) skills and defensive (fielding) skills for each player using formulas that are kept as simple and understandable as possible.

As will be explained in detail, I discovered that an offensive score of 600 and a defensive score of 400 define a "great" year at bat or in the field. A total score of 1000 defines an outstanding year overall.

I believe that the most significant contribution of this study is the work that I have done with the defensive numbers. The outstanding fielders like Brooks Robinson, Richie Ashburn, Rabbit Maranville, Nellie Fox and Ray Schalk finally get the recognition that they deserve. And the great all-around players like Willie Mays, Charlie Gehringer, Stan Musial, Joe DiMaggio and Ty Cobb come into much clearer focus.

Great Player/Great Team

Among the first questions to arise when comparing great players are those concerning the relationship of the player to the team. How much does a great player contribute to the quality of his team? How much does a great team contribute to the quality of the individual player?

Common sense and experience tell us that it is extremely difficult (if not impossible) to answer either of these questions for a sport as complex as baseball. Yet some observers of the game insist on measuring the greatness of an individual player, in part, by his impact on his team. Is it really possible to do this in a convincing manner? I think not.

If someone suggests that the number of All Star games that a player participates in or how he does in voting for the MVP award tells us something about how good he is, I would be inclined to agree since players are presumably selected for these honors on the basis of their individual achievement.

But to say that the number of playoff games or World Series games that someone participates in has any significance as to how good a player is, is pure conjecture and cannot be established in a quantitative manner. As I point out in a later chapter, the concept of attributing team wins to an individual player is an unrealistic and fruitless endeavor.

It seems to me that a great player is a great player on his own. That is to say, he would be a standout player no matter what team he played for. He may be fortunate to play on a championship team, but even if he is not his accomplishments will distinguish him from his contemporaries.

Therefore, I will resist any temptation here to base a player's greatness on any concept other than the numbers that he put into the record book for his team during the regular season. No post-season activity will be considered.

The Park Factor

Perhaps one of the most intriguing concepts that I discovered in my research is that of the "park factor." This is a statistic which attempts to adjust a player's performance based on the ballpark in which he played. I am in awe of the research that has evidently gone into this idea.

However, I must confess that I am uncomfortable with an attempt to "adjust" a player's actual performance numbers in this way. We all may agree that the park in which a player performed had an influence on his performance. Perhaps the best example of this is Chuck Klein's incredible year in 1930, where the Baker Bowl in Philadelphia helped him both at bat and in the field. And the recent offensive fireworks taking place in Coors Field in Denver are drawing much attention. We may admire the thought and work that has gone into this concept of park factor. But for me there is simply too great a leap from there to a suggestion that it is really possible to manipulate numbers in order to "balance this out."

I believe that this is an example of attempting to use numbers to support an argument where the entire premise is questionable. As a mathematician, I prefer to compare one player to another by examining their actual performance numbers which, I believe, does the job quite nicely. If the luck of the draw had one player perform in a park that gave him an advantage, so be it. We cannot change that after the fact. It seems to me to be somewhat silly to suggest, for example, that a player's actual accomplishments should be downgraded because he played in "an easy park." Therefore, in this study I deal only with a player's actual performance and compare players on that basis alone.

It is not my intent to suggest that concepts such as park factor have no value. But this is essentially a subjective notion. What I am saying is that the most objective way (and, therefore, the fairest way) to compare players is by looking at their performance numbers at bat and in the field as the sole basis for the comparison.

The Problem

In examining who were the greatest players to play the game we must be sure that the focus is on the appropriate things.

Different statistics have varying degrees of value for various purposes. But when we are comparing baseball players, the bottom line has to be:

a) How did they produce at the plate and
b) How did they perform in the field

Certainly, to attempt to compare players without some systematic way to quantify defensive skills is essentially non-productive. It may be true that a player's batting performance dominates the way people look at the player, but I do not believe that anyone would suggest that fielding performance should not be counted if there is a way to do so in a reasonable manner.

For example, we will see that Ted Williams was a more effective hitter than Stan Musial — career 655 compared to 630. But Stan the Man was the more effective total ballplayer — career 1017 compared to 993.

Essentially, we want to know the *sum* of the player's offensive and defensive contributions. We also need some reasonable way to level out the playing field since many of the great players played a few years too long — that is, at a greatly reduced level.

Since eligibility for the Hall of Fame requires that a player have played for ten seasons, I have judged a player's "career" on the *10 best years* that the player enjoyed and found the sum of his contributions during that time.

Clearly, this method will favor the "everyday player" who averaged 130 or more games per season for at least ten years. And that is as it should be. What could be more obvious than to say that a measure of a player's greatness is his durability and consistency? No player ever directly helped to win a game while sitting on the bench.

One of the results of the study which was somewhat surprising was that only one player in the Hall of Fame (even those who played for twenty years or more) had ten "1000" seasons. That player was Willie Mays.

In fact, very few players had more than five or six such years. Babe Ruth, who emerges as the greatest hitter of all time and #1 on the HEQ/HOF List, had nine 1000 seasons.

What I have accomplished is to create a reasonable process by which we can translate a player's actual performance numbers into a single understandable score that can be appreciated (and duplicated) by any serious fan.

To summarize, we are interested in measuring the sum of each player's performance in some fair, reasonable and accurate way. Statistics that are averages or percentages or that measure things per at bat or per game may be interesting for some reason but have little value in a consideration of ranking great players.

As I became acquainted with some of the attempts that have been made in the past to determine who were the "best players," several problems became apparent about these attempts:

1. The statistical methods used by some writers may not be appropriate for the job.

Most of the mathematical manipulations that I have seen have some value in the broad area of baseball research, but in some cases are not helpful (by themselves) in determining whether someone had a great year or a great career.

A good example of this is the "batting average" (BA) — probably the most common statistic familiar to the average fan. Every follower of the game knows that a .300 BA implies that a hitter had a good (and perhaps a great) year. And, as a crude indicator of a player's hitting performance, the BA has a revered and valuable place in baseball lore.

But, if we are attempting to measure how productive a player was at the plate over an entire season, we must recognize that there are more effective ways of doing this than to use the BA. In fact, as the following example illustrates, the BA can even be misleading as far as batting production is concerned.

Let us consider the case of Hall of Fame catcher Bill Dickey who is generally considered to be one of the best catchers in history. The record books show that Dickey played for 17 seasons and had a career BA of .313. This is very impressive.

Johnny Bench is also a Hall of Fame catcher. He also played for 17 seasons but his career BA is .267. Not as impressive, right? For the average fan this might appear to be an "open and shut case" of who was the better player.

However, a more serious look at the performance of the two players reveals that Bench was by far the more effective performer.

Consider the following:

1. In 1930 Dickey hit .339. Forty years later in 1970 Bench hit .293. Would you believe that Bench's offensive production for 1970 is 632, more than double that of Dickey's 306 in 1930.

The primary reason for this is that Dickey played in only 109 games while Bench played in 158 — a fact that the BA does not take into account.

2. Bench had four seasons when his offensive score was better than 500 while Dickey had one.

3. Bench had eight seasons when his defensive score was better than 400 while Dickey had three.

For their careers, Bench's total score (offensive and defensive) is 929 while Dickey's is 780.

The point of this example, of course, is to illustrate how easy it is to be mislead by a statistic if we do not take proper care to ensure that we are measuring what we think we are measuring! A baseball player's "greatness" should be measured by the sum of his accomplishments. I believe that it would be desirable to have a more thorough way to arrive at this sum than to use other statistics that were never intended for this purpose.

The baseball numbers leave no doubt that, based on their accomplishments, Johnny Bench was a more effective player than Bill Dickey. In fact, he was more effective than any other catcher in the Hall of Fame.

2. Too much importance is given to people's opinions.

The perceptions of certain people as to who were the greatest players in baseball history may be of some interest to some fans but must be secondary to the performance numbers that the player put into the record book.

It is certainly reasonable to say that the opinions of a player's contemporaries may be a reflection of how good a player was. But we must be very careful here because people's perceptions of what they have seen are notoriously inaccurate. I am reminded of the story of the three eye-witnesses to a daylight bank robbery. After questioning each of the three, the police had three different descriptions of the perpetrators as well as three different versions of the sequence of events.

An example seems appropriate here. The numbers show that Richie Ashburn was the most effective defensive outfielder of all time. But how many of his contemporaries would have realized this in the 1950s when Mays, Mantle, and Snider (among others) were roaming the outfields? I suspect very few, if any.

3. All fans (myself included) are overwhelmed by too many numbers.

How many people can understand (let alone appreciate or use) some of the complicated statistics that have been developed over the past ten to fifteen years? As a mathematician, I find myself struggling at times with these formulas in order to understand how a researcher did something, not to mention *why* they did it!

What is really needed is an attempt to create a reasonable process by which we can translate a player's actual performance numbers into a single understandable score that can be appreciated (and duplicated) by any serious fan.

This is what I have attempted to do in this study.

The "What If" Factor

In addition to the problems stated above, the concept of baseball greatness is further complicated by the desire of many fans (and writers) to speculate on "what if." For example,

1. What if Ty Cobb had played his whole career in the "live-ball era"?
2. What if Ted Williams, Joe DiMaggio or Willie Mays had not lost those years to military service?
3. What if Hank Aaron had played in a different ball park?
4. What if Mickey Mantle had not injured his knee in his prime?
5. What if Babe Ruth had not spent his early years as a pitcher?

It has always surprised me to see how some people who write about the sport seem to love to engage in this sort of fantasizing. And that would be all right as long as this daydreaming does not affect their judgment of reality.

The reality is that the players put certain numbers into the record book. And it seems obvious to conclude that to be truly objective in saying who was better than whom we want to make our judgments based on the numbers alone. (Or as Sergeant Friday used to say on the program *Dragnet*, "Just the facts, ma'am.")

They Came to Play

As indicated above, the formulas that I have developed favor those players who were "everyday players." That is, the player who played 130 or more games a season for ten or more seasons. And this is as it should be.

There were some great players who played hurt or who did not play at times because they were hurt. Mickey Mantle, for example, is a great player who was injured at various times in his career.

I assume that it is obvious to most people that Mantle never achieved his full potential because of these injuries. So we should not be surprised to learn that Mantle's place on the HEQ/HOF List (#16) is affected by this fact.

To summarize what we have been saying, we are interested in measuring the sum of each player's performance in some fair, reasonable and accurate way. Therefore, statistics that measure things per at bat or per game may be interesting for some reason but have little value in a consideration of ranking great players. These statistics always seem to be saying: "See, he would have been great if..."

Our study is not interested in "what ifs" — only in actual performance!

We are not trying to measure potential — but achievement.

Chapter 2

The Ground Rules

Given the considerations from chapter one, I have developed a set of relatively simple formulas to determine whether a player had a great season or, carrying the idea further, a great career.

My goal was as follows:

1. Using the raw baseball numbers *alone*, create a set of formulas to translate a player's season (offensive and defensive) into a single score.

2. Keep the formulas simple so that an average fan with access to the numbers can easily determine (in a few minutes) whether any player had a great season, and how that season compares to the best seasons enjoyed by the best players.

3. Use the formulas to determine which players had the best careers and who really were the most effective players of the twentieth century.

For example, we are able to say that Chuck Klein (believe it or not) had the single most effective season in baseball history in 1930 when he had a season score of 1348 (804 offensive and 544 defensive). Of course, he had the advantage of competing in a "hitting era" and in "an easy ballpark," but that does not change the numbers that he put into the books. The *only other* 1300 season in history was achieved by Babe Ruth in 1921 with a season score of 1308 (894 offensive and 414 defensive). Ruth's 894 is the best offensive season ever.

In fact, very few players ever had a 1200 season. They were:

Joe DiMaggio	1937	1257
Babe Ruth	1923	1228
Ty Cobb	1911	1222
Lou Gehrig	1927	1222
Willie Mays	1955	1211
Rogers Hornsby	1922	1203

And, as was mentioned above, only Willie Mays had as many as ten 1000 seasons even though there have been ten players who have averaged 1000 over ten seasons.

The Ground Rules

When I began the task of trying to create the formulas, I decided that the following ground rules would apply:

1. Only the numbers commonly found in a baseball encyclopedia would be used. That is, the simple offensive and defensive categories detailed below. I would not attempt to deal with pitchers at all.

2. Complicated mathematical manipulations would be avoided. Only the "pure baseball numbers" would be used. That is, those things that a player *actually does* that can be found directly in a player's record:

Offense	*Defense*
Runs Scored	Putouts
Singles	Assists
Doubles	Errors
Triples	Double Plays
Home Runs	
Runs Batted In	
Walks	
Stolen Bases	

Even a concept as common as the "batting average" (as valuable as it may be for some purposes) represents a manipulation of the numbers and would not be used.

It is not my intent to suggest that these mathematical manipulations do not have some value. Many of these statistical concepts are both intriguing and interesting. My point is that in establishing whether a player had a great year these statistics are not necessary and at times can be downright misleading.

Offensively, for example, we are interested in examining what a batter actually *did* (his raw offensive *production*) rather than seeing his comparison *per inning* or *per game* or *per at bat*.

3. I decided to concentrate on those position players (not pitchers) in the Hall of Fame who played most of their careers after 1900 (105 players in all). I wanted to include all the players from the twentieth century even though

there might be some disagreement about comparing players from the "dead-ball era" with those from the "live-ball era."

The game of baseball changed so dramatically with the livelier ball that I was not sure that offensive and defensive numbers really could be compared between the two eras.

As evidence of this, consider the following situation regarding Ty Cobb. As outfielders get older, they slow down somewhat (just like the rest of us). And so the number of putouts they make in their later years generally decreases to some extent. This is normal.

However, consider the following. In 1907 Ty Cobb played in 150 games and had 238 putouts. In 1924, some seventeen years later, he played in 155 games and had 417 putouts (his most putouts ever).

Even allowing for the fact that Cobb was an extraordinary player, this anomaly is at least partially related to the fact that the ball had gotten "livelier" and more fly balls were being hit to the outfield. Therefore, I thought that it *might not be fair* to attempt to compare Ty Cobb's fielding numbers with someone who played the outfield exclusively in the livelier ball era. And, of course, this reservation does not extend to outfielders only.

Once I began to calculate the numbers, however, I discovered that defensively, at least, the outstanding "old-timers" could compare quite well with more modern players. For example, compare Tris Speaker to Willie Mays, Rabbit Maranville to Luis Aparicio, or Ray Schalk to Johnny Bench. In each case (see Appendix A) the earlier player proves to be the more effective fielder.

Some fans may still feel that the comparisons are inappropriate, but I have moved ahead with them in any case.

The following Hall of Famers are not included in the study because they played most of their seasons before 1900 (16 players in all):

Cap Anson	Billy Hamilton
Jake Beckley	Hugh Jennings
Dan Brouthers	Joe Kelley
Jesse Burkett	King Kelly
Roger Connor	Tommy McCarthy
Ed Delehanty	Jim O'Rourke
Hugh Duffy	Sam Thompson
Buck Ewing	Monte Ward

4. I have examined all other players (non-pitchers) who have been inducted into the Hall of Fame by 1998 (105 in all) to see what their numbers indicated. I ultimately ranked them as complete ballplayers over their careers as described below based on pure baseball numbers alone and not influenced by any other criteria (such as people's opinions) which often serve to confuse rather than to enlighten. (See Appendix A for this ranking.)

Many fans may argue that induction into the Hall of Fame by itself already tells us who were the great players. And, of course, this is true to a certain extent. But would it not be interesting to be able to say definitively that even for those in the Hall of Fame, "this player who played in the 50s and 60s was more effective than that player who played in the 20s and 30s"?

Some people would argue that such comparisons are essentially impossible, and they may be right. But I figured that I would give it a shot and let the fans decide.

And what about the thought that such a formula could, in fact, be used to determine whether a player currently being considered for the Hall of Fame deserves to be there? (Or whether some players currently enshrined do not deserve to be there!)

Of course, where the Hall of Fame is concerned, it is accurate to say that a player's numbers alone are not the only consideration for induction (nor should they be). Other contributions to the game can be equally (or more) significant. Jackie Robinson would certainly be a case in point here. Robinson was a great player who did not have the opportunity to show what he could do in the major leagues in his early twenties. His contributions to baseball go far beyond the numbers that he put into the record book.

In any case, I ultimately ranked all the Hall of Famers by the numbers alone. Keep in mind that we are not talking only about hitting here, but the best complete players when both offensive and defensive skills are considered. And I did this using only the pure baseball numbers referred to above—no opinions, no awards, no media hype, *no nothing*—only performance.

5. I first created a formula to quantify offensive skills and then a set of formulas to quantify defensive skills for the different positions.

Since I wanted to be able to compare players with one another who played different positions, I created a way to come up with a single defensive score for any position. As I will explain later, we will be able to say that if Player X had a defensive score of 400 he had a great year in the field no matter what position he played!

I then combined the offensive and defensive scores into a single number as the player's total score for that season. So we will be able to say something like the following:

"If Player Y had a score of 700, he had a year that was FAIR."

800	Good
900	Great
1000	Super
1100	Spectacular
1200	Incredible

6. Ultimately, I wanted to compare the "careers" of the greatest players. Obviously, this word is usually understood to mean the total amount of time

that the man played in the major leagues. So, for example, Hank Aaron is the career home run leader in baseball history because he hit more home runs in his career than anyone else.

Does this mean then that Hank Aaron was a "better player" than Babe Ruth, who held the career home run title before Aaron surpassed him? The obvious answer is, not necessarily.

The point is, how important is longevity to the concept of "greatness"? Is a player who played for twenty or more years in the major leagues a greater player than Joe DiMaggio who played for thirteen years?

And what of someone like Ted Williams or Hank Greenberg or Willie Mays who missed two or more of what might have been their finest years due to military service?

Let me make it clear that I am not trying to diminish the significance of the longevity records such as Aaron's 755 home runs or Rose's 4256 hits or Mays' 7095 putouts. These are monumental accomplishments.

The question is: Is there any other way that we can fairly compare players' "careers" without looking at their complete playing time?

The Hall of Fame requires ten years of playing time to be considered eligible for induction. So, therefore, in order to *level out the playing field* in an effort to compare the careers of the best players, we defined a new term:

Career Effectiveness = The Best Ten Years That a Player Enjoyed

What I have done is to compare the "careers" of the greatest players by comparing their performance during the best ten years that each played.

Note that built into this definition of *an effective season* is the premise that the *sum* of the offensive and defensive contributions is the most significant factor. Therefore, as I explained in the Prologue, I will be using the phrase *more effective player* where most fans would simply use the phrase *greater player*.

7. Finally, I gave the score for defining baseball effectiveness a name. I called it the "Hoban Effectiveness Quotient," "HEQ" (although mathematically speaking, the HEQ is not actually a quotient at all but a sum).

8. In summary, in order to compare the careers of the players I proceeded as follows for each player in the Hall of Fame who played most of his career since 1900:

a) Find the HEQ offensive score for each season
b) Choose the best ten seasons
c) Find the HEQ defensive scores for these seasons

d) Find the total HEQ score for each of the ten seasons

e) Find the average HEQ score for the ten seasons

This is the player's HEQ Career Score.

I use this score to determine who among the Hall of Famers (or candidates for the HOF) were the most effective players of the twentieth century.

9. In the Epilogue, I do take career longevity into account in the PCT (player career total).

Chapter 3

The HEQ
Offensive Score

As I begin my explanation for how I created the HEQ offensive score and the HEQ defensive score, it is important to realize that some of these decisions were somewhat arbitrary on my part. When putting the numbers together in this manner, it is necessary to assign a weight to each category such as "triple" or "assist." I have opted for the simplest possible approach, and it is my hope that the open-minded fan will at least agree that my conclusions are reasonable — even if he or she does not agree with every decision.

I have indicated above my belief that the best way to determine how good a year a player has had is to calculate the *sum* of his accomplishments (both offensive and defensive) in as simple and accurate a manner as possible.

In keeping the HEQ procedures simple I wanted to use those numbers that all fans understand and can find in any baseball encyclopedia. I did not create any new statistics (other than the HEQ scores themselves), only a new way to work with the traditional categories in order to shed new light on the existing data.

The HEQ offensive formula uses only the following categories:

Single	S	1 point
Double	D	2
Triple	T	3
Home Run	HR	4
Walk	BB	0.5
Run Scored	R	1
Run Batted In	RBI	1
Stolen Base	SB	1

I start with the concept of Total Bases (S + 2D + 3T + 4HR) and add to it (R + RBI + SB + .5BB) creating a sum of the player's offensive output for the year.

Therefore, a player's HEQ offensive score for the year would be:

$$S + 2D + 3T + 4HR + R + RBI + SB + .5BB$$

Obviously, I considered and rejected a number of alternatives or variations on this formula. I will mention three of them here. The first was the question as to whether the number of times a player was caught stealing should be subtracted from the number of stolen bases — that is (SB-CS). Even though this idea had some appeal, it was not possible to do this since this statistic (caught stealing) does not exist for every HOF player who played in the twentieth century.

A second consideration was as follows. Since we are giving a weight of four for each home run, does it not mean that we are already, in some way, counting the run scored? That is, in order to avoid counting something twice, should we not subtract the number of home runs from the runs scored — that is (R-HR)? In examining this from all angles it became obvious that a similar question could be raised regarding the RBI that results directly from a home run. In fact someone might suggest that this means that a home run is actually worth six and not four. I finally determined that the home run is the ultimate offensive weapon and ought to be very special.

A third question was whether to subtract an amount to account for the "outs" that a player made – for example, .1(AB-Hits). There were a number of reasons why this thought was rejected. "Outs" have not been kept uniformly since 1900. For example, sacrifice flies have not been viewed uniformly during the century. Secondly, this would tend to lower the offensive score in comparison to the defensive score and give too much weight to defense (a point that some observers may feel is already the case). Finally, after experimenting with the concept on a number of the more famous "great players," it was determined that subtracting outs would not have a significant impact on the players' career rating. And so, for the sake of simplicity, I left the formula as it is above.

When I began to calculate the HEQ offensive scores for the Hall of Famers, it soon became obvious that a score of 600 meant that a particular player had an outstanding year at bat. In order to get some idea of how good a 600 offensive season is imagine that you produced the following numbers in a season: 145 singles, 30 home runs, 20 doubles , 5 triples, 80 walks, 100 runs scored, 120 RBIs, and 20 stolen bases. Very impressive numbers indeed! A career season for many players. These numbers yield a HEQ offensive score of exactly 600.

Babe Ruth and Lou Gehrig, generally considered two of the greatest hitters ever, were the only players who each had ten 600 offensive seasons. Ted Williams, Jimmie Foxx and Willie Mays had nine such seasons while Hank Aaron had eight.

In fact, only fifteen players in the Hall of Fame have had at least five 600 offensive seasons (number of seasons indicated):

Lou Gehrig	10	Earl Averill	6
Babe Ruth	10	Rogers Hornsby	6
Willie Mays	9	Stan Musial	6
Jimmie Foxx	9	Ty Cobb	5
Ted Williams	9	Joe DiMaggio	5
Hank Aaron	8	Hank Greenberg	5
Mel Ott	7	Chuck Klein	5
		Mickey Mantle	5

Of these outstanding hitters, only eleven have averaged better than 600 offensively over their ten best seasons:

The Most Effective Hitters — Career

1.	Babe Ruth	RF	767
2.	Lou Gehrig	1B	750
3.	Jimmie Foxx	1B	686
4.	Ted Williams	LF	655
5.	Willie Mays	CF	645
6.	Stan Musial	LF	630
7.	Hank Aaron	RF	628
8.	Rogers Hornsby	2B	625
9.	Joe DiMaggio	CF	613
10.	Ty Cobb	CF	608
11.	Mel Ott	RF	604

At the end of the 1998 season Barry Bonds became the first player since these eleven to attain a HEQ career offensive total over 600. He currently has a total of 606.

Besides these eleven outstanding hitters, here are the other players who would qualify among the top 25 hitters in the HOF:

12.	Al Simmons	LF	596
13.	Charlie Gehringer	2B	592
14.	Mickey Mantle	CF	589
15.	Frank Robinson	RF	584
16.	Earl Averill	CF	582
17.	Hank Greenberg	1B	579
18.	Mike Schmidt	3B	578
19.	Goose Goslin	LF	570
20.	Billy Williams	LF	566
21.	Eddie Mathews	3B	565
22.	Duke Snider	CF	562
23.	Harmon Killebrew	1B	561
24.	Chuck Klein	RF	552
25.	Paul Waner	RF	551

Note that twenty-one of the top twenty-five hitters are either outfielders or first basemen.

To see exactly how many 600 seasons each HOF had in his career, see the HEQ/HOF List in Appendix A. Note that 54 players (more than 50%) never had a 600 offensive season.

If a HEQ offensive score of 600 is considered a great offensive season, how many HOF have ever had a season of 700 or better? The answer is seventeen.

These seventeen players and their forty-one 700 seasons are shown here:

The Best Offensive Seasons: HEQ > 700

1.	Babe Ruth	1921	894
2.	Lou Gehrig	1927	836
	Lou Gehrig	1931	833
3.	Jimmie Foxx	1932	819
	Babe Ruth	1927	815
4.	Hack Wilson	1930	815
5.	Chuck Klein	1930	804
	Lou Gehrig	1930	799
6.	Rogers Hornsby	1922	793
	Lou Gehrig	1936	790
	Babe Ruth	1923	782
	Jimmie Foxx	1938	777
	Lou Gehrig	1936	776
7.	Hank Greenberg	1937	776
8.	Joe DiMaggio	1937	771
	Babe Ruth	1929	771
	Rogers Hornsby	1929	760
	Babe Ruth	1930	760
	Chuck Klein	1932	759
9.	Ted Williams	1949	759
	Babe Ruth	1928	757
	Babe Ruth	1931	755
10.	Ty Cobb	1911	746
11.	Stan Musial	1948	742
	Jimmie Foxx	1933	741
12.	Al Simmons	1930	738
	Hank Greenberg	1938	737
	Babe Ruth	1924	735
	Babe Ruth	1926	733
	Lou Gehrig	1937	731
	Hank Greenberg	1935	728
13.	George Sisler	1920	723
	Lou Gehrig	1932	718
	Hank Greenberg	1940	716
14.	Kiki Cuyler	1930	713
15.	Willie Mays	1962	710
	Jimmie Foxx	1936	708
	Chuck Klein	1929	708
16.	Frank Robinson	1962	706
	Rogers Hornsby	1925	704
17.	Mickey Mantle	1956	704

There are at least three interesting comments to make about these outstanding seasons:

1. Only five of the forty-one seasons (or 12%) came after 1940.
2. Only five players ever had an 800 offensive season.
3. Ruth (9) and Gehrig (7) claim sixteen of the best offensive seasons between them and they had four of the seven 800 seasons.

Note that both Willie Mays and Frank Robinson had 700 seasons in 1962. The only 700 seasons that have been recorded since 1962 are (ten of these eleven seasons have come in the 90s):

Jim Rice	1978	702
Barry Bonds	1993	709
Albert Belle	1996	708
Ellis Burks	1996	725
Larry Walker	1997	754
Ken Griffey Jr.	1997	718
Sammy Sosa	1998	763
Mark McGwire	1998	742
Ken Griffey Jr.	1998	711
Albert Belle	1998	711
Alex Rodriguez	1998	700

Here is a summary of some outstanding offensive achievements by players in the HOF:

1. Only Babe Ruth and Lou Gehrig had HEQ offensive averages over 700 for their ten best seasons.
2. Only nine other players had HEQ offensive career averages over 600.
3. Only Ruth and Gehrig had ten 600 offensive seasons.
4. Ruth had the best offensive season in 1921 with a HEQ offensive score of 894.
5. There were only 40 other seasons of 700 or better by HOF in the twentieth century.

Chapter 4

The HEQ
Defensive Score

Now for the toughest part of all — creating defensive scores that make sense!

The first consideration is that of an appropriate weight to give to the four defensive categories. For example, an assist or a double play by an outfielder requires more skill than a simple putout. The same is true for a catcher. It is probably true to say that the position of catcher is the most difficult to quantify because of the many intangibles involved, not the least of which is the ability to "handle" the pitchers. A putout by a first baseman generally requires so little skill that we will discount its value. We will assign a weight of (-2) for an error at any position.

The defensive formulas use only the following categories:

Putouts	PO
Assists	A
Errors	E
Double Plays	DP

The HEQ defensive formulas are as follows:

		MF
For outfielders:	PO + 4A - 2E + 4DP	1.00
For second basemen:	PO + A - 2E + DP	.460
For third basemen:	PO + A - 2E + DP	.888
For shortstops:	PO + A - 2E + DP	.548
For catchers:	PO + 3A - 2E + 2DP	.445
For first basemen:	.25PO + 3A - 2E + DP	.510

These weights seem reasonable even though arguments could be made for different assignments. As explained below, PO for catchers is capped at 800.

The multiplication factor (MF) indicated is the number by which each sum is multiplied in order to make the different positions equivalent. It is based on a defensive benchmark of 400. As explained in the following section, this benchmark derived initially from an analysis of Gold Glove winners together with a comparison of outstanding defensive seasons at each position.

Setting Fielding Comparison Standards

The last task that I had to perform before putting the numbers into the HEQ formulas was to figure out a reasonable and fair way to compare the HEQ fielding scores for the different positions. In my mind this is perhaps the most controversial aspect of the HEQ study. That is, can you really compare the fielding ability of an outfielder to that of a third baseman? The answer is no, but to compare the players I will attempt to do something reasonable.

Are we prepared to say that Willie Mays, whose HEQ defensive score in center field is 456, is a *better fielder* than Brooks Robinson, whose HEQ defensive score at third base is 451? I am not prepared to go that far. However, I do believe that the HEQ scores do tell us that both were extremely gifted fielders at their positions and that, for example, Robinson was the best fielding third baseman of this century.

There are at least two reasons why we needed the comparable scores no matter what position was played:

1. If we just wanted to compare outfielders to outfielders or shortstops to shortstops, this would not be necessary. However, in striving for a *single* ranking of the best players we have to be able to compare players who played at different positions.

2. Some of the great players (such as Ernie Banks and Stan Musial) played at more than one position during their careers. In fact, some played at different positions during a single season. In 1951 Musial played 91 games in the outfield and 60 at first base. So we must be able to come up with a single defensive score for such a year no matter how many different positions were played.

The big question was: How to do this?

Consider the following. Since 1957 Gold Gloves have been awarded to the "best" defensive players at each position in each league. It is true that these awards are very subjective and that in some cases they appear to be influenced by a player's offensive skills. Nevertheless, they do give us a basis by which to make comparisons.

I initially chose two years (1961 and 1974) to begin the investigation and used those years as the basis for establishing the defensive benchmark. I then tested the formulas for additional Gold Glove winners to assure myself that the outcomes seemed reasonable.

I proceeded as follows:

1. Since there are six outfielders chosen for the Gold Gloves each year and only two at each of the other positions, I found the average HEQ defensive score for the outfielders (406.4) and set the

Defensive Benchmark For A Great Season = 400 based on this score.

2. I then found the average HEQ defensive score for each position based on the performance of the four winners.

3. I compared this average score for each position to the performance of Gold Glove winners in other years to assure myself that I was being as fair as possible. I then established a score to represent a "great season" at each position.

4. Finally, I calculated the multiplication factor for each position to make it equivalent to the HEQ Benchmark for the outfielders. The MFs indicated above are those numbers.

The rationale behind step #3 above is as follows: I had to examine the players' numbers very carefully to ensure that a player who won the award at a particular position in 1961 or 1974 did not have such a spectacular year in the field that the use of his numbers would create a disadvantage for any other player at the same position. Or, if he did, to compensate accordingly.

It is interesting to note that for the players honored in 1961 all but one of these players won the Gold Glove more than once (Vada Pinson is the exception), and as a group they won a total of 106 Gold Gloves. The players selected in 1974 each won the Gold Glove at least three times and had a total of 94 Gold Gloves among them.

The 1961 recipients of the Gold Glove awards were (the numbers in parentheses are the total number of awards won by that player):

	National League	*American League*
First Baseman	Bill White, SL (7)	Vic Power, CLE (7)
Second Baseman	Bill Mazeroski, PIT (8)	Bobby Richardson, NY (5)
Third Baseman	Ken Boyer, SL (5)	Brooks Robinson, BAL (16)
Shortstop	Maury Wills, LA (2)	Luis Aparicio, CHI (9)
Catcher	John Roseboro, LA (2)	Earl Battey, MIN (3)
Outfielder	Willie Mays, SF (12)	Al Kaline, DET (10)
	Roberto Clemente, PIT (12)	Jimmy Piersall, CLE (2)
	Vada Pinson, CIN (1)	Jim Landis, CHI (5)

The 1974 recipients were:

	National League	*American League*
First Baseman	Steve Garvey, LA (4)	George Scott, MIL (8)
Second Baseman	Joe Morgan, CIN (5)	Bobby Grich, BAL (4)

	National League	*American League*
Third Baseman	Doug Rader, HOU (5)	Brooks Robinson, BAL (16)
Shortstop	Dave Concepcion, CIN (5)	Mark Belanger, BAL (8)
Catcher	Johnny Bench, CIN (10)	Thurman Munson, NY (3)
Outfielder	Cesar Cedano, HOU, (5)	Paul Blair, BAL (8)
	Cesar Geronimo, CIN (4)	Amos Otis, KC (3)
	Bobby Bonds, SF (3)	Joe Rudi, OAK (3)

As I outlined above, I first calculated the HEQ defensive score for each of the outfielders using the formula: PO + 4A - E + 4DP

	1961		*1974*
Mays	409	Cedeno	500
Clemente	366	Geronimo	405
Pinson	463	Bonds	339
Kaline	418	Blair	469
Piersall	370	Otis	457
Landis	427	Rudi	254
This yields	2453 + 2424 = 4877 / 12 = 406.4		

As you can see, the average HEQ score for the twelve outfielders is 406.4. Also note that eight of the outfielders had HEQ scores better than 400 while four had a HEQ of less than 400. Since these were the "best" outfielders for those years, I set the HEQ defensive score of 400 as the *benchmark* for a great defensive year.

When I compared the performances of these outfielders with other Gold Glove winners in other years, I concluded that a 400 score by an outfielder does indeed seem to indicate that the player had an outstanding season in the field. For example, if you were to examine the scores for the outfielders who won the Gold Gloves in the following eight years: 1962, 63, 72, 73, 82, 83, 92, 93, you would find an average HEQ score of 373 — indicating that 400 does indeed represent an outstanding defensive season by an outfielder.

I then found the average HEQ score for each of the other positions and calculated the multiplication factor that made that average equivalent to the benchmark of 400.

For the second basemen (PO + A — 2E + DP), we get the following:

Mazeroski	1013	Morgan	795
Richardson	889	Grich	1029
This yields	1902 + 1824 = 3726 / 4 = 931.5		

As you can see, the average score for the four second baseman is 932.

Proceeding in a similar manner for the other positions, I found the average score for each position.

First basemen:	1546 + 1453 = 2999 / 4 = 750
Third basemen:	930 + 1002 = 1932 / 4 = 483
Shortstop:	1504 + 1683 = 3187 / 4 = 797
Catcher:	1960 + 1925 = 3885 / 4 = 971

Using these scores as a frame of reference, I compared them to the HEQ defensive scores for other Gold Glove winners as I did for the outfielders. I concluded that the following HEQ score represents a "great" defensive season at the position indicated:

First base	784
Second base	870
Third base	450
Shortstop	730
Catcher	899

I then calculated the Multiplication Factor (MF) that made each of these scores equivalent to the defensive benchmark of 400 which defines a great defensive season.

For example, for first base, we divide 400 by 784 and we get .510 as the MF. To check this, we multiply 784 by .510 = 399.8. This procedure yields the following MF for each position:

First base	$.510 \times 784 = 399.8$
Second base	$.460 \times 870 = 400.2$
Third base	$.888 \times 450 = 399.6$
Shortstop	$.548 \times 730 = 400.0$
Catcher	$.445 \times 899 = 400.1$

I applied the MFs to the 1961 and 1974 Gold Glove winners and got the following results:

		HEQ Score
Mays		409
Clemente		366
Pinson		463
Kaline		418
Piersall		370
Landis		427
Cedeno		500
Geronimo		405
Bonds		339
Blair		469
Otis		457
Rudi		254
White	$746 \times .510 =$	380
Power	$800 \times .510 =$	408

HEQ Score

Garvey	662 × .510 =	338
Scott	791 × .510 =	403
Mazeroski	1013 × .460 =	466
Richardson	889 × .460 =	409
Morgan	795 × .460 =	366
Grich	1029 × .460 =	473
Boyer	438 × .888 =	389
Robinson	492 × .888 =	437
Rader	469 × .888 =	416
Robinson	533 x .888 =	473
Wills	727 × .548 =	398
Aparicio	777 × .548 =	426
Concepcion	814 × .548 =	446
Belanger	869 × .548 =	476
Roseboro	974 × .445 =	433
Battey	986 × .445 =	439
Bench	981 × .445 =	437
Munson	944 × .445 =	420

As you can see, of the thirty-two players who won Gold Gloves in 1961 and 1974, twenty-three of them had HEQ scores over 400 and would be said to have had great years in the field. This certainly seems appropriate. If all thirty-two had 400 seasons, we would have to wonder whether we had set the criterion for a great defensive season at a level that was too low.

Of course, any attempt to create formulas to quantify defensive accomplishments in a season is going to come up with some seasons which could be considered aberrations because a fielder has a very unusual season. One such season might be the 1930 season of Chuck Klein in right field when he set the modern record of assists by an outfielder at 44 because he had become so adept at playing the friendly confines of the Baker Bowl in Philadelphia. And, perhaps, another such season was the 1985 season of Bill Buckner when he set the modern assist record for first basemen at 184. It is said that his bad ankles slowed him down so he threw more than was necessary to the pitcher covering the base.

As I mentioned above, the position of catcher is probably the most difficult to quantify in any sort of reasonable way. The four catchers who won the Gold Gloves in 1961 and 1974 averaged 137 games behind the plate. If a catcher should catch more games than that and or catch one or two high-strikeout pitchers, then his HEQ defensive season score could soar. After examining the numbers for catchers in the different eras, it was decided to cap the number of putouts allowed in the formula for a season at 800 — in order to attempt to control for those seasons when a catcher caught more than about 135 games and had one or more high-strikeout pitchers on the staff. It is interesting to note that of the catchers in the Hall of Fame only two of them, Johnny

Bench and Roy Campanella, had any season in which they had more than 800 putouts (and each had only one such season).

The obvious question at this point is: How accurate are these procedures going to be for players at the different positions?

Consider the following:

1. Only nine outstanding fielders in the Hall of Fame have had ten 400 defensive seasons: three center fielders, three shortstops, two second basemen, and one third baseman. They are Richie Ashburn, Max Carey, Tris Speaker, Rabbit Maranville, Luis Aparicio, Luke Appling, Nellie Fox, Charlie Gehringer, and Brooks Robinson. (See Appendix A.)

2. There have been seventeen Hall of Famers who had a 500 fielding season. The season indicated is their best season while the number in parenthesis represents the number of 500 seasons that each had:

Richie Ashburn (8)	center field	1951	608
Max Carey (4)	center field	1916	571
Lloyd Waner (2)	center field	1931	564
Tris Speaker (2)	center field	1914	557
Chuck Klein (1)	right field	1930	544
Dave Bancroft (3)	shortstop	1921	531
Sam Rice (1)	right field	1920	530
Ray Schalk (2)	catcher	1916	526
Willie Mays (2)	center field	1954	522
Lou Boudreau (1)	shortstop	1944	521
Rabbit Maranville (2)	shortstop	1914	517
Luis Aparicio (1)	shortstop	1960	513
Travis Jackson (2)	shortstop	1929	512
Frankie Frisch (1)	second base	1927	506
Edd Roush (1)	center field	1920	506
Brooks Robinson (1)	third base	1967	503
Johnny Bench (1)	catcher	1974	502

Note that Ashburn is the only Hall of Famer to ever have a 600 defensive season. He also had *seven* other 500 seasons — a truly remarkable achievement! Here are four other 500 seasons by some non–Hall of Famers.

Ozzie Smith	shortstop	1980	534
Cal Ripkin	shortstop	1984	521
Gary Carter	catcher	1983	507
Bill Mazeroski	second baseman	1966	503

When you consider both lists, only first base and left field is not represented by at least one 500 season. Which means that no first baseman or left fielder in the HOF ever had a 500 defensive season. Not too surprising if you agree with the commonly held belief that first basemen and left fielders are voted into the HOF primarily for their hitting, not their fielding.

3. There were thirty-eight Hall of Famers who had at least five 400 seasons in the field (number of seasons indicated):

Luis Aparicio	shortstop	10
Luke Appling	shortstop	10
Richie Ashburn	center field	10
Max Carey	center field	10
Nellie Fox	second base	10
Charlie Gehringer	second base	10
Rabbit Maranville	shortstop	10
Brooks Robinson	third base	10
Tris Speaker	center field	10
Dave Bancroft	shortstop	9
Willie Mays	center field	9
Joe Sewell	shortstop	9
Johnny Bench	catcher	8
Yogi Berra	catcher	8
Lou Boudreau	shortstop	8
Joe Cronin	shortstop	8
Bobby Doerr	second base	8
Ray Schalk	catcher	8
Red Schoendienst	second base	8
Bobby Wallace	shortstop	8
Ernie Banks	shortstop	7
Billy Herman	second base	7
Pee Wee Reese	shortstop	7
Lloyd Waner	center field	7
Frank Baker	third base	6
Joe DiMaggio	center field	6
Frankie Frisch	second base	6
Travis Jackson	shortstop	6
Sam Rice	right field	6
Phil Rizzuto	shortstop	6
Mike Schmidt	third base	6
Arky Vaughan	shortstop	6
Honus Wagner	shortstop	6
Jimmy Collins	third base	5
Rogers Hornsby	second base	5
Mickey Mantle	center field	5
Bill Terry	first base	5
Paul Waner	right field	5

Note the distribution of these thirty-eight players among the different positions:

Shortstop	14	Catcher	3
Second base	7	Right field	2
Center field	7	First base	1
Third base	4	Left Field	0

It is not too surprising that shortstops, center fielders and second basemen dominate this list since it is generally recognized that the most mobile athletes are usually found at these positions.

4. Here are the Hall of Famers who were the best fielders at each position:

Outfield:	Richie Ashburn (529), Max Carey (490), Tris Speaker (484), Willie Mays (456)
Third base:	Brooks Robinson (451), Mike Schmidt (415)
Shortstop:	Rabbit Maranville (471), Dave Bancroft (445), Luis Aparicio (442)
Second base:	Nellie Fox (433), Charlie Gehringer (432)
First Base:	Bill Terry (393), George Sisler (387)
Catcher:	Ray Schalk (457), Johnny Bench (436), Yogi Berra (399)

In doing research on some of the candidates for the HOF (more about this in chapter thirteen) I discovered some outstanding fielders who have not yet been inducted. Consider the following career HEQ defensive scores and compare them to those above.

Outfield:	Kirby Puckett (453)
Third base:	Ron Santo (431)
Shortstop:	Ozzie Smith (465.4), Cal Ripken (464.5)
Second base:	Bill Mazeroski (444)
First base:	Keith Hernandez (440), Eddie Murray (416)
Catcher:	Gary Carter (474), Bob Boone (419), Carlton Fisk (403)

5. Finally, here is a cumulative list of the Hall of Fame players with the best HEQ career defensive average (over 380):

The Most Effective Fielders — Career

Richie Ashburn	center field	529
Max Carey	center field	490
Tris Speaker	center field	484
Rabbit Maranville	shortstop	471
Ray Schalk	catcher	457
Willie Mays	center field	456
Brooks Robinson	third base	451
Dave Bancroft	shortstop	445
Luis Aparicio	shortstop	442
Luke Appling	shortstop	442
Joe Sewell	shortstop	437
Johnny Bench	catcher	436
Lou Boudreau	shortstop	435
Nellie Fox	second base	433
Charlie Gehringer	second base	432
Lloyd Waner	center field	429
Billy Herman	second base	427
Bobby Doerr	second base	425
Joe Cronin	shortstop	424

Ernie Banks	shortstop	423
Joe DiMaggio	center field	423
Phil Rizzuto	shortstop	423
Bobby Wallace	shortstop	422
PeeWee Reese	shortstop	420
Travis Jackson	shortstop	420
Red Schoendienst	second base	419
Arky Vaughan	shortstop	417
Mike Schmidt	third base	415
Sam Rice	right field	413
Ty Cobb	center field	411
Frankie Frisch	second base	409
Earl Averill	center field	408
Honus Wagner	shortstop	408
Frank Baker	third base	402
Paul Waner	right field	402
Joe Tinker	shortstop	400
Yogi Berra	catcher	399
Jimmy Collins	third base	395
Bill Terry	first base	393
Pie Traynor	third base	392
Edd Roush	center field	389
George Davis	shortstop	388
Rogers Hornsby	second base	388
Stan Musial	left field	387
George Sisler	first base	387
Eddie Collins	second base	384
Joe Morgan	second base	382
Mickey Mantle	center field	382
Goose Goslin	left field	380

Here is the distribution of the best fielders by position. Again, the list is dominated by shortstops, center fielders and second basemen.

Shortstop	16	First base	2
Center field	10	Right field	2
Second base	9	Left field	2
Third base	5	Catcher	3

I believe that the HEQ formulas that quantify defensive skills may be the most significant contribution of the study. To my knowledge no previous study has successfully and accurately portrayed fielding skills in this way.

It appears that this lack of attention to defensive ability on the part of researchers is due, at least in part, to the statement made by Branch Rickey in *Life Magazine* in 1954 to the effect that no one could do much with fielding. It does seem that statements such as this, and a general lack of respect for fielding skills by many baseball observers, have made prospective researchers leery of attempting to quantify defensive skills over the years. This is clearly unfortunate since fielding ability has to be considered in judging the greatest players.

Here is a summary of some outstanding defensive achievements by the Hall of Famers:

1. Richie Ashburn is the only player in the Hall of Fame to have a HEQ defensive average over 500.

2. There are nine players who had ten 400 defensive seasons: three center fielders, three shortstops, two second basemen, and a third baseman. They were Luis Aparicio, Luke Appling, Richie Ashburn, Max Carey, Nellie Fox, Charlie Gehringer, Rabbit Maranville, Brooks Robinson and Tris Speaker.

3. Richie Ashburn had the greatest defensive season ever in 1951 when he had 538 putouts, 15 assists, and 6 double plays with only 7 errors in center field for a score of 608 — the only 600 defensive season by a Hall of Famer.

4. Ray Schalk and Johnny Bench are two HOF catchers who had a 500 defensive season. Surprisingly, the next most effective defensive season by another catcher in the Hall of Fame is 438 by Bill Dickey in 1933.

Of the catchers in the HOF only Schalk (457), Bench (436) and Yogi Berra (399) have a "respectable" HEQ defensive career score. This is due in part to the fact that the others simply did not play enough! Only these three averaged better than 130 games during their ten best seasons.

5. Ernie Banks has the very unusual distinction of having a truly great defensive season at two different positions. He had a 472 year at shortstop in 1959 and a 454 year at first base in 1964.

6. Rabbit Maranville (471), Ray Schalk (457) and Brooks Robinson (451) have the highest career defensive HEQs of any non-outfielder. Robinson is also the highest ranking Hall of Famer (# 31) who had no 1000 HEQ seasons.

7. No first baseman in the HOF had a HEQ defensive career score better than 400. Bill Terry at 393 and George Sisler at 387 come closest. Not too surprising since most first basemen were elected mainly for their bat.

8. Fifteen of the sixteen shortstops on the list have a defensive score of 400 or better. This is not very surprising either since virtually all the shortstops were elected because of their glove, although Ernie Banks, Joe Cronin and Honus Wagner could hit quite well also (HEQ career offensive score over 500).

Chapter 5

The Complete Players

The HEQ/HOF List which appears in Appendix A contains the scores for each Hall of Famer based on his ten best seasons. In this chapter we will look at some of the interesting numbers which emerge from combining the HEQ offensive and defensive scores. That is, I will make some comments regarding the *complete ballplayers*.

Here is a look at some of the greatest years that the game has seen.

Only two Hall of Famers have ever had a HEQ season of 1300:

1.	Chuck Klein	1930	544 + 804	1348
2.	Babe Ruth	1921	414 + 894	1308

Some writers who have commented on the best seasons have suggested that Chuck Klein's 1930 season is the best example of a ball park helping a player both at bat and in the field. This may be true. But however you interpret the numbers, they are very impressive. Not only did he hit a ton, but he set the modern record for assists by an outfielder in a single season (44).

Babe Ruth's HEQ offensive score of 894 in 1921 is the best in history. And even though he was not known as a particularly good fielder, his 414 fielding HEQ was one of the three times that he had a defensive score greater than 400. It is obvious that the younger Babe was a better fielder than he is usually depicted.

Only six 1200 seasons have ever been recorded and only one of those came after 1940:

3.	Joe DiMaggio	1937	486 + 771	1257
4.	Babe Ruth	1923	446 + 782	1228
5.	Ty Cobb	1911	476 + 746	1222
6.	Lou Gehrig	1927	386 + 836	1222
7.	Willie Mays	1955	515 + 696	1211
8.	Rogers Hornsby	1922	410 + 793	1203

You will note that in the five 1200 seasons before 1940 the player combined an offensive score over 700 with a defensive score in the 400s. Mays in 1955 did it differently by getting a defensive score over 500.

Besides these best eight seasons, the following years round out the top forty-six seasons — all of the 1100 HEQ seasons recorded by the Hall of Famers:

9. Babe Ruth	1927	374 + 815	1189
10. Chuck Klein	1932	429 + 759	1188
11. Kiki Cuyler	1930	473 + 713	1186
12. Jimmie Foxx	1932	365 + 819	1184
13. Hack Wilson	1930	363 + 815	1178
14. Jimmie Foxx	1938	400 + 777	1177
15. Hank Greenberg	1937	399 + 776	1175
16. Rogers Hornsby	1929	411 + 760	1171
17. Hank Greenberg	1938	433 + 737	1170
18. Willie Mays	1954	522 + 647	1169
19. Mel Ott	1929	470 + 698	1168
20. Tris Speaker	1912	512 + 648	1160
21. Willie Mays	1962	449 + 710	1159
22. George Sisler	1920	431 + 723	1154
23. Lou Gehrig	1936	357 + 790	1147
24. Tris Speaker	1923	475 + 670	1145
25. Ted Williams	1949	385 + 759	1144
26. Lou Gehrig	1931	309 + 833	1142
27. Lou Gehrig	1930	342 + 799	1141
28. Bill Terry	1930	440 + 697	1137
29. Babe Ruth	1924	400 + 735	1135
30. Stan Musial	1948	390 + 742	1132
31. Willie Mays	1957	480 + 651	1131
32. Ty Cobb	1917	495 + 630	1125
33. Willie Mays	1958	487 + 637	1124
34. Al Simmons	1925	455 + 668	1123
35. Hank Greenberg	1935	394 + 728	1122
36. Kiki Cuyler	1925	436 + 685	1121
37. Hack Wilson	1929	428 + 691	1119
38. Mickey Mantle	1956	414 + 704	1118
39. Joe DiMaggio	1948	462 + 655	1117
40. Charlie Gehringer	1936	454 + 662	1116
41. Tris Speaker	1914	557 + 559	1116
42. Earl Averill	1931	426 + 687	1113
43. Max Carey	1922	523 + 590	1113
44. Lou Gehrig	1934	342 + 766	1108
45. Johnny Bench	1970	473 + 632	1105
46. Lloyd Waner	1929	550 + 550	1100

Only five players had three or more of the top 46 seasons: Willie Mays and Lou Gehrig had five each, Babe Ruth had four, and Hank Greenberg and Tris Speaker had three each. Of these forty-six exceptional seasons, only seven (15%) came after 1950.

In looking for the complete ballplayers it is interesting to note that there are only twenty players in the HOF who had four or more 1000 seasons (number of seasons indicated):

Willie Mays	10	Stan Musial	5
Babe Ruth	9	Ted Williams	5
Lou Gehrig	9	Hank Aaron	4
Jimmie Foxx	7	Earl Averill	4
Charlie Gehringer	7	Ty Cobb	4
Joe DiMaggio	6	Chuck Klein	4
Rogers Hornsby	6	Mel Ott	4
Mike Schmidt	6	Al Simmons	4
Ernie Banks	5	Duke Snider	4
Hank Greenberg	5	Tris Speaker	4

Of particular interest here is the fact that Willie Mays is the only player in history to have ten 1000 seasons.

You may recall from chapters three and four that there were fifteen players who had at least five 600 seasons at bat and thirty-eight who had at least five 400 seasons in the field. But how many are on *both lists*— that is, have at least five 600 offensive *and* five 400 defensive seasons? Only four players have demonstrated this degree of *both* offensive and defensive ability.

Willie Mays	CF	9 offensive	+	9 defensive	=	18
Joe DiMaggio	CF	5	+	6	=	11
Rogers Hornsby	2B	6	+	5	=	11
Mickey Mantle	CF	5	+	5	=	10

You can see that when examined from this perspective, Willie Mays' total is far ahead of anyone else.

If you examine the list of *best hitters* from chapter three and *best fielders* from chapter four, you will note that, besides the four players above, seven others do appear on both lists: Ty Cobb, Stan Musial, Charlie Gehringer, Earl Averill, Mike Schmidt, Goose Goslin and Paul Waner. Obviously, these players also combined outstanding hitting with solid fielding performances.

It seems appropriate at this point to indicate from the HEQ/HOF List in Appendix A those individuals who emerge as the twenty-five most effective players of this century who are in the HOF. We will call this list of best players the *List of the Elite.*

The List of the Elite — The 25 Most Effective Players

1. Babe Ruth	RF	343 + 767	1110
2. Willie Mays	CF	456 + 645	1101
3. Lou Gehrig	1B	340 + 750	1090
4. Jimmie Foxx	1B	366 + 686	1052

5.	Joe DiMaggio	CF	423 + 613	1036
6.	Tris Speaker	CF	484 + 542	1026
7.	Charlie Gehringer	2B	432 + 592	1024
8.	Ty Cobb	CF	411 + 608	1019
9.	Stan Musial	LF	387 + 630	1017
10.	Rogers Hornsby	2B	388 + 625	1013
11.	Hank Aaron	RF	367 + 628	995
12.	Mike Schmidt	3B	415 + 578	993
13.	Ted Williams	LF	338 + 655	993
14.	Earl Averill	CF	408 + 582	990
15.	Mel Ott	RF	379 + 604	983
16.	Mickey Mantle	CF	382 + 589	971
17.	Max Carey *	CF	490 + 480	970
18.	Ernie Banks	SS	423 + 545	968
19.	Richie Ashburn*	CF	529 + 434	963
20.	Al Simmons	LF	366 + 596	962
21.	Joe Cronin	SS	424 + 530	954
22.	Paul Waner	RF	402 + 551	953
23.	Goose Goslin	LF	380 + 570	950
24.	Honus Wagner	SS	408 + 534	942
25.	Eddie Mathews	3B	373 + 565	938

* Max Carey and Richie Ashburn are on this list primarily because they were extraordinary fielders. Note that they are the only ones whose defensive HEQ is greater than the offensive HEQ. It would certainly be reasonable for a fan to question whether they were *better players* than those below them on the list or the next three players who would have been on the list:

26.	Duke Snider	CF	368 + 562	930
27.	Johnny Bench	C	436 + 493	929
28.	Frank Robinson	RF	341 + 584	925

Note the following about the top twenty-five players in the Hall of Fame:

1. Only two players, Babe Ruth and Willie Mays, averaged an 1100 HEQ over their ten best seasons. As I will point out in chapter twelve, if we were to consider *the 12 best years*, Mays would actually come out higher than Ruth.

2. Only eight other players have achieved a career HEQ score of 1000 or better.

3. The distribution of the twenty-five most effective players by position looks like this:

Center field	8	Second base	2
Right field	4	Third base	2
Left Field	4	First base	2
Shortstop	3	Catcher	0

You will note that the majority of players on this list played before 1950. The question may be asked whether there is any possibility that anyone who played during the last twenty years has any chance (like Mike Schmidt) of ranking among the top 25 players of all time.

Actually, the answer is yes. As we will see in chapter thirteen, some of the more recent players who have not yet been inducted into the HOF have the numbers to break into the *List of the Elite*— most notably Cal Ripken Jr., Barry Bonds, Eddie Murray and Kirby Puckett.

I noted above two ways to establish who among the Hall of Famers were both outstanding hitters and equally good fielders. Another more systematic way to do this is to find those players on the *List of the Elite* who had a career defensive HEQ of 350 and a career offensive HEQ of 550. As you can see below, such great hitters as Ruth, Gehrig, and Ted Williams do not make this list.

The 350/550 Club

1.	Willie Mays	CF	456 + 645	1101
2.	Jimmie Foxx	1B	366 + 686	1052
3.	Joe DiMaggio	CF	423 + 613	1036
4.	Charlie Gehringer	2B	432 + 592	1024
5.	Ty Cobb	CF	411 + 608	1019
6.	Stan Musial	LF	387 + 630	1017
7.	Rogers Hornsby	2B	388 + 625	1013
8.	Hank Aaron	RF	367 + 628	995
9.	Mike Schmidt	3B	415 + 578	993
10.	Earl Averill	CF	408 + 582	990
11.	Mel Ott	RF	379 + 604	983
12.	Mickey Mantle	CF	382 + 589	971
13.	Al Simmons	LF	366 + 596	962
14.	Paul Waner	RF	402 + 551	953
15.	Goose Goslin	LF	380 + 570	950
16.	Eddie Mathews	3B	373 + 565	938
17.	Duke Snider	CF	368 + 562	930

It is interesting to note that there are no shortstops or catchers on this list and only one first baseman.

Finally, only three players in history make the most exclusive baseball club of all. They are the players who have achieved the *ultimate complete ballplayer* status of averaging 400 in the field and 600 at bat over ten seasons. A very exclusive club indeed!

The 400/600 Club

1.	Willie Mays	CF	456 + 645	1101
2.	Joe DiMaggio	CF	423 + 613	1036
3.	Ty Cobb	CF	411 + 608	1019

If someone were to suggest that these were the three greatest all-around baseball players in history, I would have difficulty debating the point.

Some Significant Achievements

Let us summarize here some of the interesting facts that the HEQ study reveals regarding the complete players in the Hall of Fame:

1. Only Babe Ruth and Willie Mays had career HEQ averages over 1100.
2. Only eight other players have achieved a career HEQ score of 1000 or better.
3. Only Willie Mays had ten 1000 seasons.
4. Only Willie Mays, Joe DiMaggio, and Ty Cobb averaged better than 400 defensively and 600 offensively over ten years.
5. The two greatest seasons in modern history were Chuck Klein's 1930 season with a score of 1348 and Babe Ruth's 1921 season with a score of 1308.
6. There have been only six 1200 seasons recorded by Hall of Famers — the last (1211) was by Willie Mays in 1955. There have been thirty-eight 1100 seasons recorded — the last (1159) by Willie Mays in 1962.
7. The following players are the highest ranking at their respective positions in the Hall of Fame. I have included a designated hitter in recognition of Foxx's extraordinary hitting ability.

The HEQ/Hall Of Fame All-Star Team

		Def	*Off*	*HEQ*	*400*	*600*	*1000*
Babe Ruth	RF	343 +	767 =	1110	3	10	9
Willie Mays	CF	456 +	645 =	1101	9	9	10
Lou Gehrig	1B	340 +	750 =	1090	0	10	9
Jimmie Foxx	DH	366 +	686 =	1052	1	9	7
Charlie Gehringer	2B	432 +	592 =	1024	10	4	7
Stan Musial	LF	387 +	630 =	1017	4	6	5
Mike Schmidt	3B	415 +	578 =	993	6	2	6
Ernie Banks	SS	421 +	545 =	968	7	4	5
Johnny Bench	C	436 +	493 =	929	8	1	2

It is interesting to note that when Cal Ripken Jr. is elected to the HOF he will replace Ernie Banks as the shortstop on this *dream team* (see chapter thirteen).

Chapter 6

The Catchers

We are now ready to examine the HEQ/HOF List and analyze the performance of the players by the position that they played. Since some players in the HOF played more than one position during their careers, we will consider the player's position for our purposes to be that position where he played the greatest number of games.

As a result of our analysis, we will create three designations for each position: *most effective hitters*, *most effective fielders* and *most effective players*.

We will begin our look at each position by looking at the catchers who have been elected to the HOF. Ten of the 105 players on the HEQ list are catchers: Johnny Bench, Yogi Berra, Roger Bresnahan, Roy Campanella, Mickey Cochrane, Bill Dickey, Rich Ferrell, Gabby Hartnett, Ernie Lombardi and Ray Schalk.

I have chosen to begin with the catchers because, after examining the numbers that they have put into the record books, it is obvious that this is the group that has put the "poorest numbers" of players in the HOF. Of the twenty lowest HEQ career scores on the list, eight are catchers. Only Johnny Bench and Yogi Berra, of all the catchers, have "respectable" HEQ scores. Is there some explanation for this?

First, let me state very clearly that Roy Campanella's numbers (and his three MVPs) leave no doubt that he would have been in the class of Bench and Berra had baseball's color barrier not prevented him from playing in the majors until the age of twenty-six. By that time he had already played for ten seasons in professional baseball in the Negro Leagues. He only played for ten seasons in the major leagues.

One important consideration in the case of catchers is that, defensively, this is the most difficult of the positions to quantify. This is true because, among other reasons, it is not possible to quantify such things as "calling the game" and "handling the pitcher," the keys to the effectiveness of many of the great catchers. It is quite possible that some of these players whose HEQ scores look poor were quite good at the *intangible* aspects of the catcher's craft.

This is, of course, one reason why I am not advocating that the numbers alone should be the deciding factor for election to the HOF. Rather I propose that the HEQ scores should be *one* of the factors considered.

Having established these points, it is necessary to say that there appears to be another reason why seven of the ten catchers in the HOF do so poorly on the HEQ ratings. This is related essentially to the number of games that they played during their ten best seasons.

Before I had examined Ray Schalk's numbers carefully, I had always bought the argument that "catchers just did not catch many games in the early days." And so I thought that a catcher who played before 1940 could not have a great defensive HEQ. But Schalk's defensive numbers show that this argument does not hold water. It is true that he played some of his best seasons during the "dead-ball era" when catchers often had many more assists, but it is also true that he averaged more games per season than any of the other catchers besides Bench and Berra. His defensive HEQ is more than one hundred points better than that of Mickey Cochrane or Bill Dickey. Ray Schalk is a man whose defensive skills have not gotten the respect they deserve because of baseball's preoccupation with offensive statistics.

In this sense Schalk joins Richie Ashburn, Rabbit Maranville and Bill Mazeroski (among others) as probably the most unappreciated defensive wizards in baseball history. Brooks Robinson was in the same class of fielding giants, but I believe that he has received his due credit for this.

If Ray Schalk had been able to hit, he too would be in the class of Bench and Berra. But, alas, as you can see from the HEQ/HOF List, his offensive HEQ is the lowest of anyone. Of course, in the same vein one could also say that if Cochrane or Dickey had played more, they too would have been as effective as Bench and Berra. But we are not looking at potential, just achievement.

The numbers clearly show that the other six catchers in the HOF: Bresnahan, Cochrane, Dickey, Ferrell, Hartnett and Lombardi may have been the "best catchers" during the times in which they played, but compared to players at other positions and compared to Bench and Berra they simply do not measure up in terms of "effectiveness."

Schalk's defensive numbers seem to suggest that hype and bias (and a misunderstanding of statistics) can sometimes work to exaggerate the actual accomplishments of some players — in this case Dickey and Cochrane because each has a lifetime BA above .300. Only a completely objective look at the numbers can at times put the players into true perspective. It appears that the batting average of some of these players has been misinterpreted to mean that they were truly effective players when there appears to be some question about how much they played.

Here are the HEQ rankings for the HOF catchers as hitters, fielders and players.

Most Effective Hitters

	Off. HEQ	# of 600 seasons
Johnny Bench	493	1
Yogi Berra	469	0
Mickey Cochrane	435	0
Bill Dickey	426	0
Roy Campanella	384	1
Gabby Hartnett	377	0
Ernie Lombardi	320	0
Rick Ferrell	297	0
Roger Bresnahan	280	0
Ray Schalk	264	0
Avg. off. HEQ = 374.5		

Note that none of the catchers has an offensive HEQ over 500 even though 48 of the 105 players (46%) on the HEQ/HOF List achieved this score. And only Bench and Berra have a HEQ over 450. The average offensive HEQ for catchers in the HOF (374.5) is by far the lowest of any of the eight fielding positions. The next lowest is shortstop at 437.

It is also interesting to note that Ferrell, Bresnahan and Schalk are the *only players* on the HEQ/HOF List with a HEQ offensive score less than 300. This would certainly seem to suggest that some voters may be using a different standard for catchers than for anyone else when voting for the HOF takes place.

Most Effective Fielders

	Def. HEQ	# of 400 seasons
Ray Schalk	457	8
Johnny Bench	436	8
Yogi Berra	399	8
Roy Campanella	363	2
Bill Dickey	354	3
Mickey Cochrane	348	1
Gabby Hartnett	336	0
Roger Bresnahan	330	2
Rick Ferrell	310	0
Ernie Lombardi	258	0
Avg. def. HEQ = 359.1		

Ray Schalk's defensive HEQ is one of the biggest surprises that I encountered during the study. Note that only Schalk and Bench have HEQ defensive scores over 400 (Berra at 399 is so close that we will certainly consider him an outstanding defensive catcher). The average defensive HEQ for catchers in the HOF (359.1) is in fifth place in comparison to the other positions, ahead of left fielders, right fielders and first basemen.

Most Effective Catchers

	HEQ	# of 1000 seasons
Johnny Bench	929	2
Yogi Berra	868	1
Mickey Cochrane	783	0
Bill Dickey	780	0
Roy Campanella	747	1
Ray Schalk	721	0
Gabby Hartnett	713	0
Roger Bresnahan	610	0
Rick Ferrell	607	0
Ernie Lombardi	578	0
Avg. HEQ =	733.6	

The average HEQ score for catchers (733.6) is by far the lowest average for any of the eight positions. The next lowest is that of the right fielders at 862. Perhaps more significant is that only Bench and Berra have a career HEQ greater than 800!

Given the effectiveness of these players, it is reasonable to state that only Johnny Bench and Yogi Berra of the catchers in the HOF can be considered *great effective players*. In fact, given these numbers, it would not be surprising to hear some observers question whether a number of these catchers should be in the HOF at all. One has to wonder whether the induction of some of these players was due to a sentiment that might be expressed: "Well, we have to have *some* catchers in the HOF."

Besides Johnny Bench and Yogi Berra being the only truly effective catchers in the HOF, the biggest surprise for me (and I am sure for most fans) is just how good a defensive catcher Ray Schalk really was. As stated above, it sometimes takes a truly objective tool like the HEQ to help us realize how well some players really performed.

As mentioned earlier, a key to the performance of some of these catchers under the HEQ system is the number of games that each played during his ten best seasons.

You will recall that the HEQ method favors those players who were everyday players — that is, the players who averaged 130 games or more each season for at least ten seasons. And that is how it should be. It is probably accurate to say that the catchers in the HOF, more than any other position, are affected negatively by this reality. Look at the average number of games played during the ten best seasons for each catcher. And note that these numbers represent games in which the player *batted*. The number of games played *in the field* would often be less.

	Games	BA
Johnny Bench	148.2	.267
Yogi Berra	139.6	.285
Ray Schalk	134.4	.253
Mickey Cochrane	129.1	.320
Bill Dickey	123.4	.313
Gabby Hartnett	123.3	.297
Rick Ferrell	123.0	.281
Roy Campanella	121.5	.276
Ernie Lombardi	120.8	.306
Roger Bresnahan	108.6	.279

As you can see, only Bench, Berra and Schalk averaged more than 130 games per season during their ten best seasons. Schalk played in the time frame from 1912 to 1929. From various sources that I read I thought that no catcher ever caught as many games as he did per season "in the old days." He obviously demonstrates that even back then there were catchers like Johnny Bench and Yogi Berra who were *everyday players*.

It would appear that one reason why players like Mickey Cochrane and Bill Dickey are held in the esteem that they are by some observers (even though their career HEQ is quite low) is because of their career batting average (listed above). Because of this fact, I will make some comments at this point about the BA and the HEQ even though I will elaborate more on this point in chapter ten.

Misinterpreting the "Batting Average"

Read any article or book having to do with baseball and you will almost certainly find that the principal measure of a player's achievement mentioned most often is the "batting average."

For example, as we mentioned in chapter one, you might run into a statement such as: "Bill Dickey and Johnny Bench are both Hall of Fame catchers who played for 17 seasons. But Dickey batted .313 lifetime while Bench batted only .269."

Such statements are often made in the context of *comparing* ballplayers for one reason or another.

As baseball fans, we have become so accustomed to seeing this statistic quoted that I wonder if we ever pause to ask ourselves exactly what it means. Very often the statement above is meant to imply that Bill Dickey was a "better player" than Johnny Bench.

As we have seen, Bench was not only a more effective player than Dickey, but a *much more effective player.*

How can this be? How can our most familiar statistic apparently lead us astray? The answer is quite simple. The key concept is that of *production.* If you are going to *compare players* in a fair manner, then you must look at their overall production at bat and in the field.

The concept of "batting average" was never meant to be a measure of a player's production at the plate, but rather a way of indicating how many hits a player gets in relation to the number of times at bat. It makes no distinction, for example, as to the kind of hit — single, double, triple or home run. Nor does it address in any way other kinds of offensive output such as walks, runs scored, runs batted in or stolen bases.

If the batting average is used in some way to *compare* players' years or careers, it is a good example of using the wrong tool for a job — like trying to drive a nail into a wall using a screwdriver.

The concept of batting average has endured since 1874 because it is a simple way of getting a *rough idea* of how a player is doing at bat *while the season is in progress.* The problem with the concept only arises when someone is inclined to give too much importance to this statistic without taking other aspects of performance into account.

As a mathematician, I realize that there is another reason why the BA is used so commonly even if it is mis-used at times. And that is the simplicity of being able to "compare" two players by using a *single number* for each.

That is one of the reasons why I have endeavored to express a true comparative statistic, the HEQ, as a single number.

Let us recall once again how it can be that Bench's 17-year BA of .269 could be more productive than Dickey's 17-year BA of .313.

The answer, of course, is that the HEQ score is a sum (not a percentage) and is affected by the number of games played. That is, the more you play the more you produce (assuming that you are a good player). Therefore, the player who plays virtually every day is going to produce more and get a higher HEQ score. And this is as it should be.

Let us look at the following example to illustrate this point.

| Bill Dickey | 1930 | BA = .339 | HEQ offense = 306 |
| Johnny Bench | 1970 | BA = .293 | HEQ offense = 632 |

You will note that Bench had a great season at bat in 1970 with a HEQ of 632, more than double that of Dickey in 1930. Bench was far more productive even though Dickey batted .339. Part of the answer lies in the fact that Bench played in 158 games in 1970 and Dickey played in only 109 games in 1930. The BA does not reflect this fact at all, but the HEQ does. And this is one reason why the BA is so inadequate for comparing players.

As noted above, Bench averaged 148 games per season for his ten best seasons while Dickey averaged only 124. It is really not too surprising then that Bench's career HEQ score of 929 is 19% higher than Dickey's 780.

Finally, look at the best offensive and defensive year that each had.

1. The best offensive year:	Bench	1970	632
	Dickey	1937	562
2. The best defensive year:	Bench	1974	502
	Dickey	1933	415

Given these considerations, I hope it is clear that the lifetime BA for these two players is *clearly misleading* as an indicator of who was the more effective player.

The bottom line is that the BA has a role to play as a rough indicator of hitting ability. But we must be careful to use it appropriately. If it is our purpose to *compare players*, then we must measure overall player production in some organized manner — as the HEQ does.

When all the numbers are evaluated, Johnny Bench and Yogi Berra emerge as the two most effective catchers in the Hall of Fame.

Chapter 7

The Outfielders

Now let us examine the outfielders and analyze their results from the HEQ/HOF List in Appendix A. As we did for the catchers in the previous chapter, we will present three different rankings for each group of outfielders: most effective hitters, most effective fielders and most effective players. The center fielders turn out to be the best fielders (as expected), the left fielders the best hitters (as a group) and the center fielders the most effective players.

Center Fielders

There are fourteen center fielders from the twentieth century in the Hall of Fame. This is the strongest group in the HOF in that the average HEQ score of the group is 937, higher than for any other position. In fact, the next highest career HEQ is that of the left fielders at 879. This is to be expected since the center fielders generally hit well like most outfielders in the HOF while their defensive scores are much higher than the left fielders or right fielders.

The average defensive HEQ of the thirteen center fielders is 415, second only to the shortstops at 426. This is not too surprising since the most mobile athletes on the diamond are usually found at shortstop and center field. Their average offensive HEQ of 522 is fourth of the eight positions behind the first basemen, left fielders and right fielders. But the difference between the first basemen at 541 and the center fielders at 522 is only 19 points.

It is probably accurate to say that the position of center fielder has produced some of the most famous men to play the game. Aside from Babe Ruth, the first four players on the following list are among the most famous and the most "glamorous" in baseball history. And as we noted in chapter five, Willie Mays, Joe DiMaggio and Ty Cobb are probably the greatest all-around players to ever play the game — given that they are the only three players to ever average a 400 HEQ defensive score and a 600 HEQ offensive score.

Most Effective Hitters

	Off. HEQ	# of 600 seasons
Willie Mays	645	9
Joe DiMaggio	613	5
Ty Cobb	608	5
Mickey Mantle	589	5
Earl Averill	582	6
Duke Snider	562	4
Tris Speaker	542	3
Max Carey	480	0
Larry Doby	475	0
Hack Wilson	470	3
Earle Combs	467	0
Richie Ashburn	434	0
Edd Roush	431	0
Lloyd Waner	410	0
Avg. off. HEQ =	521.9	

As you can see, Willie Mays, Joe DiMaggio and Ty Cobb each have an offensive HEQ greater than 600. Only eleven players in the HOF have accomplished this and the only other position where there were three players who did it was right field.

Seven of the fourteen center fielders have an offensive HEQ greater than 500 and could be considered to be *very good* hitters.

The fact that Ty Cobb emerges as a more effective offensive player than Mickey Mantle (which some fans may consider something of a surprise) is due in part to the fact that base stealing plays a role in the offensive HEQ, as it must.

Most Effective Fielders

	Def. HEQ	# of 400 seasons
Richie Ashburn	529	10
Max Carey	490	10
Tris Speaker	484	10
Willie Mays	456	9
Lloyd Waner	429	7
Joe DiMaggio	423	6
Ty Cobb	411	4
Earl Averill	408	4
Edd Roush	389	4
Mickey Mantle	382	5
Larry Doby	373	2
Duke Snider	368	3
Earle Combs	347	3
Hack Wilson	325	2
Avg. def. HEQ =	415.3	

Note that eight of the fourteen center fielders have a defensive HEQ of 400 or more and, therefore, could be called *great* defensive players. Richie Ashburn at 529 has the highest defensive HEQ of anyone in the HOF. In fact, he is the only player who has a defensive HEQ greater than 500.

Ashburn, Max Carey and Tris Speaker each had ten 400 defensive seasons. Only six other HOF accomplished this feat. And every center fielder had at least two 400 defensive seasons. The only other positions where this is the case are shortstop and third base.

Before doing the study I had always considered Tris Speaker and Willie Mays to be the best defensive outfielders. But one of the strengths of the HEQ system is that it can establish players like Ashburn and Max Carey as the two most effective defensive outfielders in history. And also demonstrate that Lloyd Waner, a player always overshadowed by his brother Paul (for good reason), was a very effective defensive player.

In case you are wondering whether defensive skills in the outfield are a lost art it is interesting to note that Kirby Puckett's defensive HEQ is 453 — only three points lower than Willie Mays.

Most Effective Center Fielders

	HEQ	*# of 1000 seasons*
Willie Mays	1101	10
Joe DiMaggio	1036	6
Tris Speaker	1026	4
Ty Cobb	1019	4
Earl Averill	990	4
Mickey Mantle	971	3
Max Carey	970	3
Richie Ashburn	963	3
Duke Snider	930	4
Larry Doby	848	1
Lloyd Waner	839	2
Edd Roush	820	0
Earle Combs	814	0
Hack Wilson	795	3
Avg. HEQ =	937.3	

Only ten players in this century have averaged over 1000 as a HEQ score and four of them are center fielders (Willie Mays, Joe DiMaggio, Tris Speaker and Ty Cobb) — by far the largest group. It is interesting to note that Earl Averill, a player known only to the most ardent of fans, emerges as a more effective player than Mickey Mantle over his ten best seasons. As we will see in chapter twelve, Mantle surpasses Averill easily when the *twelve best seasons* are considered.

Nine of the fourteen center fielders have a HEQ score greater than 900 which means that each of these was a *very effective player*.

Right Fielders

Now we examine that group of players dominated by Babe Ruth, the most charismatic player to ever play the game and the #1 player on the HEQ/HOF List.

There are more right fielders in the HOF (19) who played in the twentieth century than there are for any other position. Shortstop with fifteen players is the second largest group.

Offensively, the right fielders have a HEQ average of 528, in third place behind the first basemen and the left fielders. Defensively their average HEQ is 334, last among the positions. Their HEQ average of 862 is next to last ahead of only the catchers.

Most Effective Hitters

	Off. HEQ	*# of 600 seasons*
Babe Ruth	767	10
Hank Aaron	628	8
Mel Ott	604	7
Frank Robinson	584	3
Chuck Klein	552	5
Paul Waner	551	3
Harry Heilmann	548	2
Reggie Jackson	533	1
Kiki Cuyler	524	2
Sam Crawford	507	0
Al Kaline	507	0
Willie Keeler	505	2
Sam Rice	492	0
Willie Stargell	490	1
Roberto Clemente	486	0
Enos Slaughter	483	0
Elmer Flick	463	0
Harry Hooper	422	0
Ross Youngs	387	0
Avg. off. HEQ =	528.1	

Offensively, of course, Babe Ruth was by far the most effective outfielder. He and Lou Gehrig were the only players in history to average better than a 700 offensive HEQ. And as you can see from this list, he was an amazing 139 points higher than Hank Aaron!

Only two other right fielders averaged better than 600 offensively: Hank Aaron and Mel Ott. When you consider that only eleven players have accomplished this, you can say that they also were *truly great hitters.* Nine other right fielders have an offensive HEQ greater than 500 and can be considered very good hitters.

Most Effective Fielders

	Def. HEQ	*# of 400 seasons*
Sam Rice	413	6
Paul Waner	402	5
Mel Ott	379	4
Kiki Cuyler	373	3
Hank Aaron	367	2
Al Kaline	357	3
Harry Hooper	344	0
Babe Ruth	343	3
Frank Robinson	341	1
Roberto Clemente	339	1
Enos Slaughter	338	1
Chuck Klein	337	3
Harry Heilmann	305	1
Elmer Flick	297	0
Sam Crawford	291	0
Reggie Jackson	288	0
Willie Keeler	285	0
Ross Youngs	280	0
Willie Stargell	258	0
Avg. def. HEQ =	333.5	

Only two right fielders, Sam Rice and Paul Waner, had HEQ defensive averages greater than 400 and can be considered great defensive players. It is also interesting to note that Babe Ruth, not generally known for his glove work, had three 400 seasons and ranks ahead of eleven of the right fielders defensively.

Perhaps the most interesting observation to make about this list is to point out the relative positions of Al Kaline and Roberto Clemente. Both of these players won multiple Gold Gloves (Clemente won twelve and Kaline won ten) and yet neither was a really effective fielder according to the defensive numbers — as was, for example, Willie Mays who played during the same time frame. Note that Kaline had three 400 seasons while Clemente had only one. What this illustrates more than anything else is that the Gold Glove award is often given to the best all-around performer at a given position (which both Kaline and Clemente were) regardless of whether they were the best fielder at that position.

As far as the numbers are concerned, one of the strangest defensive aberrations of all times occurred in 1930 when Chuck Klein set the modern assist record for outfielders at 44 and had a 544 defensive HEQ, one of the best defensive seasons by an outfielder. He had two more 400 defensive seasons indicating that this was not a complete fluke. However, once he left the friendly confines of the Baker Bowl, he was not nearly as effective. His HEQ defensive score of 337 is just mediocre.

In fact, Klein seems to have had one of the strangest careers in history. He is the only HOF with four 1000 HEQ seasons who does not have a career HEQ greater than 900. This is due to the fact that he had five sensational seasons from 1929 to 1933. However, once he was traded in 1934, he became at best an average player.

Most Effective Right Fielders

	HEQ	# 0f 1000 seasons
Babe Ruth	1110	9
Hank Aaron	995	4
Mel Ott	983	4
Paul Wane	. 953	2
Frank Robinson	925	1
Sam Rice	905	1
Kiki Cuyler	897	3
Chuck Klein	889	4
Al Kaline	864	1
Harry Heilmann	853	0
Roberto Clemente	825	0
Reggie Jackson	821	0
Enos Slaughter	821	0
Sam Crawford	798	0
Willie Keeler	790	0
Harry Hooper	766	0
Elmer Flick	760	0
Willie Stargell	748	0
Ross Youngs	667	0
Avg. HEQ =	861.6	

Babe Ruth's HEQ score of 1110 is the best ever recorded. Only six right fielders out of nineteen have scores greater than 900 (32%), compared to 64% for the center fielders.

Perhaps a more significant fact is that 39 of the 105 players on the HEQ/HOF List had HEQ scores over 900 (37%). I am surprised that the percentage for the right fielders is lower than this overall average.

Left Fielders

There are thirteen left fielders in the Hall of Fame of whom Stan Musial and Ted Williams are the dominant players. As you can see below, Williams is the best hitter in the group while Musial is the best fielder and all-around player.

As a group, the average offensive HEQ of the left fielders is 538 — second only to the first basemen (541). Defensively, their average HEQ is 340 — ahead of only the first basemen (335) and the right fielders (334). The average HEQ of the left fielders is 878 — second only to the center fielders at 937.

The Most Effective Hitters

	Off. HEQ	*# of 600 seasons*
Ted Williams	655	9
Stan Musial	630	6
Al Simmons	596	4
Goose Goslin	570	4
Billy Williams	566	2
Joe Medwick	549	3
Lou Brock	534	0
Carl Yastrzemski	533	2
Ralph Kiner	527	4
Heinie Manush	501	1
Zack Wheat	466	0
Fred Clarke	462	0
Chick Hafey	400	0
Avg. off. HEQ =	538.4	

Ted Williams' offensive HEQ of 655 is the fourth best in history — behind Babe Ruth, Lou Gehrig and Jimmie Foxx. Stan Musial at 630 is not far behind in seventh place among the most effective hitters in the HOF. Keep in mind that only eleven players have ever averaged better than a 600 offensive HEQ.

Ten of the thirteen left fielders (77%) have an offensive HEQ greater than 500 and can be considered very good hitters. This compares to 50% of the center fielders and 63% of the right fielders.

The Most Effective Fielders

	Def. HEQ	*# of 400 seasons*
Stan Musial	387	4
Goose Goslin	380	3
Zack Wheat	371	3
Al Simmons	366	3

	Def. HEQ	# of 400 seasons
Carl Yastrzemski	364	1
Joe Medwick	358	1
Fred Clarke	356	1
Ted Williams	338	0
Heinie Manush	326	0
Ralph Kiner	321	1
Billy Williams	301	0
Lou Brock	286	0
Chick Hafey	267	1
Avg. def. HEQ =	340.1	

Fielding is not the forte of the left fielders. None of the thirteen left fielders averaged a 400 defensive HEQ, and so none can be called a great fielder. Musial's case is debatable since he came so close at 387 and also had four 400 seasons. It should be noted that his play at first base added significantly to his achieving 400 or better in some of those four seasons.

As noted above, the left fielders' defensive average of 340 is ahead of only the right fielders and the first basemen.

The Most Effective Left Fielders

	HEQ	# of 1000 seasons
Stan Musial	1017	5
Ted Williams	993	5
Al Simmons	962	4
Goose Goslin	950	3
Joe Medwick	907	3
Carl Yastrzemski	898	0
Billy Williams	867	0
Ralph Kiner	858	2
Zack Wheat	837	0
Heinie Manush	827	0
Lou Brock	820	0
Fred Clarke	818	0
Chick Hafey	667	0
Avg. HEQ =	878.5	

Stan Musial is the best left fielder to ever play the game. His career HEQ of 1017 makes him one of only ten players who have ever averaged 1000 or better and establishes him as the ninth most effective player of this century.

Five of the thirteen left fielders (38%) had a HEQ career average of 900 or better — denoting a very effective player. This compares with 64% of the center fielders and 32% of the right fielders.

Having examined the numbers that the outfielders have put into the record book, we can say with some confidence that the most effective outfielder at each position in this century was:

Babe Ruth	right field
Willie Mays	center field
Stan Musial	left field

Chapter 8

The Infielders

We will now look at the infielders who have played in this century and who have been elected to the HOF. As we did for the catchers and the outfielders, we will present three different rankings for each position: *most effective hitters, most effective fielders* and *most effective players*. There are eleven first basemen on our list, fourteen second basemen, fifteen shortstops and only eight third basemen (the least at any position).

In 1946 three infielders were inducted into the HOF at the same time: Joe Tinker, shortstop; Johnny Evers, second base; and Frank Chance, first base. There are some commentators who have expressed the view that the *only reason* that they are in the HOF is because of a poem written by F. P. Adams. The reason that I mention this here is to point out that if you examine the lists below, you will find that these three players are each ranked last in every category of their respective positions. None of them has the numbers to be elected to the HOF *as a player* which would seem to support the allegation that they are there primarily as literary figures.

Offensively, the first basemen turn out to be the most productive of all the positions while the second basemen, third basemen and shortstops emerge as numbers five, six and seven of the eight positions (the catchers are the least effective hitters). Defensively, the shortstops are ahead of everyone while the third basemen and second basemen are in a virtual dead heat for third and fourth place. The first basemen are ahead of only the right fielders as a defensive group. Perhaps surprisingly, the second basemen emerge as the most effective players in the infield with a career average HEQ of 874.

First Basemen

The average HEQ offensive score for the first basemen is 541—the best of any position (the left fielders are second at 538). This establishes the first basemen as the most effective hitters in the HOF.

The Most Effective Hitters

	Off. HEQ	*# of 600 seasons*
Lou Gehrig	750	10
Jimmie Foxx	686	9
Hank Greenberg	579	5
Harmon Killebrew	561	1
Johnny Mize	549	4
Bill Terry	528	2
George Sisler	525	3
Jim Bottomley	517	3
Willie McCovey	488	1
George Kelly	442	0
Frank Chance	327	0
Avg. off. HEQ =	541.1	

The first basemen emerge as the best hitters of any of the eight position groups. It is easy to see why. Lou Gehrig and Jimmie Foxx are the two most effective hitters in baseball history after Babe Ruth, and six other first basemen have an offensive HEQ better than 500.

It is interesting to note that Willie McCovey, who was known as a slugger and had 521 career home runs, still did not achieve a HEQ offensive average of 500. This gives us some appreciation of the stature of a 500 offensive HEQ.

The Most Effective Fielders

	Def. HEQ	*# of 400 seasons*
Bill Terry	393	5
George Sisler	387	3
Jimmie Foxx	366	1
George Kelly	363	2
Lou Gehrig	340	0
Johnny Mize	333	1
Hank Greenberg	328	1
Jim Bottomley	317	0
Willie McCovey	312	1
Harmon Killebrew	303	0
Frank Chance	245	0
Avg. def. HEQ =	335.1	

The first basemen as a group are not noted for their fielding prowess. In fact, no one achieved a defensive HEQ of 400 and so there is no first baseman in the HOF who can be called a very effective fielder. Their average HEQ of 335 is the lowest of any of the groups except the right fielders at 334.

Lest anyone infer from this that it is unlikely that a first baseman can attain a 400 fielding HEQ, we will see in a later chapter that there are at least two candidates for the HOF who have in fact done this. They are Keith Hernandez and Eddie Murray. Hernandez's defensive HEQ of 440 is particularly impressive, making him the most effective defensive first baseman of the twentieth century.

The Most Effective First Basemen

	HEQ	# of 1000 seasons
Lou Gehrig	1090	9
Jimmie Foxx	1052	7
Bill Terry	921	3
George Sisler	912	2
Hank Greenberg	907	5
Johnny Mize	882	2
Harmon Killebrew	864	1
Jim Bottomley	834	0
George Kelly	805	0
Willie McCovey	800	1
Frank Chance	572	0
Avg. HEQ =	876.3	

Lou Gehrig emerges as the most effective first baseman in the HOF with Jimmie Foxx close behind. They are two of only ten players in this century who have averaged better than a 1000 HEQ over ten seasons.

Three other first basemen averaged better than a 900 HEQ, meaning that only five of eleven (45%) did so. The average HEQ of 876 for the first basemen ranks them as third in comparison with the other positions — behind the center fielders and the left fielders.

It seems appropriate to say a word about Hank Greenberg at this point since he is perhaps the only player on our list whose HEQ score may not truly reflect his effectiveness as a player *mainly because* of the time he lost due to his military service.

It is true that other outstanding players spent two or more years in the service. Ted Williams, Willie Mays and Joe DiMaggio come to mind. But none of these players was as negatively affected as Greenberg because each of them was still able to put at least ten impressive seasons into the record book. Greenberg, however, played only nine full seasons, having lost all or most of five seasons to the service at the height of his career.

You will note from the HEQ/HOF List that only twelve players had five or more 1000 seasons. Greenberg's 907 HEQ is the lowest of these. It seems rather obvious that his HEQ would have been substantially higher had he not been inducted into military service. In 1940, at the age of thirty, he had an offensive HEQ of 716 and enjoyed his fifth season with a total HEQ of 1000 or more and was one of the dominant sluggers in the game. In early 1941 he entered the service and did not return until midway through the 1945 season. At thirty-six he could not regain his former greatness.

Second Basemen

As a group, the second basemen rank fifth offensively among the eight positions — ahead of the third basemen, shortstops and catchers. Defensively, they are virtually tied with the third basemen for third place behind the shortstops and center fielders. They emerge as a surprising fourth in career HEQ (874) behind the center fielders (937), left fielders (878) and first basemen (876).

Most Effective Hitters

	Off. HEQ	*# of 600 seasons*
Rogers Hornsby	625	6
Charlie Gehringer	592	4
Joe Morgan	527	2
Eddie Collins	521	0
Frankie Frisch	506	0
Nap Lajoie	503	1
Bobby Doerr	482	0
Tony Lazzeri	479	0
Rod Carew	470	1
Jackie Robinson	456	1
Billy Herman	434	0
Nellie Fox	424	0
Red Schoendienst	423	0
Johnny Evers	337	0
Avg. off. HEQ =	484.2	

Rogers Hornsby is clearly the best hitting second baseman in history. Only eleven players have averaged a career 600 offensive HEQ and all of the others were outfielders or first basemen. Five other second basemen averaged 500 or more offensively (43%) compared to 46% for the entire list of 105 players. Joe Morgan is the only modern second baseman in the HOF to manage this feat. However, as we will see in a later chapter, Ryne Sandberg has also accomplished this with an offensive HEQ of 517.

The Most Effective Fielders

	Def. HEQ	# of 400 seasons
Nellie Fox	433	10
Charlie Gehringer	432	10
Billy Herman	427	7
Bobby Doerr	425	8
Red Schoendienst	419	8
Frankie Frisch	409	6
Rogers Hornsby	388	5
Eddie Collins	384	4
Joe Morgan	382	3
Rod Carew	373	3
Nap Lajoie	372	3
Tony Lazzeri	361	2
Jackie Robinson	340	2
Johnny Evers	322	0
Avg. def. HEQ =	390.3	

Nellie Fox and Charlie Gehringer emerge not only as the best fielding second basemen in the HOF but also as two of only nine players who had ten 400 fielding seasons. We will see in a later chapter that Bill Mazeroski had a higher HEQ fielding score (444) but had only eight 400 seasons.

Four other second basemen had HEQ fielding scores over 400 and therefore could be regarded as great fielding second basemen: Billy Herman, Bobby Doerr, Red Schoendienst and Frankie Frisch.

The Most Effective Second Basemen

	HEQ	# of 1000 seasons
Charlie Gehringer	1024	7
Rogers Hornsby	1013	6
Frankie Frisch	915	2
Joe Morgan	909	1
Bobby Doerr	907	1
Eddie Collins	905	0
Nap Lajoie	875	1
Billy Herman	861	0
Nellie Fox	857	0
Rod Carew	843	1
Red Schoendienst	842	0
Tony Lazzeri	840	0
Jackie Robinson	796	1
Johnny Evers	659	0
Avg. HEQ =	874.4	

As a result of this study, I have come to regard Charlie Gehringer as the "forgotten superstar" of baseball history. As you can see above, he is the most effective second baseman to ever play the game. He is one of only ten players in history to average a career 1000 HEQ. He is #7 on the HEQ/HOF List ahead of such renowned players as Stan Musial, Ty Cobb, Ted Williams and Hank Aaron.

Everything that I have read about him describes him as a low-key, quiet and conservative gentleman. He was not flashy or charismatic in any sense of the term and so received virtually no publicity while he played — except, of course, from the most discerning of baseball observers (he was the American League MVP in 1937). Evidently he was so smooth and efficient at bat and in the field that reporters of his day labeled him the "mechanical man." It would be interesting to see how many casual baseball fans have ever even heard of him, even though he is one of the most effective players to ever play the game.

Rogers Hornsby also has a career HEQ of 1000 and is among the ten most effective players ever. But, of course, he is a much more famous baseball legend than Gehringer since he was the more effective offensive player. Four other second basemen achieved career HEQ scores over 900: Frankie Frisch, Joe Morgan, Bobby Doerr and Eddie Collins. Only 37% of our 105 HOF achieved this distinction, so these players are in very good company indeed.

It is necessary to make the point here that Jackie Robinson is one of the few players on our list of HOF for whom the HEQ scores do not do justice. The only two players mentioned to this point in a similar context are Hank Greenberg and Roy Campanella (Greenberg for his military service).

The HEQ score is based on a player's ten best seasons. Robinson only played for ten seasons for reasons having nothing to do with talent or desire. As with Campanella, the color barrier in baseball prevented Robinson from playing in the major leagues until much later than his talent warranted. When he "broke the color line" in 1947, he was already twenty-eight years old and, obviously, many of what would have been his best seasons were behind him. And so his HEQ score suffers because of his playing time, but his reputation as a great player and as a great baseball figure do not.

Shortstops

As might be expected, the shortstops emerge as the best fielding position with an average defensive HEQ of 426. Offensively, they rank seventh ahead of only the catchers. Their average career HEQ score of 863.3 is ahead of only the right fielders and the catchers.

The Most Effective Hitters

	Off. HEQ	# of 600 seasons
Ernie Banks	545	4
Honus Wagner	534	0
Joe Cronin	530	1
Arky Vaughan	485	0
George Davis	474	0
Joe Sewell	460	0
Luke Appling	450	0
PeeWee Reese	445	0
Lou Boudreau	408	0
Bobby Wallace	401	0
Luis Aparicio	400	0
Travis Jackson	400	0
Rabbit Maranville	391	0
Phil Rizzuto	367	0
Dave Bancroft	362	0
Joe Tinker	353	0

Avg. off. HEQ   =   437.3

Only three shortstops have a HEQ offensive score over 500 and can be considered very effective hitters: Ernie Banks, Honus Wagner and Joe Cronin. Since it would be fair to say that most observers consider shortstop to be primarily a defensive position, it is not too surprising to find this to be the case. But it does mean that a shortstop who can hit at this level is probably as valuable a player as a team can get.

The Most Effective Fielders

	Def. HEQ	# of 400 seasons
Rabbit Maranville	471	10
Dave Bancroft	445	9
Luis Aparicio	442	10
Luke Appling	442	10
Joe Sewell	437	9
Lou Boudreau	435	8
Joe Cronin	424	8
Phil Rizzuto	423	6
Ernie Banks	423	8
Bobby Wallace	422	8
Travis Jackson	420	6
PeeWee Reese	420	7
Arky Vaughan	417	6
Honus Wagner	408	6
Joe Tinker	400	4
George Davis	388	4

Avg. def. HEQ   =   426.0

Note that every shortstop in the HOF except for George Davis has a fielding HEQ of 400 or better and the average of 426 is the highest for any position — center fielders are next at 415. This is not too surprising since it is probably fair to say that with a few exceptions, every shortstop was elected primarily for his fielding ability. This cannot be said for any other position.

Three shortstops are among the nine players in the HOF who have ten 400 fielding seasons: Rabbit Maranville, Luis Aparicio and Luke Appling. Maranville's 471 defensive HEQ is the best by any non–center fielder (Ashburn, Carey and Speaker are higher).

Most Effective Shortstops

	HEQ	*# of 1000 seasons*
Ernie Banks	968	5
Joe Cronin	954	2
Honus Wagner	942	2
Arky Vaughan	902	1
Joe Sewell	897	0
Luke Appling	892	1
PeeWee Reese	865	0
George Davis	862	0
Rabbit Maranville	862	0
Lou Boudreau	843	1
Luis Aparicio	842	0
Bobby Wallace	823	0
Travis Jackson	820	1
Dave Bancroft	807	2
Phil Rizzuto	783	0
Joe Tinker	753	0
Avg. HEQ =	863.4	

Ernie Banks is the most effective shortstop of the twentieth century (in the HOF) followed fairly closely by Joe Cronin and Honus Wagner. These results surprised me a bit because from what I read I was mentally prepared for Honus Wagner to head the field. In fact, I find that Wagner provides an interesting counter-point to Charlie Gehringer. Gehringer is virtually "unknown" and emerges as a superstar, whereas Wagner has the big reputation but emerges as a great player but not quite up to Gehringer's stature. Wagner is #24 on the HEQ/HOF List and only the third most effective shortstop.

The only other shortstop in the HOF to crack the 900 HEQ level is Arky Vaughn although Joe Sewell and Luke Appling come very close.

It should be noted here that one modern player will be taking his place among the most effective shortstops of the twentieth century. Cal Ripken Jr. has put together the numbers to be the most effective shortstop of all time: 465 defensive + 529 offensive = 994 HEQ.

Third Basemen

The eight third basemen from the twentieth century in the HOF represent the smallest group at any position. Their average HEQ scores rank sixth offensively, third defensively and fifth overall.

Most Effective Hitters

	Off. HEQ	# of 600 seasons
Mike Schmidt	578	2
Eddie Mathews	565	2
Pie Traynor	484	0
Brooks Robinson	462	0
Frank Baker	451	1
Jimmy Collins	437	0
Freddy Lindstrom	420	1
George Kell	391	0
Avg. off. HEQ =	473.5	

Two third basemen, Mike Schmidt and Eddie Mathews, have offensive HEQ scores greater than 500 (well over 500 in both cases) and can be considered outstanding hitters. I was somewhat surprised to find that the average offensive HEQ of 474 was less than that for the second basemen (484).

The Most Effective Fielders

	Def. HEQ	# of 400 seasons
Brooks Robinson	451	10
Mike Schmidt	415	6
Frank Baker	402	6
Jimmy Collins	395	5
Pie Traynor	392	4
Eddie Mathews	373	0
George Kell	366	4
Freddy Lindstrom	327	3
Avg. def. HEQ =	390.1	

Brooks Robinson emerges as the most effective fielding third baseman in the HOF — as, indeed, virtually anyone who saw him play would expect. What is very impressive for me (but not exactly unexpected) is that his defensive 451 is better than any other infielder except Rabbit Maranville at 471. This is one of those instances in baseball (similar to Ruth's offensive numbers) where the expectation proves to be completely accurate.

Two other third basemen, Mike Schmidt and Frank Baker, had a defensive HEQ greater than 400 and can be considered great fielders. Actually, Jimmy Collins and Pie Traynor come very close also.

The Most Effective Third Basemen

	HEQ	# of 1000 seasons
Mike Schmidt	993	6
Eddie Mathews	938	2
Brooks Robinson	913	0
Pie Traynor	876	1
Frank Baker	853	1
Jimmy Collins	832	0
George Kell	757	1
Freddy Lindstrom	747	0
Avg. HEQ =	863.6	

Mike Schmidt emerges as the most effective third baseman of the century. In fact he is #12 on the HEQ/HOF List and thereby qualifies as the "greatest modern player" in the HOF if we think of "modern" as meaning since 1975. Eddie Mathews and Brooks Robinson also have HEQ scores greater than 900 and qualify as truly great all-around players.

The most striking example that I have encountered during this study of "Why isn't he in the HOF?" is the case of Ron Santo. Santo was an outstanding third baseman who played from 1960 to 1974 mainly for the Chicago Cubs. He was an outstanding fielder (defensive HEQ of 431) and a consistent hitter (offensive HEQ of 520). His career HEQ of 951 is second only to Mike Schmidt making him the second most effective third baseman of the 20th century. That 951 would place him as #23 on the HEQ/HOF List . His case is by far the greatest oversight that I have encountered in my research. When you realize that George Brett's career HEQ is 892, you begin to realize just how good Ron Santo really was!

Chapter 9

Hall of Fame Numbers — A New Meaning

Induction into the Baseball Hall of Fame is supposed to be reserved for those individuals whose contributions to baseball are considered to be outstanding. Most fans think of the Hall as being populated by those people who distinguished themselves on the playing field such as Babe Ruth or Hank Aaron. But, of course, there are any number of other inductees such as umpires like Al Barlick or executives like Branch Rickey. And there are a few, like Jackie Robinson, who have been inducted for a combination of playing skill and other contributions to the game.

Each year the individuals who vote for the candidates who are eligible primarily for their playing skills are faced with having to determine who are the most worthy. Presumably, in the case of non-pitchers, they do so based on their perception of how good a hitter and or how good a fielder a player was. They would consider such things as whether the player ever led the league in various categories such as batting average, slugging percentage or fielding percentage. Did the player ever win such awards as the MVP, Gold Glove or selection to the All Star team.

Having weighed these considerations, the voter then casts a ballot in favor of or against induction. Some voters may even have "pet numbers" which automatically trigger a yes vote. For example, a voter may believe that any player who accumulates 3000 hits in the majors deserves to be in the HOF and votes yes for all such players who appear on the ballot. And this is as it should be. Diversity and independent thinking among the voters should be welcomed.

As we all recognize, some of these considerations are based on someone's *perception* of the player's ability, and this is unavoidable given the task at hand.

As the HEQ study progressed, it occurred to me that one of the possible side effects of the research might be to assist the HOF voters to determine whether a particular player who had none of the "special numbers" such as 3000 hits or 500 home runs really did have "HOF numbers." That is, perhaps we could shed some new light on what this phrase might mean.

Would it not be desirable to have at least one completely *objective* criterion (based on *all* of a player's numbers) that the voters could consider as they examine all the other aspects? The HEQ score is based *solely* on the numbers and reflects (in an objective manner) the player's accomplishments during his career both at bat *and* in the field and can be compared with a similar score for every Hall of Famer who played in this century. It seems to me that such a comparison might be valuable for those who vote for the candidates.

In his 1994 book on the Baseball Hall of Fame, *The Politics of Glory*, Bill James makes a very important point when he is discussing whether there should be *strict* statistical standards for induction into the Hall. He indicates that he does not support strict standards and he says, "So, statistical standards are useful for certain purposes — spotting the best candidates, focusing on anomalies, evaluating groups of selectees" (184).

This is an excellent point. The numbers alone are not the sole criterion for election to the Hall of Fame, nor should they be. But an objective look at the player's numbers can be an extremely helpful ingredient in decision making. That is, if the voter knows definitively that John Doe did or did not have HOF numbers, it almost certainly would help in the decision on how to vote.

The problem is how to define the term"HOF numbers."

We will now examine the results of the HEQ study and make some suggestions regarding a definition of this term.

In *The Politics of Glory* James presents a series of eleven questions that he suggests can be used to establish who belongs in the HOF and, perhaps, who does not. The questions are rather interesting but two problems immediately jump out at a mathematician like myself. Ten of the eleven questions have to do with hitting accomplishments and only one with fielding. And because of the heavy reliance on traditional baseball statistics (six of the questions deal with career hits, batting average, slugging percentage, on-base percentage, home runs and extra base hits) some hitting feats are counted two or three times (174).

One of the important aspects of the HEQ study is that it deals with both hitting and fielding in a straightforward and objective manner. No one sat down ahead of time and said, "Now how much weight should we give to hitting and how much to fielding?" The HEQ offensive and defensive scores *grow from the numbers themselves*. And so we see that in the case of Babe Ruth (the most effective hitter) his HEQ score of 1110 is made up of a HEQ offensive score of 767 (69%) and a HEQ defensive score of 343 (31%). But Richie Ashburn (the most effective fielder) has a very different ratio since his HEQ score of 963 is made up of a HEQ offensive score of 434 (45%) and a HEQ defensive score of 529 (55%). This is extremely important to note because we want to honor the great fielders and the great all-around players just as we want to honor the great hitters.

The following aspects of the HEQ system are significant:

1. This score gives a much better picture of how good a season a player had than any existing comprehensive statistic. And, because it is so easily understood and fan-friendly, it has the potential to become the most popular statistic for comparing players' seasons.

2. Since the career numbers of all the Hall of Famers of the twentieth century (105 in all) have been quantified, the method can be helpful in answering the question of whether a potential candidate has "Hall of Fame numbers."

3. Since the method quantifies both hitting and fielding accomplishments, it can also be helpful in comparing players for such awards as the MVP or the Gold Gloves. We will consider these awards in later chapters.

4. Perhaps the most significant aspect of the study is that it represents the most ambitious attempt to date to quantify *defensive* skills in a logical and accurate manner. This makes it possible to create a single score to represent both hitting and fielding accomplishments for the season.

5. Since the HEQ scores are based on the players' numbers *alone*, the system represents the most *objective* and therefore the fairest assessment of a player's total achievements.

Let us now analyze the HEQ/HOF List in Appendix A to see what it tells us regarding a possible definition of HOF numbers. Keep in mind that we are only trying to establish whether a player has the numbers for induction into the HOF. We are not dealing with any other qualifications that a particular voter may have in mind for a positive vote. It could be that a voter might vote *against* a player who *does* have the numbers because he lacks some other qualification that the voter considers important.

One place to start is to look at those players who have achieved a career HEQ of 920 or greater over their ten best seasons. These, of course, are the highest ranked players in the HOF. Only 29 of the 105 players on the list (28%) have done this. There can be no question that such a score means that a player has HOF numbers. We will call such players Group A players.

The next appropriate cut-off point appears to be at 860. There are a total of fifty-five players on our list (52%) who have scores above 860. I assume that there would be no objection to saying that these players certainly have HOF numbers since they represent only a little more than half of the position players in the HOF. We will designate this group between 860 and 919 as Group B players.

Group C players would be those on our list whose HEQ score is between 820 and 859. There are 22 players in this group. Players such as Ralph Kiner, Rod Carew, Roberto Clemente and Reggie Jackson are spread across this spectrum. A total of seventy-seven of our 105 players (73%) have HEQ scores greater than 820. If a player is a candidate for the HOF and falls into the Group C range, especially into the lower end of the range, it would be reasonable for a voter to question whether such a player clearly has HOF numbers. I would say that at least in the lower end of this group the players have "questionable" HOF numbers.

Group D consists of those players whose career HEQ score falls below 820. There are twenty-eight players on our list (27%) who fall into this range. It seems clear to me that we can say that these players *do not have* HOF numbers. That does not mean that I am saying that none of these players belongs in the HOF. These are not the same statements.

The two players in this group who, in my mind, definitely belong in the HOF are Jackie Robinson and Roy Campanella. As we discussed previously, both of these players clearly had the talent and desire to put very impressive numbers into the record book and demonstrated this in the majors. However, both had limited careers and lost some of their prime years because they were prevented from coming to the majors by the color barrier.

I suspect that some other observers might be inclined to say that Mickey Cochrane and Bill Dickey are clearly Hall of Famers also, and I would not dispute this. It is possible that one or both of these players (as well as others in Group D) have equally persuasive reasons why they did not put HOF numbers into the record book and should be in the HOF. All I am saying is that they clearly *do not have HOF numbers.*

Let us summarize the suggestions above regarding guidelines for establishing HOF numbers.

Group A — the player's career HEQ is 920 or above. These are the truly great effective players.

Group B — the player's career HEQ is between 860 and 919. Very effective players who clearly have HOF numbers.

There are fifty-five players in Groups A and B on the HEQ/HOF List. It is interesting to note how they are distributed by position: 9 right fielders, 9 center fielders, 9 shortstops, 8 second basemen, 7 left fielders, 7 first basemen, 4 third basemen and 2 catchers. A rather balanced spread among the "obvious Hall of Famers" (see Appendix A).

Group C — the player's career HEQ is between 820 and 859. Questionable HOF numbers — especially in the lower range. Some other justification for election to the HOF (other than performance numbers) may be needed.

Group D — the player's career HEQ is lower than 820. Does not have HOF performance numbers. Some other justification for election to the HOF is clearly needed.

When I speak of "other justification," it seems to me that it is possible that a player might have some other quality or achievement that a voter considers significant enough to justify a positive vote even though the player does not have HOF numbers. Winning an MVP award, winning a number of Gold Gloves or repeated selection to the All Star team might be such achievements. For example, some voters may have voted for Willie Stargell because they remembered his outstanding leadership qualities. Or for Phil Rizzuto because he played on a number of championship teams or because he was a baseball broadcaster for many years. Rightly or wrongly, I assume that such considerations do influence some voters.

We will use these HEQ guidelines in a later chapter when we examine the numbers for those players who are considered candidates for the HOF. At this time I want to use just one player as an example of how the HEQ system might work to help the HOF voters to clarify in their own minds whether a particular player has HOF numbers.

Ron Santo was a third baseman who played principally for the Chicago Cubs from 1960 to 1974, fifteen seasons. As we pointed out in chapter eight when discussing the third basemen, he was an outstanding fielder (defensive HEQ of 431) and a consistent hitter (offensive HEQ of 520). His career HEQ of 951 puts him solidly into Group A. In fact he would be #27 on the list of the most effective players of this century (see chapter seventeen).

Santo emerges from the HEQ study as the most extreme case of a great player being denied induction into the HOF. He may be the most under-rated player of the sixties and seventies. He emerges as the second best third baseman in history (after Mike Schmidt) and his accomplishments are comparable to such greats as Joe Cronin and Paul Waner. I suspect that he has not yet been inducted into the Hall of Fame because, up until the present time, no clearly objective system such as the HEQ has been available to cut through the confusion and point out a player's true numbers. It may help some readers to appreciate just how good he was to realize that his HEQ of 951 compares to George Brett's HEQ of 892. So, if you think that Brett is HOF material, then Santo certainly is.

Let me repeat once again that I am not suggesting that a player's numbers alone should be the only criterion or even the most important criterion for induction into the Hall of Fame. What I am suggesting, however, is that a truly objective tool like the HEQ system may have some value in assisting the voters to assess a player's true effectiveness.

Chapter 10

The Problem with the "Batting Average"

In speaking of the 1980 season in his wonderful one-volume history of baseball entitled *Our Game,* Charles Alexander makes the following comment: "For the Royals, the gifted George Brett threatened the .400 mark almost to the end of the season before finishing at .390. Besides achieving the highest average since Ted Williams's .406 thirty-nine years earlier, Brett connected for twenty-four home runs and drove in 118 runs — an indubitably Most Valuable Player performance"(310).

This statement by an astute historian points out as well as any what is the essential problem with the batting average and most other baseball statistics if they are used to *compare* the seasons of different players. And that is that the statistic is misunderstood and over-estimated.

The implication of the comment is that Brett's 1980 season is somehow comparable to Williams' 1941 season and that it was one of the best years in baseball since that time. Unfortunately, neither of these implications is accurate. Brett's .390 batting average in 1980 is somewhat misleading in terms of his overall productivity because of the number of games that he played. And this is the key difference between many of the common baseball statistics and the HEQ score.

The problem with the batting average (and all percentage-based statistics) is that they do not take *playing time* into account. And any comparison of seasons that is to be fair must be based on a *total assessment* of all of a player's accomplishments during a season. The HEQ method is a sum of key offensive and defensive factors and *automatically takes playing time into account.*

One of the major problems with baseball statistics in general is that their creators have always appeared to be somewhat obsessed with expressing things as a *percentage* as if this were, somehow, the best way to do things. (Part of the motivation for this is to be able to see how a player is doing *as the season progresses.)* From a mathematical point of view a percentage is not a good way to compare players' achievements *once the season is over.* All a percentage tells us is how often something happens in relation to something else. For example, the fielding percentage tells us how often a player makes an error in relation to the number of chances he attempts. It does not have anything to do with a fielder's range which is a most significant factor in how good a fielder the person is. A shortstop's assists, putouts, double plays and errors tell us a great deal more about his fielding ability than his fielding percentage. Whoever first developed the concept of *total bases* (adding things together) was on the right track but simply did not go far enough.

The fact of the matter is that Brett's 1980 season (despite his .390 BA) falls far short of Williams' 1941 season. Keep in mind that Ted Williams is the fourth most effective hitter of all time behind only Babe Ruth, Lou Gehrig and Jimmie Foxx.

Look at Brett's offensive HEQ for 1980 compared to Williams' for 1941.

	Games	At Bats	BA	Off. HEQ
Williams	143	456	.406	665
Brett	117	449	.390	547

As you can see, Brett does not achieve the 600 offensive HEQ needed for a great season whereas Williams does. Do not be mislead by the at bats since Williams drew 145 walks in 1941 to lead the league (Brett had 58 walks in 1980).

Brett's failure to get a 600 offensive HEQ means that, despite his .390 BA, he did not have a *great* season at bat because he just did not play enough! And his season really does not compare to Williams' since Williams' HEQ is a full 22% better.

Perhaps a better illustration of the shortcomings of the BA as a comparative tool is to indicate that Williams' 1941 season was not his best despite his .406 BA. In 1949 Williams hit .343, not too shabby by any means, but a long way from .406. However, he played in 155 games and tore the cover off the ball to produce his best offensive season with a HEQ of 759 — 14% better than in 1941. Once again demonstrating that the BA is not a valid indicator of how good a season a player had.

It may be even more informative to compare Brett's 1980 season with that of Mike Schmidt who was the MVP in the National League that year. Schmidt hit "only .286" compared to Brett's .390. Some people might think that this makes it obvious that Brett had the better season. But as you can see below, it is not even close. Since both players were third baseman, we give both the offensive and defensive HEQ scores.

		Defensive		*Offensive*		*HEQ*
Schmidt	1980	397	+	624	=	1021
Brett	1980	313	+	547	=	860

As you can see, Schmidt had a great season in 1980 with a HEQ greater than 1000 while Brett's HEQ falls far short of this mark. In fact, Schmidt's HEQ score is 19% better than Brett's. But how is this possible if Brett had a batting average of .390, the best in thirty-nine years? The answer is quite simple and straightforward. Schmidt played in 150 games while Brett played in only 117. And it seems rather obvious to observe that if you have two great players and one plays many more games than the other, then the one who plays more is going to be more productive. Unfortunately, the BA does not necessarily have a direct relationship to a player's offensive effectiveness as these examples illustrate.

The most important lesson here is that Brett's BA of .390 simply means that he got a hit 39% of the time, and that is all it means. The BA was *never designed* to tell us *how good a hitter a player is* but rather how often he gets a hit. Understood in this way the BA can be a valuable *piece* in the puzzle of how good a hitter is. However, when it is used inappropriately, it can be quite misleading.

Another important lesson is that a player cannot have a *truly great season* (a HEQ offensive score of 600 or a total HEQ of 1000) unless he plays enough, no matter how high his BA is. Playing time must be an element in a fair comparison of players' seasons.

As was mentioned in an earlier chapter, an even better illustration of the shortcomings of the BA as an indicator of player effectiveness is to consider the careers of Johnny Bench and Bill Dickey, two HOF catchers.

Consider the following statements:

In 1930 Hall of Fame catcher Bill Dickey had a batting average (BA) of .339.

In 1930 Hall of Fame catcher Bill Dickey had a HEQ score of 540.

Both statements are true. The first might lead a baseball fan to believe that Dickey had quite a good season in 1930. This would be completely misleading and is a good example of the confusion that the batting average can cause.

As soon as the fan becomes acquainted with the HEQ system, he will immediately recognize that a score of 540 means that Dickey had a very disappointing season in 1930. (800 would be a good season and 900 a great season).

The point is that any statistic that is "percentage-based," such as the batting average, the fielding percentage, etc., cannot, by itself, give you a clear idea of how good a season a player had. In fact they can be downright misleading. If you want to *compare* players' seasons, you need a more sophisticated tool.

The problem with a percentage-based statistic is quite simple. All it is intended to tell you is how "frequently" a player does something. A BA of .339 means that if Dickey came to bat in 1930 exactly 1000 times, he would have gotten 339 hits. In reality, he came to bat 366 times and got 124 hits. The BA was never intended to indicate "how good a season" a player had! It is our misuse of this and other statistics that causes some confusion.

The batting average, for example, makes no distinction as to the kind of hit — single, double, triple or home run. Nor does it address in any way other kinds of offensive output such as walks, runs scored, runs batted in or stolen bases. If it is used in some way to compare players' seasons or careers, it is a good example of using the wrong tool for a job.

The concept of the BA has endured since 1874 because it is a simple way of getting a rough idea of how a player is doing at bat during the season. The problem with the concept only arises when someone is inclined to give too much importance to this statistic. It is very tempting to be able to compare the performance of two players by using a *single number* for each.

There is something within us all that yearns for simplicity. Sabermetricians such as Bill James and Pete Palmer have suggested better ways to compare baseball players, but their formulas are quite complicated and difficult to understand even for a mathematician like myself.

Until the present time there has not existed a relatively simple method that produces a single number that tells a fan how good a season a player had, a method that a fan could easily understand and use. Such a system would have to have built into it some fair way to represent a player's hitting accomplishments *and* his fielding accomplishments *and* how much he played during the season.

This last point is extremely important. If Dickey had played 130–140 games in 1930 and batted .339, then his HEQ score probably would have been in the 900 range. But, in fact, he only batted in 109 games and caught 101 games. The percentage-based statistics do not (and cannot) take this point into consideration because they were never intended to do so. And that is their essential shortcoming.

The HEQ system takes all three elements into account: hitting, fielding and playing time and creates a single score to represent each season. And the accuracy of the system is uncanny. For example, in 1937 Dickey batted .332 and had a truly great season because he batted in 140 games and caught 137 games. He had a hitting HEQ of 562 and a fielding HEQ of 396 for a total HEQ of 958 (compared to his 540 in 1930).

Look at the comparison between Dickey's 1930 season and Bench's 1970 season:

Bill Dickey	1930	BA = .339	HEQ offense = 306
Johnny Bench	1970	BA = .293	HEQ offense = 632

You will note that Bench had a great season at bat in 1970 with a HEQ of 632, more than double that of Dickey in 1930. Bench was far more productive even though Dickey batted .339!

Part of the answer lies in the fact that Bench played in 158 games in 1970 and Dickey played in only 109 games in 1930. The BA does not reflect this fact at all, but the HEQ does. And this is one reason why the BA is so inadequate for comparing players.

But is it possible that the BA can be misleading not over a single season but over a player's entire career? This is a more interesting question.

Bill Dickey and Johnny Bench each played for 17 seasons. Dickey batted .313 lifetime while Bench batted .269. What is the conclusion that most fans might reach? There would almost certainly be a "knee-jerk" reaction to say that Dickey's numbers are more impressive. It is almost as if the baseball public has been "brainwashed" into accepting an interpretation of the BA that is totally inappropriate. But anyone who really digs into the numbers will come away with the following conclusion. Bench was by far the more effective player. Consider their career HEQ scores:

	Def.		Off.	HEQ
Johnny Bench	436	+	493	929
Bill Dickey	354	+	426	780

Let us recall once again how it can be that Bench's 17-year BA of .269 could be more productive than Dickey's 17-year BA of .313.

The answer, of course, is that the HEQ score is a sum (not a percentage) and is affected by the number of games played. That is, the more you play the more you produce (assuming that you are a good player). Therefore, the player who plays virtually every day is going to produce more and get a higher HEQ score. And this is as it should be.

Bench averaged 148 games per season for his ten best seasons while Dickey averaged only 123. It is really not too surprising then that Bench's HEQ score of 929 is 19% higher than Dickey's 780.

Bench had four seasons when his offensive HEQ score was better than 500 while Dickey had only one. Bench had eight seasons when his defensive HEQ score was better than 400 while Dickey had only three.

Finally, look at the best offensive and defensive year that each had.

1. The best offensive year:	Bench	1970	632
	Dickey	1937	562
2. The best defensive year:	Bench	1974	502
	Dickey	1933	415

Given these considerations, I hope it is clear that the lifetime BA for these two players is *clearly misleading* as an indicator of who was the more effective player.

The bottom line is that the BA has a role to play as a rough indicator of hitting ability. But we must be careful to use it appropriately. If it is our purpose to *compare players*, then we must measure overall player production in some organized manner as the HEQ does.

The crucial point is that, over his career, Bill Dickey simply did not play enough to be as effective as Bench. It seems reasonable to say that to be a *truly* great player you must *play*!

The Strange Case of "Shoeless Joe" Jackson

Early in 1998 Hall of Famers Ted Williams and Bob Feller re-opened the question as to whether the ban on "Shoeless Joe" Jackson should be lifted and he should be made eligible for consideration for induction into the Hall of Fame. Most fans who follow the history of the game would know that Jackson was banned from consideration for the Hall because of his role in the infamous "Black Sox" scandal of 1919.

My concern about this question has nothing to do with the scandal of 1919. My view is that baseball decided to ban him so baseball can also decide to lift the ban if circumstances appear to warrant this. What I fear is that if the ban is lifted, there may be a "rush to judgment" and an *assumption* that Jackson belongs in the HOF. It seems fair to say that there are few figures in baseball history more surrounded by myth and hype than "Say it ain't so, Joe" Jackson.

My point is that if the ban is lifted, we have to step back and examine Jackson's career and his numbers carefully and ask ourselves whether he truly has HOF numbers or whether another Chick Hafey is about to go into the HOF. In fact, given that he has been banned from the Hall for a long period of time, some may argue that he would need truly outstanding numbers in order to be admitted.

And given the myth that has built up around him over the years, it is surprising to learn that when looked at in a completely objective way, Joe Jackson does not have the numbers to be inducted into the Hall of Fame. That is, even if he had no part whatsoever in the 1919 scandal, his time spent in the major leagues does not justify his election. And this is not directly related to the fact that his career was relatively short. As we will soon see, there have been a number of great players who have established their credentials in the same length of time that Jackson was in the major leagues.

Joe Jackson is probably the best example in baseball history of how misleading the concept of "batting average" can be. The statement that his supporters seem to favor the most is the following: "Joe Jackson has the third highest career batting average in baseball history after Ty Cobb and Rogers Hornsby." The implication of the statement is that this fact somehow establishes his credentials to be considered in the same class as these two great players. Unfortunately for Shoeless Joe, a more careful analysis of his numbers reveals that in no way does he come close to the stature of these superstars.

Using the HEQ system, we can compare Joe Jackson to other players to see just how good his numbers really were. Since the system is based on a player's ten best seasons, the fact that Jackson did not have a long career is not as relevant as it might at first appear.

First, let us compare Jackson's numbers to those of Cobb and Hornsby. The HEQ system ranks Ty Cobb as the eighth most effective player in baseball history and Rogers Hornsby close behind him in tenth place, two of the greatest superstars that the game has ever seen (Babe Ruth is #1 on the HEQ list). There are 105 position players in the HOF who have played in this century. Using the same criteria as was used for these players, Joe Jackson would rank as #93 of 106 players, not good at all.

Here are the numbers:

	Off		*Def*		*HEQ*
1. Babe Ruth	767	+	343	=	1110
8. Ty Cobb	608	+	411	=	1019
10. Rogers Hornsby	625	+	388	=	1013
93. Joe Jackson	461	+	292	=	753

Jackson's career HEQ score of 753 comes out well below the minimum score of 820 considered to be needed to say that a player has HOF numbers.

Joe Jackson is credited with having played thirteen years in the major leagues. There is no doubt that his poor HEQ showing has to do with the fact that he played in 100 or more games in only nine of those seasons. But there have been other players who have played in thirteen or fewer seasons who had sufficient time to establish their credentials for the HOF beyond any doubt. Four such players are Joe DiMaggio, Earl Averill and Hank Greenberg who are in the HOF and Kirby Puckett who is not yet eligible. Consider these career scores:

Joe DiMaggio	13 seasons	613	+	423	=	1036
Earl Averill	13 seasons	582	+	408	=	990
Kirby Puckett	12 seasons	503	+	453	=	956
Hank Greenberg	13 seasons	579	+	328	=	907
Joe Jackson	13 seasons	461	+	292	=	753

Like Jackson, Hank Greenberg only had nine seasons in which he played more than 100 games, but as you can see, Greenberg posted much better numbers.

Even though he played the same number of seasons as these players, Jackson played the least number of games. He had only seven seasons in which he played more than 130 games while Earl Averill, Joe DiMaggio and Kirby Puckett each had ten such seasons. Here are the total number of games that each played: Puckett (1783), DiMaggio (1736), Averill (1668), Greenberg (1394) and Jackson (1332). If Jackson's numbers rivaled Greenberg's, then perhaps a valid argument might be made for his candidacy for the Hall of Fame. But as you can see above they do not.

Joe Jackson's enduring myth is based on his batting average and the fact that he did have a few very good seasons. But the HEQ analysis (which is based on a player's ten best seasons) reveals that he did not have *enough* good seasons to accumulate Hall of Fame numbers. In this sense his career is somewhat similar to Hack Wilson's. Wilson played for only twelve years (1348 games). Like Jackson, he had only nine seasons in which he played more than 100 games. And, like Jackson, he had only a few good seasons. However, his best season (1930) was one of the best of all time when he hit 56 home runs and had 191 RBIs (a record that still stands). He had three 1000 HEQ seasons when Jackson had none. And yet, because he had so few really good seasons, he does not have Hall of Fame numbers. Here is his career HEQ score:

Hack Wilson   478   +   302   =   780

Like Jackson, Hack Wilson falls below the 820 benchmark. However, he is in the Hall of Fame. In fact, of the 105 twentieth century position players in the HOF, twenty-eight (26.7%) fall below the 820 level.

The myth surrounding Shoeless Joe is interesting. Before I looked seriously at the numbers, I had the impression that he was one of the outstanding players of the game. Now I know that his actual production does not justify this. He had only two truly outstanding hitting seasons in which his HEQ offensive score was 600 or more: 1911 = 615 and 1912 = 604 (he also came close in 1920 with a score of 599). Cobb had five such seasons, Hornsby had six, Ted Williams had nine and Hank Aaron had eight — to name just a few.

Jackson had only one 400 defensive season in the outfield. Tris Speaker had ten such seasons, Puckett had seven, DiMaggio had six and even Babe Ruth had three. So his reputation as a good fielder is somewhat questionable.

And finally, Jackson never had a 1000 HEQ season — a truly great all-around season. Willie Mays had ten 1000 seasons, the Babe and Lou Gehrig had nine and Jimmie Foxx had seven.

Joe Jackson may be the best example in baseball history of "unfulfilled potential" (or, perhaps, of "form over substance"). That is, so many people were so sure that he *would be* one of the greats that they convinced themselves and most other people that he really was. But the numbers really do tell the tale. Shoeless Joe failed to live up to his potential, even though, as we have demonstrated above, thirteen seasons should have been enough time to put Hall of Fame numbers into the record books for a truly great player.

If Joe Jackson is elected to the Hall of Fame, it will mark at least the second time in history when myth rather than reality was the key element in the election. In 1946 Joe Tinker, Johnny Evers and Frank Chance were inducted into the Hall essentially on the strength of a poem by F.P. Adams. None of the three had Hall of Fame numbers; in fact, they were not even close! Their career HEQ scores were: Tinker (753), Evers (659) and Chance (572) — well below the 820 level. Tinker is the lowest-ranked shortstop in the Hall of Fame while Evers and Chance are the lowest-ranked second baseman and first baseman respectively.

How does Jackson compare with that other HOF outcast Pete Rose? Here are Pete's numbers:

Pete Rose	507	+	390	=	897
Joe Jackson	461	+	292	=	753

Pete Rose clearly has Hall of Fame numbers while Jackson does not.

How does Shoeless Joe's numbers compare to those of the two players selected by the Veterans Committee in 1998 for induction into the Hall of Fame?

George Davis	474	+	388	=	862
Larry Doby	475	+	373	=	848
Joe Jackson	461	+	292	=	753

Both Davis and Doby have career HEQ scores greater than 820 and have legitimate Hall of Fame numbers.

One last note about Joe Jackson. If one were looking for a modern day candidate for the Hall of Fame with whom to compare Jackson, the numbers indicate that Dwight Evans might be the choice. Look at their career HEQ numbers:

Dwight Evans	491	+	342	=	833
Joe Jackson	461	+	292	=	753

Evans and Jackson were both right fielders. Each player had two 600 offensive seasons among his ten best seasons and no 1000 seasons. The numbers indicate that Evans was a more effective offensive player by thirty points and a more effective defensive player by fifty points. With a HEQ score of 833, Evans has Hall of Fame numbers. Even so, in the 1998 balloting for the Hall, Dwight Evans got only 49 votes (10.4%). His chances for election do not look good.

In conclusion, I am not saying that Joe Jackson should not be in the Hall of Fame. I am saying that he *does not have Hall of Fame numbers*. It may be that those who vote for the inductees will see other factors that will convince them to vote for him. Shoeless Joe's story is the stuff of which legends are made. In his case it appears that the legend may be greater than the ballplayer.

Chapter 11

How Best to Measure the Performance of Baseball Players?

In this chapter I want to mention another player rating system (the Total Player Rating — TPR) and see how this system compares to the HEQ method of comparing the performance of the players. To set the stage for this comparison, let us review briefly why the HEQ was developed.

The basic premise of the HEQ method is that the simplest and fairest way to determine how good a season a player had is to add together his offensive and defensive accomplishments (taking playing time into account) in a consistent and logical manner. And, since many players had virtually no control over the team for which they played, this should be done as independently as possible from the team's statistics.

We all know that if we want to determine who is the career home run king, we simply add up all the home runs that each player hit. Hank Aaron hit 755, so he is number one. What could be more simple or more fair? Whether Aaron played on a championship team is irrelevant to this consideration.

What has been achieved in the HEQ study is to design a relatively simple method of finding the *sum* of a player's accomplishments during a season and representing them by a single number. Then, finding the player's *ten best years* and assigning a "career" score.

So, for example, we can say that Babe Ruth had the ten best years in history with a career score of 1110. Willie Mays was a close second with 1101. (See Appendix A for the HEQ/HOF List.)

Because this method is essentially so simple, understandable and fair, and produces a single number score, it has the potential to replace other statistics as the simplest description of a player's *complete* season or career. When a fan becomes familiar with the HEQ method, he or she will know (better than at the present time) exactly how good a season a particular player had.

For example, when a fan hears that the 1997 National League MVP, Larry Walker, had a season HEQ of 1059 he will know that Walker had a super season. After all, in an eighteen year career, Mickey Mantle only had three 1000 seasons. But when the fan hears that the 1997 American League MVP, Ken Griffey Jr., had a season HEQ of 1142, he will be stunned since this was the greatest season in thirty-five years — since Willie Mays in 1962 (Mantle's highest season was a score of 1118 in 1956).

As I have said previously, the comparison of accomplishments by baseball players is *not an exact science.* That is, there is no right way or wrong way to do this. Different writers and statisticians have suggested various approaches to comparing baseball players and these approaches have been embraced or denounced by others depending on their view of baseball "greatness." A goal of any comparison system should be to produce the simplest *accurate* method so that the average fan can understand what has been done and *replicate* it if he wishes to do so.

Writers such as Bill James and Pete Palmer have made significant contributions to the game through their research into baseball history. The Society for American Baseball Research (SABR) and its many committees are dedicated to advancing the state of baseball knowledge.

What we must keep in mind is that these efforts (especially where they are concerned with the comparison of players' seasons or careers) are simply attempts to shed new light on the existing numbers. That is, the players did what they did — we cannot change that. But we can suggest new ways of looking at what they did in order to make those accomplishments more meaningful to the fans of the game.

For example, some writers and commentators like to point out that even though Aaron is the career home run king, Babe Ruth hit more home runs per-times-at-bat than any other player. Such tidbits of information are generally of interest to fans and do help to put players' accomplishments into an appropriate context. The attempt to develop a whole new approach to examining a player's career is obviously quite a different undertaking.

In this context I hope (and believe) that the HEQ study will shed some new light on how we look at a baseball player's accomplishments. It represents an attempt by a mathematician to return the enjoyment of comparing players' numbers to the fans. A pleasure that some statisticians (by their overly complicated manipulations) may have inadvertently taken from the fans.

Essentially, what the study advocates is that the fairest way to compare players' seasons is by computing a sum of their actual offensive and defensive achievements. Any use of "averages," "percentages" or theoretical "estimates" or "projections" can be misleading. Only the players' *real* numbers such as hits, runs, assists, errors, etc. should be used. Artificially contrived concepts such as "park factor," "runs created" or "wins" tend to favor (and excuse) those players who did not in fact accomplish as much as others.

Only a system that is completely *objective* and *comprehensive* — and based on *real numbers* — can be completely *fair* to the players.

How misleading can some of these statistics be? The batting average certainly represents an objective look at a player's batting performance. However, because it is not a comprehensive statistic, it cannot be used to *compare* performances. One of the better examples of this, which I have mentioned earlier, is the comparison of the 1980 MVP seasons of George Brett and Mike Schmidt.

Both Brett and Schmidt were third basemen who had really good seasons in 1980 and were voted the MVP in their respective leagues. If I told you that Brett hit .390 that season and Schmidt hit .286, you might conclude that Brett had a much better season. But, in fact, the opposite is true. Schmidt had a great season whereas Brett had a very good but not a great season. How can this be?

When we look at the objective scores generated by the HEQ system, we can see this clearly.

Schmidt had an offensive score of 624 + a defensive score of 397 = HEQ score of 1021.

Brett had an offensive score of 547 + a defensive score of 313 = HEQ score of 860.

One of the main differences between Brett and Schmidt in 1980 was that Brett played in only 117 games while Schmidt played in 150. The batting average is not a comprehensive statistic and does not take playing time into account while the HEQ system does. Mike Schmidt was a much more effective player in 1980 than George Brett despite batting averages of .286 compared to .390.

Earlier I made the point that there is no right way or wrong way to measure player performance. Anyone involved in baseball research, particularly in trying to compare the seasons or the careers of the players, is simply trying to shed new light on the accomplishments that the players have put into the record book.

The nature of such research means that there will be times when a new suggested approach (such as the HEQ) will raise questions about an existing approach in order to focus the discussion for other researchers and fans in general. The raising of such questions is, of course, what research of this type is all about.

The author of this study owes a tremendous debt of gratitude to the wonderful, monumental work entitled *Total Baseball — Second Edition* by John Thorn and Pete Palmer. Among other things, their Fielding Register initially helped me to do the in-depth analysis of fielding numbers which is at the heart of the HEQ approach. More than any other single source, this volume has brought me "up to date" regarding the crucial role that sabermetrics has played in baseball research.

But as we know, true progress is made when we are able to stand on the shoulders of giants in order to see more clearly. And, if what we see appears to be in conflict with some of the beliefs of the giants, it is the role of valid research to point that out as clearly as possible.

For example, in 1954 Branch Rickey is reported to have said that "There is nothing on earth anyone can do with fielding." Rickey was a baseball genius, but that does not necessarily mean that he was always right. As I have demonstrated in the HEQ study, it is possible to do something reasonable with defensive numbers beyond what has been attempted in the past, and in so doing shed new light on the accomplishments of the great players.

Now let us look at the approach of using "runs" and "wins" as the best measure of player performance.

In their "Introduction To Part Two" of *Total Baseball*, Thorn and Palmer give a marvelous overview of the role that statistics have played and do play in baseball research. Towards the end of this section they state:

> For everyday position players, add Fielding Runs to Stolen Base Runs toBatting Runs, then convert those combined Runs to Wins, and you havethe best measure of the complete ballplayer: the Total Player Rating [678].

A few pages later the authors state that "because the object of the game is to win, runs are the best measure of player performance, just as they are of team performance at the end of a game"(682). This statement appears at the beginning of the chapter on "Sabermetrics" and points to a problem that I have with this approach to comparing players.

It is true that runs are the best measure of a *team's* performance because runs are a *real* statistic for a team. It is *not* true that runs are the best measure of a *player's* performance because runs are not a real statistic for a player. For a player the concept of runs is essentially a projection. That is, we are not counting the runs (or wins) for which an individual player is, in fact, responsible. Since baseball is a team sport, this is not possible. But rather the concept is based on using real numbers to create projected numbers.

You can *count* the runs that a team produces (just look at the box score) but you cannot count the runs produced (in the sabermetric sense) that a player produces. *Teams* score runs and win games in a sport like baseball, not individual players. To attempt to attribute "wins" to individual players is a stretch of the imagination that is highly questionable and *totally unnecessary*! As with all such "contrived statistics," it tends to cloud the issue of a player's true accomplishments.

No statistic based on percentages or projections can be an appropriate way to *fairly* measure a player's performance or to establish that player's place among the greats of the game.

The only fair way to measure a player's performance is to find the sum of his actual production at bat and in the field in a manner similar to that of the HEQ. The use of percentages, averages or projections may have some relevance in baseball research but *not* in a comparison of players' performances to determine who was better than whom.

As an example of the basis for my concern regarding the TPR, consider the following numbers that Rickey Henderson put into the record books for 1985 and 1990:

Offensive	G	R	H	2B	3B	HR	RBI	BB	SB
1985	143	146	172	28	5	24	72	99	80
1990	136	119	159	33	3	28	61	97	65

Defensive	G	PO	A	E	DP
1985	141	439	7	9	3
1990	118	289	5	5	0

Take a careful look at these offensive and defensive numbers together and decide for yourself whether Henderson had a better year in 1985 or 1990. It seems reasonable to say that, based on his actual numbers, Rickey had a more productive year in 1985 than in 1990. (One important factor is that he only played 118 games in the outfield in 1990.) It would be difficult to imagine how any reasonable fan could examine these numbers and come to any other conclusion. And, as usual, our common sense is accurate. It is only when someone attempts to put an unrealistic spin on the numbers that any other interpretation is possible.

Consider his HEQ scores for the two years:

1985	offensive: 630	+	defensive: 461	=	HEQ: 1091
1990	576	+	299	=	875

As you can see from the actual numbers and the HEQ scores, Henderson had a super year in 1985 and a good year in 1990. His offensive scores for the years are somewhat close, but there is no comparison between his defensive scores. We can see that Henderson can be a very good fielder *when* he plays.

To see just how good a HEQ of 1091 really is, compare it to the scores of these three players who had really good years in 1996. Ken Caminiti and Juan Gonzalez were the MVPs and Alex Rodriguez was the runner-up to Gonzalez.

Ken Caminiti (3B)	offensive: 628	+	defensive: 356	=	HEQ: 984
Juan Gonzalez (OF)	606	+	182	=	788
Alex Rodriguez (SS)	688	+	385	=	1073

All three had great seasons at bat but Gonzalez only played 102 games in the outfield and so his defensive effectiveness is sub-par. (One of the strengths of the HEQ system is that it takes playing time into account.)

Now, here is the problem regarding Henderson's two seasons. Our examination of the numbers tells us that 1985 was a better season than 1990 (and the HEQ score supports this). However, according to *Total Baseball*, in 1985 Henderson contributed 7.1 "extra wins" to his team (wins that an average player would not) while in 1990 he contributed a "whopping 7.7." Thus, making 1990 a better year for Henderson than 1985. (His TPR for 1990 was 8.2 compared to 7.4 for 1985.)

I want to emphasize that I understand quite well where these scores come from even though the manipulations are somewhat complex (I am, after all, a mathematician). The problem is that, in my view, they do not reflect *reality*. In this case at least the TPR has twisted the actual performance of Rickey Henderson into something that it is not. The point is that if you wish to *compare* different seasons, there is *no need* to undergo these mathematical contortions. The HEQ system is both simpler and more accurate.

I believe that I am as open as the next person to being convinced of a point by logical arguments. And I know that baseball numbers can be interpreted in various ways. But I have to say that I cannot conceive of any interpretation of the *actual* numbers that could convince me (or any regular fan) that Rickey Henderson had a "better year" in 1990 than he had in 1985.

The concept of runs (and wins) produced may have some valuable uses in baseball research, but *not* as a tool for *comparing* which player had a better baseball season.

Rickey Henderson's actual production at bat and in the field in 1985 was superior to that of 1990 and no amount of mathematical manipulation of the real numbers is going to produce a convincing argument to the contrary.

The sabermetricians have made some wonderful contributions to baseball research over the past two decades. But, like Branch Rickey in 1954, that does not mean that they are always right!

Chapter 12

Beyond the HEQ — The Best Twelve Years

The HEQ study has examined the careers of the Hall of Fame players by creating a score based on their ten best seasons. An interesting question that arises is: How would the ranking of the top twenty-five players change if we selected twelve instead of ten seasons as the basis for the comparison?

Clearly, every player's numbers will decrease when we include two additional seasons, but some players who were not as consistent as others will decrease proportionately more.

Would it be reasonable to assume that a player who had a longer career would fare better for comparison purposes when the number of seasons is increased? For example, would Richie Ashburn, who played for fifteen years, drop from his #19 ranking to a lower rung? Or would Stan Musial, who played for twenty-two seasons, move up from his rank of #9?

There are some people who may argue that increasing the number of years would begin to separate the "great" from the "greatest." That is, the longer you are able to play at an outstanding level the better you are. And this is, of course, another of those questions that baseball fans will probably enjoy debating.

An interesting example to consider would be to compare the relative positions of Joe DiMaggio and Ty Cobb. DiMaggio slips from #5 to #8 when we consider twelve seasons whereas Cobb moves up from #8 to #7. Does this mean that Cobb was a better player than DiMaggio?

Here is the list of the top twenty-five players in the HOF by career HEQ score for their 10 Best Years.

The columns headed Def, Off, and Total represent the average defense, offense, and total HEQ scores for a player's ten best seasons — where 400 and 600 are great defensive and offensive scores, respectively, and 1000 is an outstanding overall season.

		Def		Off	Total
1. Babe Ruth	RF	343	+	767	1110
2. Willie Mays	CF	456	+	645	1101
3. Lou Gehrig	1B	340	+	750	1090
4. Jimmie Foxx	1B	366	+	686	1052
5. Joe DiMaggio	CF	423	+	613	1036
6. Tris Speaker	CF	484	+	542	1026
7. Charlie Gehringer	2B	432	+	592	1024
8. Ty Cobb	CF	411	+	608	1019
9. Stan Musial	LF	387	+	630	1017
10. Rogers Hornsby	2B	388	+	625	1013
11. Hank Aaron	RF	367	+	628	995
12. Mike Schmidt	3B	415	+	578	993
13. Ted Williams	LF	338	+	655	993
14. Earl Averill	CF	408	+	582	990
15. Mel Ott	RF	379	+	604	983
16. Mickey Mantle	CF	382	+	589	971
17. Max Carey	CF	490	+	480	970
18. Ernie Banks	SS	423	+	545	968
19. Richie Ashburn	CF	529	+	434	963
20. Al Simmons	LF	366	+	596	962
21. Joe Cronin	SS	424	+	530	954
22. Paul Waner	RF	402	+	551	953
23. Goose Goslin	LF	380	+	570	950
24. Honus Wagner	SS	408	+	534	942
25. Eddie Mathews	3B	373	+	565	938

Here is the list of the top twenty-five players by career HEQ score for their 12 Best Years:

		Def		Off	Total
1. Willie Mays	CF	447	+	640	1087
2. Lou Gehrig	1B	345	+	727	1072
3. Babe Ruth	RF	331	+	738	1069
4. Jimmie Foxx	1B	357	+	668	1025
5. Tris Speaker	CF	472	+	531	1003
6. Stan Musial	LF	385	+	616	1001
7. Ty Cobb	CF	399	+	595	994
8. Joe DiMaggio	CF	407	+	582	989
9. Charlie Gehringer	2B	416	+	570	986
10. Hank Aaron	RF	361	+	619	980
11. Mike Schmidt	3B	406	+	570	976
12. Rogers Hornsby	2B	375	+	593	968
13. Mel Ott	RF	371	+	587	958
14. Max Carey	CF	476	+	463	939
15. Al Simmons	LF	366	+	573	939
16. Ted Williams	LF	313	+	625	938
17. Ernie Banks	SS	409	+	527	936
18. Mickey Mantle	CF	356	+	575	931
19. Paul Waner	RF	391	+	538	929

		Def	*Off*	*Total*
20. Joe Cronin	SS	419 +	509	928
21. Goose Goslin	LF	371 +	556	927
22. Honus Wagner	SS	396 +	530	926
23. Richie Ashburn	CF	500 +	422	922
24. Eddie Mathews	3B	373 +	549	922
25. Brooks Robinson	3B	446 +	453	899

Let us examine the two lists and see what happens to the top twenty-five players.

1. Only six players have achieved a career HEQ score of 1000 over twelve seasons compared to ten players who did it over ten seasons. Obviously, the more seasons that are included the more difficult it will be to sustain this level of achievement.

2. Perhaps the most significant change is that Willie Mays and Lou Gehrig move ahead of Babe Ruth at the top of the list. This appears to be a further indication that although Ruth is unquestionably the best hitter of all time, Mays may be the greatest player of all time. Of course, we must point out that Ruth spent the first few years of his major league career as an outstanding pitcher before converting to a full time outfielder.

It should be noted that Mays' HEQ score dropped by only 14 points (1.3%) compared to Ruth whose score fell 41 points (3.7%).

The other three players whose scores fell relatively little are Gehrig (18 points = 1.65%), Ty Cobb (17 points = 1.68%) and Stan Musial (19 points = 1.85%). Mays, Musial and Cobb each played for 22 or more seasons while Gehrig played for 17 seasons.

3. The most dramatic change occurs to Earl Averill. He is #14 on the HEQ/10 year list and is not in the top 25 on the HEQ/12 year list. He played only thirteen seasons and only in eleven of those did he play in more than 100 games. So when we consider the twelve best seasons, he is more seriously affected than anyone else. His HEQ score dropped by 114 points (11.5%).

All the other players remain in the top 25.

4. The only new addition to the HEQ/12 year list is Brooks Robinson at #25.

5. There is only one player whose ranking does not change at all and that is Jimmie Foxx at #4.

6. Here are the players whose rankings have increased:

	HEQ/10	*HEQ/12*	*Years played*
Willie Mays	2	1	22
Lou Gehrig	3	2	17
Tris Speaker	6	5	22
Ty Cobb	8	7	24

	HEQ/10	*HEQ/12*	*Years played*
Stan Musial	9	6	22
Hank Aaron	11	10	23
Mike Schmidt	12	11	18
Mel Ott	15	13	22
Max Carey	17	14	20
Al Simmons	20	15	20
Ernie Banks	18	17	19
Paul Waner	22	19	20
Joe Cronin	21	20	20
Goose Goslin	23	21	18
Honus Wagner	24	22	21
Eddie Mathews	25	24	17
Brooks Robinson		25	23

7. Here are the players whose rankings have decreased:

	HEQ/10	*HEQ/12*	*Years played*
Babe Ruth	1	3	22
Joe DiMaggio	5	8	13
Charlie Gehringer	7	9	19
Rogers Hornsby	10	12	23
Ted Williams	12	16	19
Earl Averill	14		13
Mickey Mantle	16	18	18
Richie Ashburn	19	23	15

8. The players whose rankings increased played an average of 20.5 seasons. Those whose rankings decreased played an average of 17.75 seasons.

9. Note that on the HEQ/10 list three players average better than 600 offensive and 400 defensive: Willie Mays, Joe DiMaggio and Ty Cobb, the most complete players of all time.

However, only one player accomplishes this feat on the HEQ/12 list: Willie Mays. It appears that if we are talking consistency over time, Mays begins to stand out even more.

10. Eleven players have an offensive score of 600 or more on the HEQ/10 list while only seven achieve this distinction on the HEQ/12 list: Willie Mays, Babe Ruth, Jimmie Foxx, Lou Gehrig, Stan Musial, Hank Aaron and Ted Williams.

11. Thirteen players have a defensive score of 400 or more on the HEQ/10 list while the number drops to ten on the HEQ/12 list: Willie Mays, Tris Speaker, Joe DiMaggio, Charlie Gehringer, Mike Schmidt, Max Carey, Ernie Banks, Joe Cronin, Richie Ashburn and Brooks Robinson.

Chapter 13

The HEQ/Hall of Fame Candidates List

How Do They Compare?

Who belongs in the Hall of Fame is one of those topics that many fans love to discuss at great length. Some fans have their personal favorites and cannot understand why they have not yet been inducted. Others are indignant that a particular player came so close but did not make it. And, of course, there are players who are still playing whom some observers believe are "a shoo-in for the HOF."

In this chapter we will examine some of these players according to the HEQ system and the guidelines that were outlined in chapter 9. And we will determine which players appear to be the strongest candidates *by their numbers alone.*

First, let us review the guidelines that we established for determining who had HOF numbers:

Group A — the player's career HEQ is 920 or above. These are the truly great effective players.

Group B — the player's career HEQ is between 860 and 919. Very effective players who clearly have HOF numbers.

Group C — the player's career HEQ is between 820 and 859. Questionable HOF numbers — especially in the lower range. Some other justification for election to the HOF (other than performance numbers) may be needed.

Group D — the player's career HEQ is lower than 820. Does not have HOF performance numbers. Some other justification for election to the HOF is clearly needed.

You may recall that when I speak of "other justification," it means that it is possible that a player might have some other quality or achievement that a voter considers significant enough to justify a positive vote even though the player does not have HOF numbers. Winning an MVP award, winning a number of Gold Gloves or repeated selection to the All Star team might be such achievements. We assume that there are other reasons why voters do vote for players whose numbers do not measure up. Otherwise, there would be far fewer players in the HOF.

We saw that there are twenty-nine players in Group A (28%) and another twenty-six players in Group B (25%) on the HEQ/HOF List. These fifty-five players were distributed by position as follows: 9 right fielders, 9 center fielders, 9 shortstops, 8 second basemen, 7 left fielders, 7 first basemen, 4 third basemen and 2 catchers.

The following list of "HOF candidates" is composed of different groups. There are twelve players who finished with more than 5% of the vote in the 1997 balloting. These are designated on our list by an asterisk (*). There are others who will become eligible over the next few years and who are listed on the major league baseball web site. There are a few players like Pete Rose, Gil Hodges and Orlando Cepeda who are retired for a number of years and are not on any current HOF list but who some observers believe should be in the HOF. And finally there are those players who are still playing like Cal Ripken Jr. who are not yet eligible but who many observers believe will be elected when their turn comes.

This list makes no pretense at being complete. Some fans will certainly come up with the names of players whom they feel should be on the list. One of the advantages of the HEQ system is that any fan can take the formulas and calculate the career HEQ score for any player who has been inadvertently omitted.

Once again I wish to emphasize the truly *objective nature* of the HEQ system. I am not suggesting that these scores alone indicate whether a player should be in the Hall of Fame. But it may be significant to see whether the numbers alone help to differentiate the candidates.

Consider the career HEQ scores for the following group of players and compare them to the list of Hall of Famers on the HEQ/HOF List in Appendix A. This format is identical to that one. Remember that the career scores are based on the *10 best seasons* for each player. Therefore, a player has to have completed at least ten seasons to be considered. Keep in mind that an active player such as Barry Bonds may yet improve on his scores. (The following list is updated through the end of the 1998 season.)

The numbers to the right indicate how many 400 defensive seasons, 600 offensive seasons and 1000 HEQ seasons each player had in his ten best seasons.

		Def		*Off*		*Total*	*400*	*600*	*1000*
Cal Ripken	SS	465	+	529	=	994	10	1	4
Kirby Puckett	CF	453	+	503	=	956	7	2	4

		Def		Off		Total	400	600	1000
Barry Bonds	LF	348	+	606	=	954	1	6	3
Eddie Murray	1B	416	+	538	=	954	7	0	2
Ron Santo*	3B	431	+	520	=	951	6	0	3
Rickey Henderson	LF	379	+	551	=	930	3	2	3
Robin Yount	SS	416	+	512	=	928	6	1	2
Keith Hernandez*	1B	440	+	485	=	925	9	0	2
Gary Carter	C	474	+	450	=	924	10	0	1
Ryne Sandberg	2B	407	+	517	=	924	6	1	2
Rafael Palmeiro	1B	394	+	529	=	923	4	3	3
Dale Murphy	CF	382	+	534	=	916	5	3	2
Vada Pinson	CF	387	+	524	=	911	3	0	2
Pete Rose	LF	390	+	507	=	897	4	0	0
Andre Dawson	LF	387	+	508	=	895	5	2	1
Gil Hodges	1B	376	+	519	=	895	3	1	2
George Brett	3B	364	+	528	=	892	3	2	2
Ken Boyer	3B	387	+	504	=	891	2	0	0
Dave Winfield	RF	350	+	538	=	888	2	1	1
Graig Nettles	3B	437	+	441	=	878	7	0	0
Steve Garvey*	1B	371	+	500	=	871	2	0	0
Orlando Cepeda	1B	337	+	533	=	870	0	1	0
Joe Torre*	C	408	+	460	=	868	6	1	0
Tony Perez*	1B	361	+	504	=	865	1	1	0
Don Mattingly	1B	364	+	500	=	864	1	2	2
Dave Parker*	RF	344	+	518	=	862	1	1	1
Minnie Minoso*	LF	349	+	507	=	856	1	0	1
Wade Boggs	3B	357	+	493	=	850	3	0	0
Jim Rice*	LF	282	+	561	=	843	3	1	1
Ozzie Smith	SS	465	+	378	=	843	10	0	0
Dwight Evans*	RF	342	+	491	=	833	0	2	0
Carlton Fisk	C	403	+	426	=	829	4	0	0
Al Oliver	CF	352	+	471	=	823	1	0	0
Tony Gwynn	RF	347	+	474	=	821	1	0	0
Willie Wilson	CF	396	+	424	=	820	4	0	1
Bobby Grich	2B	411	+	403	=	814	5	0	0
Dick Allen*	1B	292	+	519	=	811	0	1	0
Alan Trammell	SS	372	+	439	=	811	2	0	0
Dave Concepcion*	SS	418	+	390	=	808	8	0	0
Lou Whitaker	2B	362	+	439	=	801	1	0	0
Bill Mazeroski	2B	444	+	356	=	800	8	0	0
Steve Sax	2B	371	+	420	=	791	1	0	0
Curt Flood	CF	402	+	387	=	789	7	0	0
Paul Molitor	3B	217	+	536	=	753	2	1	0
Joe Jackson	RF	292	+	461	=	753	0	2	0
Willie Randolph	2B	370	+	382	=	752	2	0	0
Jack Clark	LF	304	+	442	=	746	0	0	0
Tony Oliva	LF	256	+	476	=	732	0	1	0
Carney Lansford	3B	303	+	414	=	717	0	0	0
Pedro Guerrero	1B	283	+	428	=	711	0	0	0
Bob Boone*	C	419	+	283	=	702	7	0	0
Kirk Gibson	LF	214	+	394	=	608	0	0	0

There are fifty-two players on this list of HOF candidates. They are distributed by position as follows: ten first basemen, six second basemen, five shortstops, seven third basemen, six center fielders, seven right fielders, seven left fielders and four catchers.

Here is the distribution of the candidates in Groups A, B, C and D mentioned above:

Group A — the truly great effective players — have HOF numbers — eleven players (21%): Cal Ripken, Eddie Murray, Keith Hernandez, Kirby Puckett, Ron Santo, Gary Carter, Barry Bonds, Robin Yount, Rickey Henderson, Ryne Sandberg and Rafael Palmeiro.

Group B — very effective players — have HOF numbers — fifteen players (29%): Dale Murphy, Vada Pinson, Don Mattingly, Pete Rose, Andre Dawson, George Brett, Ken Boyer, Dave Winfield, Joe Torre, Graig Nettles, Dave Parker, Orlando Cepeda, Gil Hodges, Tony Perez and Steve Garvey.

Group C — marginal HOF numbers — nine players (17%): Minnie Minoso, Wade Boggs, Jim Rice, Ozzie Smith, Dwight Evans, Carlton Fisk, Al Oliver, Tony Gwynn and Willie Wilson.

Group D — do not have HOF numbers — seventeen players (33%): Bobby Grich, Alan Trammell, Dave Concepcion, Dick Allen, Lou Whitaker, Bill Mazeroski, Steve Sax, Curt Flood, Paul Molitor, Joe Jackson, Willie Randolph, Jack Clark, Tony Oliva, Carney Lansford, Bob Boone, Pedro Guererro and Kirk Gibson.

When you consider that there are fifty-five players (52%) on the HEQ/ HOF List who have Group A or B numbers, it is significant to note that there are twenty-six players (50%) on this list who have such numbers.

Here are the lists of the ten most effective hitters and the ten most effective fielders from our list of candidates:

The Ten Most Effective Hitters

	Off. HEQ	*# of 600 seasons*
Barry Bonds	606	6
Jim Rice	561	1
Rickey Henderson	551	2
Eddie Murray	538	0
Dave Winfield	538	1
Paul Molitor	536	1
Dale Murphy	534	3
Orlando Cepeda	533	1
Rafael Palmeiro	529	3
Cal Ripken	529	1

In chapter 3 I gave the list of the 25 most effective offensive players in the HOF. Note that Barry Bonds at 606 is the 11th most effective hitter of all time. In fact, there have only been twelve players in history who have been able to average a 600 offensive score over ten seasons.

The Ten Most Effective Fielders

		Def. HEQ	*# of 400 seasons*
Gary Carter	C	474	10
Ozzie Smith	SS	465	10
Cal Ripken	SS	465	10
Kirby Puckett	CF	453	7
Bill Mazeroski	2B	444	8
Keith Hernandez	1B	440	9
Graig Nettles	3B	437	7
Ron Santo	3B	431	6
Bob Boone	C	419	7
Dave Concepcion	SS	418	8

Note that there are a number of outstanding fielders on our list of HOF candidates. Three of these players are the *most effective* fielders at their respective positions when compared to current Hall of Famers. Bill Mazeroski at second base, Keith Hernandez at first base and Gary Carter at catcher have HEQ defensive scores better than anyone on the HEQ/HOF List. Ozzie Smith at 465.4 and Cal Ripken at 464.5 are the most effective fielders at shortstop behind Rabbit Maranville at 471. Graig Nettles at 437 and Ron Santo at 431 are the most effective fielders at third base behind Brooks Robinson at 451. And Eddie Murray at 416 is the most effective fielder at first base behind Hernandez.

In chapter 4 we saw that only nine HOFs had a 400 defensive HEQ in ten different seasons. There are three players on our list who have accomplished this: Gary Carter, Ozzie Smith and Cal Ripken.

Perhaps the biggest fielding surprise of all is Kirby Puckett. He always had a reputation as a good fielder, but I did not realize exactly how good. His defensive HEQ of 453 is only three points behind Willie Mays at 456, making him the fourth most effective outfielder in the twentieth century.

Note that the only candidate on *both* the offensive and defensive top ten lists, a truly effective complete player, is Cal Ripken. Eddie Murray just misses the defensive list.

If you examine our list of candidates closely, a number of other observations come to mind:

1. Ron Santo is the Group A player who has waited longest to be elected to the Hall of Fame. Why is he not there already? As we have pointed out

previously, his numbers are clearly outstanding. In fact he would be #23 on the present HEQ/HOF List. He may be the most under-rated player of the sixties and seventies. He emerges as the second best third baseman in history (after Mike Schmidt) and his accomplishments are comparable to such greats as Joe Cronin and Paul Waner. I suspect that he has not yet been inducted into the Hall of Fame because no clearly objective criterion such as the HEQ has been available until now to point out a player's true numbers.

Vada Pinson is another very effective player (HEQ = 911) who has been passed over for selection to the HOF. How to explain this when players like Reggie Jackson (HEQ = 821), Willie McCovey (HEQ = 792) and Willie Stargell (HEQ = 745) were all *first round* selections? Is it home run power or media hype that is responsible for such anomalies? Or is it simply that the voters do not have appropriate information when voting?

2. You will note from the HEQ/HOF List that only ten players in history have achieved a HEQ career score of 1000 or more. Chronologically, Willie Mays and Stan Musial were the last to do so. This gives us some appreciation of the incredible all-around ability of Cal Ripken (994) who would be #12 on the HOF list with this score.

Cal Ripken emerges as the greatest all-around shortstop to ever play the game, supplanting Ernie Banks in this respect.

Only three players in history have accumulated both 3000 hits and 500 home runs: Hank Aaron, Willie Mays and Eddie Murray. Now, that's impressive!

3. Note that six of the candidates had three or more 1000 seasons: Ripken, Kirby Puckett, Barry Bonds, Ron Santo, Rickey Henderson and Rafael Palmeiro. When you consider that Mickey Mantle had only three such seasons in his eighteen year career, you can begin to appreciate the significance of this achievement.

4. Keep in mind that some of these players are still active and have the potential to improve further on these scores. Certainly Bonds and Palmeiro can reasonably be expected to do so. Speaking of Bonds, you can see that his offensive HEQ of 606 is the best of this group. As mentioned above, it would rank him as #11 on the HEQ/HOF List of the most effective hitters.

You will note that despite his six Gold Gloves, Bonds is just an average fielder at best (HEQ defensive score of 348). It appears that, as in the case of Roberto Clemente who had twelve Gold Gloves, the voters are making the award on the basis of all-around ability and not on fielding ability alone. Note that Babe Ruth, who was an average outfielder, had a defensive HEQ of 343. Yet Ruth had three different seasons with a defensive HEQ over 400 while Clemente and Bonds only had one each.

This is the essential beauty of a truly objective measuring tool like the HEQ. It cuts through all the hype and myth and shows us what the numbers themselves reveal.

5. At the end of 1997 both Tony Gwynn and Wade Boggs had each played for sixteen seasons and had career batting averages over .330: Gwynn at .340 and Boggs at .331. This is very impressive. However, it is significant to note that their career HEQ scores are lower than many other players with much lower batting averages, a further indication of the limited role that the batting average can play in evaluating the performance of players.

6. Kirby Puckett only played for twelve years. He is the best example on this list of a player who established his credentials with both his bat and his glove in a relatively short period of time as major league careers go. Joe DiMaggio, who played for only thirteen seasons, is another dramatic example.

7. Paul Molitor is the only example on the list of a really good hitter having a poor HEQ fielding score *mainly because* he was used so much as a designated hitter. He is one of only twenty players in this century to accumulate 3000 hits and six of them are on this list. The other five are Pete Rose (the all-time hit leader with 4256), Eddie Murray, George Brett, Robin Yount and Dave Winfield. The fact that Molitor does not come out higher in terms of his HEQ score is precisely one of the important strengths of the HEQ system — that is, to differentiate between the *complete player* and the good hitter or the good fielder.

8. Three other players on our list, Jack Clark, Tony Oliva and Kirk Gibson have their HEQ defensive score negatively affected by having been designated hitters at times. However, unlike Molitor, none of these players has the offensive numbers to be considered a really good hitter.

9. Bob Boone is an example of perhaps just the opposite type of player than Molitor — that is, a "good field/poor hit" type of player reminiscent of Ray Schalk. His defensive HEQ as a catcher is better than anyone except Gary Carter, Schalk and Johnny Bench but his offensive production is the lowest on our list.

The HEQ numbers that the HOF candidates put into the record book lead us to ask the following two questions:

1. How significant is Barry Bonds' HEQ offensive average of 606?

There are only eleven players in the Hall of Fame who have achieved this distinction — Hank Aaron having been the last to play (1976). Note from the HEQ/HOF List that each of these players had at least five 600 seasons. Also note that Mickey Mantle, who had five 600 seasons, does *not* have a career offensive score greater than 600. Just look at the names of the ten players ahead of Bonds on the list: Ruth, Gehrig, Foxx, Williams, Mays, Musial, Aaron, Hornsby, DiMaggio and Cobb. Quite a Who's Who of offensive talent.

2. Will we ever see another player who will have a career HEQ greater than 1000?

As noted previously, only ten Hall of Famers have ever averaged a 1000 career HEQ over ten seasons. However, since Cal Ripken has come close (HEQ score of 994), it seems reasonable to be optimistic that someone may achieve this distinction in the future. In order to do this, however, the player will almost certainly have to be an outstanding fielder with a HEQ defensive score better than 400.

Ken Griffey Jr. would appear to be the active player with the best shot at reaching a career HEQ of 1000. In 1997 he had the best all-around season HEQ in thirty-five years (since Willie Mays in 1962) with a HEQ score of 424 + 718 = 1142. In 1998 he had another incredible season: 450 + 711 = 1161. He already has two other 1000 seasons with 1000 in 1993 and 1090 in 1996. If he keeps improving like this, who knows?

In order to put the players from our list of HOF candidates into an appropriate perspective take a look at how they compare by position with the players on the HEQ/HOF List. The players who are candidates for the HOF are in italics.

Catchers

	Def		Off		Total	400	600	1000
Johnny Bench	436	+	493	=	929	8	1	2
Gary Carter	474	+	450	=	924	10	0	1
Yogi Berra	399	+	469	=	868	8	0	1
Joe Torre	408	+	460	=	868	6	1	0
Carlton Fisk	403	+	426	=	829	4	0	0
Mickey Cochrane	348	+	435	=	783	1	0	0
Bill Dickey	354	+	426	=	780	3	0	0
Roy Campanella	363	+	384	=	747	2	1	1
Ray Schalk	457	+	264	=	721	8	0	0
Gabby Hartnett	336	+	377	=	713	0	0	0
Bob Boone	419	+	283	=	702	7	0	0
Roger Bresnahan	330	+	280	=	610	2	0	0
Rick Ferrell	310	+	297	=	607	0	0	0
Ernie Lombardi	258	+	320	=	578	0	0	0

Johnny Bench emerges as the most effective catcher of this century with Gary Carter second. Bench and Yogi Berra are the most effective offensive catchers. However, since none of the catchers has a 500 offensive HEQ, none can be said to be a truly effective hitter.

All four of the candidates have a defensive HEQ greater than 400 and can be considered great defensive catchers. It should be noted that Joe Torre played more games behind the plate than any other position (903) but he also played a considerable number of games at first (787) and third (515). So, he may not be considered a "pure catcher" as the others were.

Gary Carter is the only candidate in Group A while Joe Torre is the only one in Group B.

Only these two of the four catchers clearly have HOF numbers. Carlton Fisk at 829 is the only catcher in Group C and can be said to have marginal HOF numbers. However, he is the fifth most effective catcher on our list.

First Basemen

Lou Gehrig	340 + 750 =	1090	0	10	9
Jimmie Foxx	366 + 686 =	1052	1	9	7
Eddie Murray	*416 + 538 =*	*954*	*7*	*0*	*2*
Keith Hernandez	*440 + 485 =*	*925*	*9*	*0*	*2*
Rafael Palmeiro	*394 + 529 =*	*923*	*4*	*3*	*3*
Bill Terry	393 + 528 =	921	5	2	3
George Sisler	387 + 525 =	912	3	3	2
Hank Greenberg	328 + 579 =	907	1	5	5
Gil Hodges	376 + 519 =	895	3	1	2
Johnny Mize	333 + 549 =	882	1	4	2
Steve Garvey	*371 + 500 =*	*871*	*2*	*0*	*0*
Orlando Cepeda	*337 + 533 =*	*870*	*0*	*1*	*0*
Tony Perez	*361 + 504 =*	*865*	*1*	*1*	*0*
Harmon Killebrew	303 + 561 =	864	0	1	1
Don Mattingly	*364 + 500 =*	*864*	*1*	*2*	*2*
Jim Bottomley	317 + 517 =	834	0	3	0
Dick Allen	*292 + 519 =*	*811*	*0*	*1*	*0*
George Kelly	363 + 442 =	805	4	0	0
Willie McCovey	312 + 488 =	800	1	1	1
Pedro Guererro	*283 + 428 =*	*711*	*0*	*0*	*0*
Frank Chance	245 + 327 =	572	0	0	0

Eddie Murray, Keith Hernandez and Rafael Palmeiro are the third, fourth and fifth most effective first basemen behind Lou Gehrig and Jimmie Foxx. They are the only three Group A candidates among the first basemen. Gil Hodges, Tony Perez, Steve Garvey, Don Mattingly and Orlando Cepeda are all Group B candidates. Dick Allen and Pedro Guererro are both in Group D.

Eight of the first base candidates have a HEQ offensive score greater than 500 and can be considered very effective offensive players: Eddie Murray, Orlando Cepeda, Dick Allen, Gil Hodges, Rafael Palmeiro, Tony Perez, Steve Garvey and Don Mattingly.

Only two have a HEQ defensive score of 400 or more and can be considered truly effective defensive players: Keith Hernandez and Eddie Murray.

Second Basemen

Charlie Gehringer	432 + 592 =	1024	10	4	7
Rogers Hornsby	388 + 625 =	1013	5	6	6
Ryne Sandberg	407 + 517 =	924	6	1	2
Frankie Frisch	409 + 506 =	915	6	0	2
Joe Morgan	382 + 527 =	909	3	2	1
Bobby Doerr	425 + 482 =	907	8	0	1
Eddie Collins	384 + 521 =	905	4	0	0
Nap Lajoie	372 + 503 =	875	3	1	1
Billy Herman	427 + 434 =	861	7	0	0
Nellie Fox	433 + 424 =	857	10	0	0
Red Schoendienst	419 + 423 =	842	8	0	0
Tony Lazzeri	361 + 479 =	840	2	0	0
Rod Carew	364 + 470 =	834	2	1	1
Bobby Grich	411 + 403 =	814	5	0	0
Lou Whitaker	362 + 439 =	801	1	0	0
Bill Mazeroski	444 + 356 =	800	8	0	0
Jackie Robinson	342 + 456 =	796	2	1	1
Steve Sax	371 + 420 =	791	1	0	0
Willie Randolph	370 + 382 =	752	2	0	0
Johnny Evers	322 + 337 =	659	0	0	0

Ryne Sandberg emerges as the third most effective second baseman of this century behind Charlie Gehringer and Rogers Hornsby. He is the only second base candidate in Group A and there are no other candidates in Group B or C. The other five candidates are all in Group D.

Only Sandberg of the five candidates has an offensive HEQ greater than 500 and can be considered a very effective offensive player.

Bill Mazeroski, Bobby Grich and Sandberg all have defensive HEQ scores above 400 and are great defensive second basemen. In fact, Mazeroski is the most effective fielding second baseman of the century.

Shortstops

Cal Ripken	465 + 529 =	994	10	1	4
Ernie Banks	423 + 545 =	968	8	4	5
Joe Cronin	424 + 530 =	954	8	1	2
Honus Wagner	408 + 534 =	942	6	0	2
Robin Yount	416 + 512 =	928	6	1	2
Arky Vaughan	417 + 485 =	902	6	0	1
Joe Sewell	437 + 460 =	897	9	0	0
Luke Appling	442 + 450 =	892	10	0	1
PeeWee Reese	420 + 445 =	865	7	0	0
George Davis	388 + 474 =	862	4	0	0
Rabbit Maranville	471 + 391 =	862	10	0	0
Lou Boudreau	435 + 408 =	843	8	0	1
Ozzie Smith	465 + 378 =	843	10	0	0

Luis Aparicio	442 + 400 =	842	10	0	0
Bobby Wallace	422 + 401 =	823	8	0	0
Travis Jackson	420 + 400 =	820	6	0	1
Alan Trammell	*372 + 439 =*	*811*	*2*	*0*	*0*
Dave Concepcion	*418 + 390 =*	*808*	*8*	*0*	*0*
Dave Bancroft	445 + 362 =	807	9	0	2
Phil Rizzuto	423 + 360 =	783	6	0	0
Joe Tinker	400 + 353 =	753	4	0	0

Cal Ripken emerges as the most effective shortstop of this century and Robin Yount as the fifth most effective. They are the only two shortstop candidates in Group A and there is no candidate in Group B. Ozzie Smith is in Group C while Alan Trammell and Dave Concepcion are in Group D.

Both Ripken and Yount have offensive HEQ scores greater than 500 and can be considered very effective hitters.

Ozzie Smith with a HEQ defensive score of 465.4 is the second most effective fielding shortstop of this century behind Rabbit Maranville. Cal Ripken at 464.5 is close behind Smith. Dave Concepcion and Robin Yount also have defensive HEQs greater than 400 and were also great defensive shortstops.

Third Basemen

Mike Schmidt	415 + 578 =	993	6	2	6
Ron Santo	*431 + 520 =*	*951*	*6*	*0*	*3*
Eddie Mathews	373 + 565 =	938	0	0	2
Brooks Robinson	451 + 462 =	913	10	0	0
George Brett	*364 + 528 =*	*892*	*3*	*2*	*2*
Ken Boyer	*387 + 504 =*	*891*	*2*	*0*	*0*
Graig Nettles	*437 + 441 =*	*878*	*7*	*0*	*0*
Pie Traynor	392 + 484 =	876	4	0	1
Frank Baker	402 + 451 =	853	6	1	1
Wade Boggs	*357 + 493 =*	*850*	*3*	*0*	*0*
Jimmy Collins	395 + 437 =	832	5	0	0
George Kell	366 + 391 =	757	4	0	1
Paul Molitor	*217 + 536 =*	*753*	*2*	*1*	*0*
Freddy Lindstrom	327 + 420 =	747	3	1	0
Carney Lansford	*303 + 414 =*	*717*	*0*	*0*	*0*

Ron Santo is the only third base candidate in Group A. He is the second most effective third baseman in this century after Mike Schmidt. George Brett, Ken Boyer and Craig Nettles are all Group B players while Wade Boggs is in the upper end of Group C. Paul Molitor and Carney Lansford are in Group D.

Molitor, Brett, Santo and Boyer all have offensive HEQ scores of 500 or better and were very effective hitters.

Graig Nettles and Ron Santo were both great defensive third basemen. Only Brooks Robinson, the most effective fielding third baseman of this century, had a defensive HEQ better than these two.

Paul Molitor (who has the best offensive HEQ in this group of candidates) is included among the third basemen only because he played more games at this position than at any other position. As mentioned above, he was a very effective hitter and his defensive HEQ score is affected by his having been a designated hitter at times.

Center Fielders

Willie Mays	456 + 645 =	1101	9	9	10
Joe DiMaggio	423 + 613 =	1036	6	5	6
Tris Speaker	484 + 542 =	1026	10	3	4
Ty Cobb	411 + 608 =	1019	4	5	4
Earl Averill	408 + 582 =	990	4	6	4
Mickey Mantle	382 + 589 =	971	5	5	3
Max Carey	490 + 480 =	970	10	0	3
Richie Ashburn	529 + 434 =	963	10	0	3
Kirby Puckett	*453 + 503 =*	*956*	*7*	*2*	*4*
Duke Snider	368 + 562 =	930	3	4	4
Dale Murphy	*381 + 534 =*	*915*	*5*	*3*	*2*
Vada Pinson	*387 + 524 =*	*911*	*3*	*0*	*2*
Larry Doby	373 + 475 =	848	2	0	1
Lloyd Waner	429 + 410 =	839	7	0	2
Al Oliver	*352 + 471 =*	*823*	*1*	*0*	*0*
Edd Roush	389 + 431 =	820	4	0	0
Willie Wilson	*396 + 424 =*	*820*	*4*	*0*	*1*
Earle Combs	347 + 467 =	814	3	0	0
Hack Wilson	325 + 470 =	795	2	3	3
Curt Flood	*402 + 387 =*	*789*	*7*	*0*	*0*

Of the center field candidates, only Kirby Puckett is a Group A player. Dale Murphy and Vada Pinson are both very strong Group B candidates. Al Oliver and Willie Wilson are close together in Group C while Curt Flood is the only center field candidate in Group D.

Three of these candidates have offensive HEQ scores of 500 or greater and were very effective hitters: Dale Murphy, Vada Pinson and Kirby Puckett.

Only Kirby Puckett and Curt Flood had HEQ defensive scores better than 400 and could be considered great defensive center fielders — although Willie Wilson at 396 came very close.

Right Fielders

Babe Ruth	343 + 767 =	1110	3	10	9
Hank Aaron	367 + 628 =	995	2	8	4
Mel Ott	379 + 604 =	983	4	7	4
Paul Waner	402 + 551 =	953	5	3	2

Frank Robinson	341 + 584 =	925	1	3	1
Sam Rice	413 + 492 =	905	6	0	1
Kiki Cuyler	373 + 524 =	897	3	2	3
Pete Rose	*390 + 507 =*	*897*	*4*	*0*	*0*
Chuck Klein	337 + 552 =	889	3	5	4
Dave Winfield	*350 + 538 =*	*888*	*2*	*1*	*1*
Al Kaline	357 + 507 =	864	3	0	1
Dave Parker	*344 + 518 =*	*862*	*1*	*1*	*1*
Harry Heilmann	305 + 548 =	853	1	2	0
Dwight Evans	*342 + 491 =*	*833*	*0*	*2*	*0*
Roberto Clemente	339 + 486 =	825	1	0	0
Tony Gwynn	*347 + 474 =*	*821*	*1*	*0*	*0*
Reggie Jackson	288 + 533 =	821	0	1	0
Enos Slaughter	338 + 483 =	821	1	0	0
Sam Crawford	298 + 507 =	805	0	0	0
Willie Keeler	285 + 505 =	790	0	2	0
Harry Hooper	344 + 422 =	766	0	0	0
Elmer Flick	297 + 463 =	760	0	0	0
Joe Jackson	*292 + 461 =*	*753*	*0*	*2*	*0*
Willie Stargell	258 + 490 =	748	0	1	0
Ross Youngs	280 + 387 =	667	0	0	0
Kirk Gibson	*214 + 394 =*	*608*	*0*	*0*	*0*

There are no Group A players among the right field candidates. Pete Rose, Dave Winfield and Dave Parker are all Group B level candidates. Dwight Evans and Tony Gwynn are in Group C while Joe Jackson and Kirk Gibson are both in Group D.

All three Group B candidates have a HEQ offensive score greater than 500 and were very effective hitters: Dave Winfield, Dave Parker and Pete Rose.

None of the seven right field candidates has a HEQ defensive score better than 400 and therefore none of them can be considered to be a great defensive player.

Left Fielders

Stan Musial	387 + 630 =	1017	4	6	5
Ted Williams	338 + 655 =	993	0	9	5
Al Simmons	366 + 596 =	962	3	4	4
Barry Bonds	*348 + 606 =*	*954*	*1*	*6*	*3*
Goose Goslin	380 + 570 =	950	3	4	3
Rickey Henderson	*379 + 551 =*	*930*	*3*	*2*	*3*
Joe Medwick	358 + 549 =	907	1	3	3
Carl Yastrzemski	364 + 533 =	897	1	2	0
Andre Dawson	*387 + 508 =*	*895*	*5*	*2*	*1*
Billy Williams	301 + 566 =	867	0	2	0
Ralph Kiner	321 + 537 =	858	1	4	2
Minnie Minoso	*349 + 507 =*	*856*	*1*	*0*	*1*

Jim Rice	*282*	+ *561*	=	*843*	*3*	*1*	*1*
Zack Wheat	371	+ 466	=	837	3	0	0
Heinie Manush	326	+ 501	=	827	0	1	0
Lou Brock	286	+ 534	=	820	0	0	0
Fred Clarke	356	+ 462	=	818	1	0	0
Jack Clark	*304*	+ *442*	=	*746*	*0*	*0*	*0*
Tony Oliva	*256*	+ *476*	=	*732*	*0*	*1*	*0*
Chick Hafey	267	+ 400	=	667	1	0	0

Barry Bonds and Rickey Henderson are the only Group A players among the left field candidates while Andre Dawson is in Group B. Minnie Minoso and Jim Rice are both in Group C while Jack Clark and Tony Oliva are Group D candidates.

There are five very effective hitters among the seven left field candidates: Barry Bonds (606), Jim Rice (561), Rickey Henderson (551), Andre Dawson (508) and Minnie Minoso (507).

There are no great defensive players among the left field candidates since no one has a HEQ defensive score greater than 400.

It seems apparent from this analysis that a number of the players who are candidates for the Hall of Fame compare quite favorably with the players already enshrined there — where their performance numbers are concerned.

But let me repeat once again that I am not suggesting that a player's numbers should be the only criterion or even the most important criterion for induction into the Hall of Fame. What I am suggesting, however, is that a truly objective tool like the HEQ system may have some value in determining who should be elected.

Chapter 14

Comparing the Players from the First Half to the Second Half of the Century

The First Half — 1900–1949
The Second Half — 1950–1998

The HEQ/HOF List in Appendix A contains the names and numbers for the 105 position players in the HOF who have played since 1900. Appendix B contains the same information for the 52 players on the *HOF Candidates List* that we discussed in chapter 13.

In this chapter we will examine the Group A, B and C players from the two lists (that is, HEQ > 820) and indicate the most effective players in each half of the 20th century. If any player spanned both eras, then he will be included in that time span in which the majority of his ten best seasons occurred. Ted Williams, for example, had eight of his ten best seasons by 1949 so he will be included in the first half of the century. Stan Musial split his ten best between the two eras but played more years after 1949 than before. So he will be counted in the second half.

As in Appendix A and B, we give the career defensive and offensive scores as well as the total career HEQ score (based on the player's ten best seasons). In addition, we indicate the number of 400 defensive seasons, 600 offensive seasons and 1000 HEQ seasons.

The First Half — 1900–1949

		Def	*Off*		*Total*	*400*	*600*	*1000*
1. Babe Ruth	RF	343	+ 767	=	1110	3	10	9
2. Lou Gehrig	1B	340	+ 750	=	1090	0	10	9

		Def Off		*Total*	*400*	*600*	*1000*
3.	Jimmie Foxx	1B	366 + 686 =	1052	1	9	7
4.	Joe DiMaggio	CF	423 + 613 =	1036	6	5	6
5.	Tris Speaker	CF	484 + 542 =	1026	10	3	4
6.	Charlie Gehringer	2B	432 + 592 =	1024	10	4	7
7.	Ty Cobb	CF	411 + 608 =	1019	4	5	4
8.	Rogers Hornsby	2B	388 + 625 =	1013	5	6	6
9.	Ted Williams	LF	338 + 655 =	993	0	9	5
10.	Earl Averill	CF	408 + 582 =	990	4	6	4
11.	Mel Ott	RF	379 + 604 =	983	4	7	4
12.	Max Carey	CF	490 + 480 =	970	10	0	3
13.	Al Simmons	LF	366 + 596 =	962	3	4	4
14.	Joe Cronin	SS	424 + 530 =	954	8	1	2
15.	Paul Waner	RF	402 + 551 =	953	5	3	2
16.	Goose Goslin	LF	380 + 570 =	950	3	4	3
17.	Honus Wagner	SS	408 + 534 =	942	6	0	2
18.	Bill Terry	1B	393 + 528 =	921	5	2	3
19.	Frankie Frisch	2B	409 + 506 =	915	6	0	2
20.	George Sisler	1B	387 + 525 =	912	3	3	2
21.	Bobby Doerr	2B	425 + 482 =	907	8	0	1
22.	Hank Greenberg	1B	328 + 579 =	907	1	5	5
23.	Joe Medwick	LF	358 + 549 =	907	1	3	3
24.	Eddie Collins	2B	384 + 521 =	905	4	0	0
25.	Sam Rice	RF	413 + 492 =	905	6	0	1
26.	Arky Vaughan	SS	417 + 485 =	902	6	0	1
27.	Kiki Cuyler	RF	373 + 524 =	897	3	2	3
28.	Joe Sewell	SS	437 + 460 =	897	9	0	0
29.	Luke Appling	SS	442 + 450 =	892	10	0	1
30.	Chuck Klein	RF	337 + 552 =	889	3	5	4
31.	Johnny Mize	1B	333 + 549 =	882	1	4	2
32.	Pie Traynor	3B	392 + 484 =	876	4	0	1
33.	Nap Lajoie	2B	372 + 503 =	875	3	1	1
34.	George Davis	SS	388 + 474 =	862	4	0	0
35.	Rabbit Maranville	SS	471 + 391 =	862	10	0	0
36.	Billy Herman	2B	427 + 434 =	861	7	0	0
37.	Frank Baker	3B	402 + 451 =	853	6	1	1
38.	Harry Heilmann	RF	305 + 548 =	853	1	2	0
39.	Lou Boudreau	SS	435 + 408 =	843	8	0	1
40.	Tony Lazzeri	2B	361 + 479 =	840	2	0	0
41.	Lloyd Waner	CF	429 + 410 =	839	7	0	2
42.	Zack Wheat	LF	371 + 466 =	837	3	0	0
43.	Jim Bottomley	1B	317 + 517 =	834	0	3	0
44.	Jimmy Collins	3B	395 + 437 =	832	5	0	0
45.	Heinie Manush	LF	326 + 501 =	827	0	1	0
46.	Bobby Wallace	SS	422 + 401 =	823	8	0	0
47.	Enos Slaughter	RF	338 + 483 =	821	1	0	0
48.	Travis Jackson	SS	420 + 400 =	820	6	0	1
49.	Edd Roush	CF	389 + 431 =	820	4	0	0
	Average score:		391 + 525 =	916			

As you can see from the first-half list, there are forty-nine position players in the HOF who played their careers primarily from 1900 to 1949 *and* who have a career HEQ of 820 or greater. There are sixty-two players on the second-half list who have played from 1950 to the present and who are either in the HOF or on our list of candidates and have a similar HEQ score.

It is important to note that there may be other players who played in the majors for at least ten seasons and who have a career HEQ of 820 or greater and who are not on either of the lists in Appendix A or B. We have not examined the credentials of every player who played in the twentieth century — only those who are in the HOF or who are considered prime candidates for the Hall.

There are a few observations that we might make about the distribution of the players by position on the two lists:

1. There are no catchers at all on the first-half list which means that no catcher in the first half of the century had a career HEQ of 820 or greater. There are five catchers on the second-half list with a career HEQ score better than 820. As I mentioned earlier, this is due (at least in part) to the fact that in the second half of the century the best catchers actually played more than their earlier predecessors.

2. Eleven of the players on the second-half list (17.7%) are shortstops or second basemen. More than twice that percentage (eighteen players = 36.7%) played those positions on the first-half list.

3. There are only three third basemen on the first-half list (6.12%) but eight (12.9%) on the second-half list.

The Second Half — 1950–1998

		Def		*Off*		*Total*	*400*	*600*	*1000*
1. Willie Mays	CF	456	+	645	=	1101	9	9	10
2. Stan Musial	LF	387	+	630	=	1017	4	6	5
3. Hank Aaron	RF	367	+	628	=	995	2	8	4
4. Cal Ripken	SS	465	+	529	=	994	10	1	4
5. Mike Schmidt	3B	415	+	578	=	993	6	2	6
6. Mickey Mantle	CF	382	+	589	=	971	5	5	3
7. Ernie Banks	SS	423	+	545	=	968	8	4	5
8. Richie Ashburn	CF	529	+	434	=	963	10	0	3
9. Kirby Puckett	CF	453	+	503	=	956	7	2	4
10. Barry Bonds	LF	348	+	606	=	954	1	6	3
11. Eddie Murray	1B	416	+	538	=	954	7	0	2
12. Ron Santo	3B	431	+	520	=	951	6	0	3
13. Eddie Mathews	3B	373	+	565	=	938	0	2	2
14. Rickey Henderson	LF	379	+	551	=	930	3	2	3
15. Duke Snider	CF	368	+	562	=	930	3	4	4
16. Johnny Bench	C	436	+	493	=	929	8	1	2
17. Robin Yount	SS	416	+	512	=	928	6	1	2

		Def		Off	Total	400	600	1000
18. Keith Hernandez	1B	440	+	485 =	925	9	0	2
19. Frank Robinson	RF	341	+	584 =	925	1	3	1
20. Gary Carter	C	474	+	450 =	924	10	0	1
21. Rafael Palmeiro	1B	394	+	529 =	924	4	3	3
22. Ryne Sandberg	2B	407	+	517 =	924	6	1	2
23. Dale Murphy	CF	381	+	534 =	915	5	3	2
24. Brooks Robinson	3B	451	+	462 =	913	10	0	0
25. Vada Pinson	CF	387	+	524 =	911	3	0	2
26. Joe Morgan	2B	382	+	527 =	909	3	2	1
27. Carl Yastrzemski	LF	364	+	533 =	897	1	2	0
28. Pete Rose	LF	390	+	507 =	897	4	0	0
29. Andre Dawson	LF	387	+	508 =	895	5	2	1
30. Gil Hodges	1B	376	+	519 =	895	3	1	2
31. George Brett	3B	364	+	528 =	892	3	2	2
32. Ken Boyer	3B	387	+	504 =	891	3	0	0
33. Dave Winfield	RF	350	+	538 =	888	2	1	1
34. Graig Nettles	3B	437	+	441 =	878	7	0	0
35. Steve Garvey	1B	371	+	500 =	871	2	0	0
36. Orlando Cepeda	1B	337	+	533 =	870	0	1	0
37. Yogi Berra	C	399	+	469 =	868	8	0	1
38. Joe Torre	C	408	+	460 =	868	6	1	0
39. Billy Williams	LF	301	+	566 =	867	0	2	0
40. Tony Perez	1B	361	+	504 =	865	1	1	0
41. PeeWee Reese	SS	420	+	445 =	865	7	0	0
42. Al Kaline	RF	357	+	507 =	864	3	0	1
43. Harmon Killebrew	1B	303	+	561 =	864	0	1	1
44. Don Mattingly	1B	364	+	500 =	864	1	2	2
45. Dave Parker	RF	344	+	518 =	862	1	1	1
46. Ralph Kiner	LF	321	+	537 =	858	1	4	2
47. Nellie Fox	2B	433	+	424 =	857	10	0	0
48. Minnie Minoso	LF	349	+	507 =	856	1	0	1
49. Wade Boggs	3B	357	+	493 =	850	3	0	0
50. Larry Doby	CF	373	+	475 =	848	4	0	0
51. Jim Rice	LF	282	+	561 =	843	3	1	1
52. Ozzie Smith	SS	465	+	378 =	843	10	0	0
53. Luis Aparicio	SS	442	+	400 =	842	10	0	0
54. Red Schoendienst	2B	419	+	423 =	842	8	0	0
55. Rod Carew	2B	364	+	470 =	834	2	1	1
56. Dwight Evans	RF	342	+	491 =	833	0	2	0
57. Carlton Fisk	C	403	+	426 =	829	4	0	0
58. Roberto Clemente	RF	339	+	486 =	825	1	0	0
59. Al Oliver	CF	352	+	471 =	823	1	0	0
60. Reggie Jackson	RF	288	+	533 =	821	0	1	0
61. Lou Brock	LF	286	+	534 =	820	0	0	0
62. Willie Wilson	CF	396	+	424 =	820	4	0	1
Average score of top 49 players:		392	+	523 =	915			

It is remarkable how close the average scores are for the forty-nine players on the first-half list compared to the top forty-nine on the second-half list:

First-half — 1900–1949:   391 +   525 =   916
Second-half — 1950–1998:   392 +   523 =   915

It is true that the list of the top fifty seasons of the century has a majority of seasons before 1950, but this is due in large part to the dominance of a few players such as Babe Ruth, Lou Gehrig, Jimmie Foxx and Hank Greenberg (see chapter 5).

On the other hand, it is informative to note that of the twenty players who have accumulated 3000 hits, fourteen of them have played in the second half of the century and only six during the first half. Of the fifteen players who have hit 500 or more home runs, eleven have played in the second half and only four during the first half. And the three players who have accomplished *both* feats have all played during the second half: Hank Aaron, Willie Mays and Eddie Murray.

Therefore, it seems reasonable to question whether the quality of the best players has changed significantly from the first half of the twentieth century to the second half.

The First Half — the 15 Most Effective Offensive Players

1.	Babe Ruth	RF	767
2.	Lou Gehrig	1B	750
3.	Jimmie Foxx	1B	686
4.	Ted Williams	LF	655
5.	Rogers Hornsby	2B	625
6.	Joe DiMaggio	CF	613
7.	Ty Cobb	CF	608
8.	Mel Ott	RF	604
9.	Al Simmons	LF	596
10.	Charlie Gehringer	2B	592
11.	Earl Averill	CF	582
12.	Hank Greenberg	1B	579
13.	Goose Goslin	LF	570
14.	Paul Waner	RF	551
15.	Chuck Klein	RF	552
	Average offensive HEQ		622

Note that there are no third basemen, shortstops or catchers among the fifteen most effective hitters of the first half of the century.

The Second Half — the 15 Most Effective Offensive Players

1.	Willie Mays	CF	645
2.	Stan Musial	LF	630

3.	Hank Aaron	RF	628
4.	Barry Bonds	LF	606
5.	Mickey Mantle	CF	589
6.	Frank Robinson	RF	584
7.	Mike Schmidt	3B	578
8.	Billy Williams	LF	566
9.	Eddie Mathews	3B	565
10.	Duke Snider	CF	562
11.	Harmon Killebrew	1B	561
12.	Jim Rice	LF	561
13.	Rickey Henderson	LF	551
14.	Ernie Banks	SS	545
15.	Eddie Murray	1B	538
	Dave Winfield	RF	538
	Average offensive HEQ		578

There are no catchers or second basemen among the fifteen most effective hitters of the second half of the century. And the average offensive HEQ of 622 for the fifteen best from the first half is clearly superior to that of 578 for the fifteen best from the second half.

The First Half — the 15 Most Effective Defensive Players

1.	Max Carey	CF	490
2.	Tris Speaker	CF	484
3.	Rabbit Maranville	SS	471
4.	Luke Appling	SS	442
5.	Joe Sewell	SS	437
6.	Lou Boudreau	SS	435
7.	Charlie Gehringer	2B	432
8.	Lloyd Waner	CF	429
9.	Billy Herman	2B	427
10.	Bobby Doerr	2B	425
11.	Joe Cronin	SS	424
12.	Joe DiMaggio	CF	423
13.	Bobby Wallace	SS	422
14.	Travis Jackson	SS	420
15.	Arky Vaughan	SS	417
	Average defensive HEQ		439

Note that there are no catchers, third basemen or first basemen among the fifteen most effective fielders for the first half of the century. And eight of the fielders (more than 50%) are shortstops.

The Second Half — the 15 Most Effective Defensive Players

1.	Richie Ashburn	CF	529
2.	Gary Carter	C	474
3.	Ozzie Smith	SS	465
4.	Cal Ripken	SS	465
5.	Willie Mays	CF	456
6.	Kirby Puckett	CF	453
7.	Brooks Robinson	3B	451
8.	Luis Aparicio	SS	442
9.	Keith Hernandez	1B	440
10.	Graig Nettles	3B	437
11.	Johnny Bench	C	436
12.	Nellie Fox	2B	433
13.	Ron Santo	3B	431
14.	Ernie Banks	SS	423
15.	PeeWee Reese	SS	420
	Average defensive HEQ		450

Besides having a higher average defensive HEQ, the fifteen most effective fielders from the second half of the century are much more evenly distributed: three outfielders, two catchers, one first basemen, one second basemen, five shortstops and three third basemen.

We will now take a look at the HEQ/All Star Teams (first and second teams) for the first half and the second half of the century. For each team, we simply choose the players at each position who have the highest career HEQ score. Clearly there is room for debate here. For example, a fan might argue that Ty Cobb should be on the first team. However, there are three outfielders who have higher career HEQ scores than Cobb so he is on the second team.

The HEQ/All Star Team: 1900–1949

First Team

Babe Ruth	RF	343	+	767	=	.	1110
Lou Gehrig	1B	340	+	750	=		1090
Joe DiMaggio	CF	423	+	613	=		1036
Tris Speaker	CF	484	+	542	=		1026
Charlie Gehringer	2B	432	+	592	=		1024
Joe Cronin	SS	424	+	530	=		954
Pie Traynor	3B	392	+	484	=		876
Mickey Cochrane	C	348	+	435	=		783
			Average HEQ				987

Second Team

Jimmie Foxx	1B	366	+	686	=	1052
Ty Cobb	CF	411	+	608	=	1019

Rogers Hornsby	2B	388 + 625	=	1013
Ted Williams	LF	338 + 655	=	993
Mel Ott	RF	379 + 604	=	983
Honus Wagner	SS	408 + 534	=	942
Frank Baker	3B	402 + 451	=	853
Bill Dickey	C	354 + 426	=	780
		Average HEQ		954

Since there are no catchers among the 49 players on the first half list, we have to choose the two most effective catchers from the HEQ/HOF List in Appendix A.

When you examine the two teams, it would not surprise me if some fans would conjecture that the second team might beat the first team in a series of any length.

It is interesting to compare the average HEQ scores for the all-star teams from the first half and the second half of the century. The first team from the second half has a better average HEQ than that of the first team from the first half (988 versus 987). But the opposite is true for the second teams (954 versus 947).

The HEQ/All Star Team: 1950–1998

First Team

Willie Mays	CF	456 + 645	=	1101
Stan Musial	LF	387 + 630	=	1017
Hank Aaron	RF	367 + 628	=	995
Cal Ripken	SS	465 + 529	=	994
Mike Schmidt	3B	415 + 578	=	993
Eddie Murray	1B	416 + 538	=	954
Gary Carter	C	474 + 450	=	924
Ryne Sandberg	2B	407 + 517	=	924
		Average HEQ		988

Second Team

Keith Hernandez	1B	440 + 485	=	925
Mickey Mantle	CF	382 + 589	=	971
Ernie Banks	SS	423 + 545	=	968
Richie Ashburn	CF	529 + 434	=	963
Kirby Puckett	CF	453 + 503	=	956
Ron Santo	3B	431 + 520	=	951
Johnny Bench	C	436 + 493	=	929
Joe Morgan	2B	382 + 527	=	909
		Average HEQ		947

Note that the first team from 1950 to 1998 is the only one of the four teams where every player is a Group A player (HEQ > 920).

Keep in mind that these teams are put together strictly by the numbers, the total HEQ score. If I were actually choosing a team that had to *play,* I am not sure that I would choose, for example, Richie Ashburn over Frank Robinson.

Perhaps the strangest development of all in comparing the players from the first half of the century to the second half is that there are no Group A, B or C catchers who played from 1900 to 1949. In addition, there are only three third baseman in any of these groups (Pie Traynor, Frank Baker and Jimmy Collins). The five most effective catchers and the seven most effective third baseman all played during the second half of the century.

Chapter 15

The MVP Awards —
A Look at the
Players' Numbers

The MVP award is intended to honor the player in each league who is the "most valuable player" for that season. Voters may define this term for themselves in slightly different ways and that presumably is their prerogative. The assumption seems to be that the writers who do the voting have the expertise to make such judgments. But there is one point that I assume few people would contest. And that is that the voters should have as much information as possible about the candidates so that they can make the most informed decision.

In this chapter we will look at the MVP awards for the 1996 season and analyze the players' numbers according to the HEQ system for comparing players. We will see whether the player with the "best performance numbers" won the award or whether another player with lesser numbers was considered to be the most valuable player.

We will be dealing exclusively with a player's performance numbers — both offensive and defensive. By doing this I do not wish to imply that the numbers alone should decide who should be named the MVP. There are other considerations which voters may weigh in deciding who they feel is the most valuable. But I have to wonder whether some of the decisions that have been made in the past were due to the fact that the voters did not have the information available *in an appropriate manner* to make a fully informed decision. How else to explain the fact that in 1996 neither of the MVP awards was won by the best performer in the league for that year. The voters appeared not to realize how well some players had done. And I believe that this was due, at least in part, to the fact that an understandable and accurate rating system for comparing the players simply did not exist. The HEQ rating system tells us simply and directly who had the best numbers each season and this information should be available to anyone who wishes to decide who was the MVP in each league.

The 1996 MVP Awards

The 1996 MVP awards went to Ken Caminiti of the San Diego Padres of the National League and Juan Gonzalez of the Texas Rangers of the American League. Both players had solid seasons but the awards certainly did not go to the player in each league who had the best season. That is, it is clear that there were players in each league who had better numbers than Caminiti or Gonzalez. Of course, someone may argue (based on his own view of the situation) that despite other players having better numbers, Caminiti and Gonzalez were still the "most valuable."

Here are the HEQ scores for the top ten vote-getters in each league. If I have found other players with a HEQ score better than 1000, I have included them and indicated their placement in the MVP voting. (Recall that under the HEQ rating system an offensive score of 600 is considered an outstanding offensive season, a defensive score of 400 a great season in the field and a total HEQ of 1000 a super all-around season.)

American League — HEQ season score for the top MVP vote-getters in 1996:

	Off	Def		HEQ
1. Juan Gonzalez	606	+ 182	=	788
2. Alex Rodriquez	688	+ 385	=	1073
3. Albert Belle	708	+ 333	=	1041
4. Ken Griffey Jr.	662	+ 428	=	1090
5. Mo Vaughn	681	+ 295	=	976
6. Rafael Palmeiro	650	+ 426	=	1076
7. Mark McGwire	584	+ 256	=	840
8. Frank Thomas	630	+ 339	=	969
9. Brady Anderson	655	+ 379	=	1034
10. Ivan Rodriguez	528	+ 467	=	995
11. Ken Lofton	600	+ 420	=	1020

National League — HEQ season score for the top MVP vote-getters in 1996:

	Off	Def		HEQ
1. Ken Caminiti	628	+ 356	=	984
2. Mike Piazza	541	+ 447	=	988
3. Ellis Burks	725	+ 301	=	1026
4. Chipper Jones	599	+ 290	=	889
5. Barry Bonds	685	+ 318	=	1003
6. Andres Galarraga	683	+ 434	=	1117

7.	Gary Sheffield	649 + 258	=	907
8.	Brian Jordan	471 + 341	=	812
9.	Jeff Bagwell	644 + 421	=	1065
10.	Steve Finley	619 + 407	=	1026

In the American League, based on the numbers alone, it is difficult to imagine how anyone could have voted for Juan Gonzalez over the other players on the list *if* they were aware of the complete contribution of the player to his team. But, of course, that is the problem. It is doubtful that the voters had the information in the appropriate format to see that at least seven other players had more effective seasons than Gonzalez. It is also possible that a voter may be defining "most valuable" in such a manner that he feels comfortable in voting for a player even though he knows that there are a number of other players in his league who had better numbers. It is possible — but quite a stretch. It is more likely that we are dealing with a lack of information.

Gonzalez came to bat in 134 games and played in the field in only 102 games. He did not even have a great season by HEQ standards (a 900 HEQ score at least) whereas a number of other players had super seasons. (One of the strong features of the HEQ rating system is its ability to separate the *complete player* from the one-dimensional player.) Does anyone else feel that unless a position player plays both ways he should not be considered seriously for the MVP award? How can someone be the "most valuable player" if he only plays part-time in the field?

As if the situation in the American League were not bad enough, consider for a moment that a similar scenario took place in the National League where at least six other players had more effective seasons than Ken Caminiti. However, since Caminiti did have a very effective season (984), his selection is not quite as surprising.

Let us look at the two players who had 700 offensive seasons in 1996 (Ellis Burks and Albert Belle) and the player who had a HEQ season of 1100 (Andres Galarraga). It is true that some baseball observers would attribute (at least in part) the outstanding offensive seasons of Burks and Galarraga to the "park factor" involved in Coors Field in Denver. However important this may be, the fact remains that the numbers are impressive.

A 700 Offensive Season

To appreciate how impressive a 700 offensive season is, consider the following:

1. By the end of the 1996 season there had only been seven 700 offensive seasons since 1950 and two of them occurred in 1996. Here they are:

Mickey Mantle	1956	704
Willie Mays	1962	710
Frank Robinson	1962	706
Jim Rice	1978	702
Barry Bonds	1993	709
Albert Belle	1996	708
Ellis Burks	1996	725

2. Only seventeen Hall of Famers have ever had a HEQ offensive season of 700 or better. These seventeen players had forty-one such seasons among them, and six players accounted for thirty of these seasons. Those who had multiple 700 seasons are Babe Ruth (9), Lou Gehrig (7), Jimmie Foxx (4), Hank Greenberg (4), Rogers Hornsby (3) and Chuck Klein (3).

Ellis Burks' 725 offensive HEQ was the best (up to that time) in the second half of the twentieth century since Ted Williams had an offensive score of 759 in 1949. In fact, it was the 32nd best offensive season of all time. And Albert Belle's offensive HEQ score of 708 was quite an accomplishment also since it represented the fourth best since 1950.

In case you are curious, here are the 25 best offensive seasons in history through 1996:

1. Babe Ruth	1921	894
2. Lou Gehrig	1927	836
3. Lou Gehrig	1931	833
4. Jimmie Foxx	1932	819
5. Babe Ruth	1927	815
6. Hack Wilson	1930	815
7. Chuck Klein	1930	804
8. Lou Gehrig	1930	799
9. Rogers Hornsby	1922	793
10. Lou Gehrig	1936	790
11. Babe Ruth	1923	782
12. Jimmie Foxx	1938	777
13. Lou Gehrig	1936	776
14. Hank Greenberg	1937	776
15. Joe DiMaggio	1937	771
16. Babe Ruth	1920	771
17. Rogers Hornsby	1929	760
18. Babe Ruth	1930	760
19. Chuck Klein	1932	759
20. Ted Williams	1949	759
21. Babe Ruth	1928	757
22. Babe Ruth	1931	755
23. Ty Cobb	1911	746
24. Stan Musial	1948	742
25. Jimmie Foxx	1933	741

An 1100 HEQ Season

Andres Galarraga's season total of 1117 in 1996 is very impressive. He certainly had the most effective numbers in the majors for the season. An 1100 HEQ season is the ultimate accomplishment of the complete ballplayer. A player must hit very well *and* have a great season in the field. It might be interesting to note that Mickey Mantle, in an eighteen year career, had only one 1100 season (1956) and had only two other 1000 seasons. And Hank Aaron never had an 1100 season at all even though he had four 1000 seasons.

From 1950 to 1996, only six players ever had an 1100 season. Here are those ten seasons:

			Off	Def		HEQ
Willie Mays	CF	1954	647 +	522	=	1169
Willie Mays	CF	1955	696 +	515	=	1211
Mickey Mantle	CF	1956	704 +	414	=	1118
Willie Mays	CF	1957	651 +	480	=	1131
Willie Mays	CF	1958	637 +	487	=	1124
Willie Mays	CF	1962	710 +	449	=	1159
Johnny Bench	C	1970	632 +	473	=	1105
Kirby Puckett	CF	1988	606 +	508	=	1114
Cal Ripken Jr.	SS	1991	614 +	486	=	1100
Andres Galarraga	1B	1996	683 +	462	=	1145

You will note that Willie Mays owns five of the ten seasons and his 1955 HEQ score of 1211 is the highest on this list. In baseball history there have only been two 1300 seasons and six 1200 seasons.

So, Galarraga's season, whether or not his hitting was inordinately helped by playing in Coors Field, was a significant achievement.

It is obvious from these numbers that the 1996 season was an extraordinary one. At least eleven different players had a HEQ score of 1000 — an amazing feat (just check the lists in Appendix A and B and see how many players in the HOF or candidates for that honor never had a single 1000 season). In light of these comments, ask yourself whether Ken Caminiti and Juan Gonzalez would have been voted the "most valuable players" in 1996 if the voters had more information of this type available to them when they cast their ballots.

As a final note and to put the 1996 season into context, consider the HEQ scores for the top three vote-getters in each of the MVP elections from 1990 to 1995. Remember that the 1994 and 1995 seasons were affected by the strike and the scores for those seasons reflect this fact. You can judge for yourself whether the HEQ scores for 1996 are within a "normal range" for a season or whether they represent unusually high productivity on the part of a number of players. At the same time, decide for yourself whether you think the correct person won the award in each of these years. (If I have found other 1000 HEQ scores in any of these seasons, I have included them.)

The 1995 MVP Awards

American League:

		Off	Def		HEQ
1.	Mo Vaughn	585 +	358	=	943
2.	Albert Belle	666 +	324	=	990
3.	Edgar Martinez	617 +	2	=	619

National League:

1.	Barry Larkin	490 +	319	=	809
2.	Dante Bichette	613 +	238	=	851
3.	Greg Maddux	pitcher			

The 1994 MVP Awards

American League:

1.	Frank Thomas	555 +	193	=	748
2.	Ken Griffey	515 +	277	=	792
3.	Kenny Lofton	494 +	336	=	830

National League:

1.	Jeff Bagwell	568 +	340	=	908
2.	Matt Williams	458 +	277	=	735
3.	Moises Alou	437 +	211	=	648

The 1993 MVP Awards

American League:

1.	Frank Thomas	627 +	331	=	958
2.	Paul Molitor	617 +	49	=	666
3.	John Olerud	603 +	341	=	944
	Rafael Palmeiro	619 +	460	=	1079
	Albert Belle	611 +	420	=	1031
	Ken Griffey Jr.	646 +	354	=	1000

National League:

	Off		Def		HEQ
1. Barry Bonds	709	+	328	=	1037
2. Len Dykstra	618	+	457	=	1075
3. Dave Justice	553	+	357	=	910
Mike Piazza	526	+	489	=	1015

The 1992 MVP Awards

American League:

1. Dennis Eckersley	pitcher				
2. Kirby Puckett	566	+	436	=	1002
3. Joe Carter	556	+	295	=	851

National League:

1. Barry Bonds	610	+	320	=	930
2. Terry Pendleton	530	+	397	=	927
3. Gary Sheffield	539	+	347	=	886
Andy Van Slyke	543	+	467	=	1010

The 1991 MVP Award

American League:

1. Cal Ripken Jr.	614	+	486	=	1100
2. Cecil Fielder	594	+	309	=	903
3. Frank Thomas	592	+	181	=	773

National League:

1. Terry Pendleton	515	+	391	=	906
2. Barry Bonds	570	+	371	=	941
3. Bobby Bonilla	533	+	363	=	896

The 1990 MVP Awards

American League:

1. Rickey Henderson	576	+	299	=	875
2. Cecil Fielder	620	+	377	=	997
3. Roger Clemens	pitcher				

National League:

		Off	Def		HEQ
1.	Barry Bonds	610 +	390	=	1000
2.	Bobby Bonilla	583 +	332	=	915
3.	Daryl Strawberry	531 +	318	=	849

Note that a HEQ score of 1000 or more is not nearly as common as the 1996 season may have led you to believe. Of the thirty-eight scores given here (presumably the "best" players during these seasons), only ten (26%) are greater than 1000. As mentioned above, Mickey Mantle only had three 1000 seasons in an eighteen year career. In fact, Willie Mays is the only player in history to have ten 1000 seasons.

Did the "most valuable player" win the award each year? You can decide that for yourself. But I do believe that it is rather obvious how valuable it would be for the voters to have this sort of comparative information available in order to make the most informed decision when they cast their ballot for the MVP.

Chapter 16

The Gold Glove Awards — A Look at the Players' Numbers

The Best Fielders of the Past Forty Years

The Gold Glove awards are given each year to the outstanding fielder at each position in each league. When the first awards were announced in the December 18, 1957, issue of *The Sporting News,* it was explained that the selections were made solely on the basis of defensive ability. But right from the start critics maintained that two problems got in the way of the awards: too much importance given to fielding average and batting performance was often counted.

This is perfectly understandable to some extent since the voters had no systematic way to measure defensive ability alone. But now the HEQ rating system is available to help to distinguish the great fielding performances. No longer should extraneous factors such as fielding average, offensive production, reputation or hype obscure the actual fielding performance.

A good example of this occurred during that first selection process in 1957. In that first year of the awards only one GG was awarded at each position, not one in each league as in every year since. Willie Mays was awarded the GG as the best defensive center fielder. Far be it from me to take away from the defensive prowess of Willie Mays. As we have discussed in earlier chapters, Mays was the greatest all-around player to ever play the game and the fourth greatest defensive outfielder in history. And so, under ordinary circumstances, he would have been the obvious choice since he had a defensive HEQ score of 480 in 1957 (an absolutely fabulous fielding season), the fourth best of Mays' long and illustrious career.

But, as fate would have it, the greatest defensive player of all time (at any position) was having the second greatest defensive season of his absolutely incredible defensive career — in center field. In 1957 Richie Ashburn had a defensive

HEQ of 588 (108 points higher than Mays). As great a center fielder as Mays was, Ashburn was even better. Mays had two 500 HEQ defensive seasons in his career while Ashburn had *eight*. No one else in the HOF had more than four.

Ashburn was in the twilight of his career in 1957 and he never won a GG. This was really a shame because it would have given some recognition to his fabulous defensive ability. But he was up against the awesome offensive production and the much deserved reputation of Willie Mays. But in 1957 Ashburn was the best defensive center fielder in baseball.

Having begun in this vein, you may be thinking that I am going to conclude that the GG awards have not fulfilled their intent. But actually I am going to demonstrate just the opposite. That is, if you examine the players who have won at least four GG (which we will do), you find that indeed, in most cases, they were all truly great defensive players.

The HEQ rating system for fielders is not concerned with who is the flashiest or the smoothest fielder or who has the best fielding average. It focuses on who is the most effective fielder — that is, who gets the job done in terms of putouts, assists, double plays and errors (see Appendix C for the HEQ defensive formulas).

In this chapter we will look at the HEQ defensive numbers for all the players at any position who have won at least four GG. We will base our analysis on the average of the four best fielding seasons that each player put into the record books — even though, in some cases, the player may not have won the GG in these particular years. Remember that in some cases the voters seem to award the GG to a player who was overlooked the previous season. Consider one example of this.

As you can see from the numbers below, Don Mattingly won nine GG — very impressive. Mattingly had his best defensive season in 1984 with a HEQ defensive score of 441. However, he did not win the GG that year — Eddie Murray did with a 479. Mattingly then went on to win his nine GG starting in 1985. It is interesting to note that Mattingly never had a 400 defensive season again. Whereas, Murray had 400 seasons in 1985, 1987 and 1989 but did not win the GG in those seasons because Mattingly did — go figure.

A word of caution. Keep in mind that the career HEQ defensive scores given in Appendix A and B are based on the *ten* best seasons that each player enjoyed. It is rather obvious that there is a big difference between displaying excellent fielding skills for four seasons as compared to ten seasons. As you examine some of the impressive fielding numbers below, glance at these appendices and compare the four-year numbers to the ten-year numbers for the following outstanding defensive players who have played during the past forty years: Keith Hernandez and Eddie Murray at first base, Bill Mazeroski and Nellie Fox at second, Ozzie Smith and Cal Ripken at short, Brooks Robinson and Graig Nettles at third, Gary Carter and Johnny Bench behind the plate and Richie Ashburn, Willie Mays and Kirby Puckett in the outfield. To sustain the fielding excellence that these players did over ten years or more is truly impressive.

The Great Fielders: 1957–1996

Here is the list of every fielder who has won four or more GG from 1957 to 1996. The defensive score listed here is based on *the best four fielding seasons* that the player had. Keep in mind that a 400 defensive season is considered a great fielding season. For reference purposes, you may want to consult Appendix A and B to see how many 400 seasons were recorded by the HOF players or candidates for the HOF who are not on this list. Note that we have included a few players (for obvious reasons) who have not won four GG.

The Average of the Four Most Effective Defensive Seasons by the "Best" Fielders

	GG	Years Won	HEQ
Second Base			
Bill Mazeroski	8	58, 60, 61, 63–67	479
Bobby Grich	4	73–76	456
Nellie Fox	3	57, 59, 60	449
Ryne Sandberg	9	83–91	435
Frank White	8	77–82, 86, 87	416
Joe Morgan	5	73–77	412
Bobby Richardson	5	61–65	410
Roberto Alomar	6	91-96	382
		Avg. =	430
Third Base			
Brooks Robinson	16	60–75	480
Graig Nettles	2	77, 78	473
Ron Santo	5	64–68	473
Buddy Bell	6	79–84	461
Mike Schmidt	10	76–84, 86	451
Gary Gaetti	4	86–89	427
Ken Boyer	5	58–61, 63	417
Doug Rader	5	70–74	409
Robin Ventura	4	91–93, 96	388
		Avg. =	442
Shortstop			
Ozzie Smith	13	80–92	499
Cal Ripken Jr	2	91, 92	496
Luis Aparicio	9	58–62, 64, 66, 68, 70	476

	GG	Years Won	HEQ
Mark Belanger	8	69, 71, 73–78	464
Dave Concepcion	5	74–77, 79	457
Tony Fernandez	4	86–89	451
Alan Trammell	4	80, 81, 83, 84	406
Omar Vizquel	4	93–96	404
		Avg. =	457

First Base

	GG	Years Won	HEQ
Mark Grace	4	92, 93, 95, 96	469
Keith Hernandez	11	78–88	465
Eddie Murray	3	82–84	459
Vic Power	7	58–64	427
Rafael Palmeiro	0		416
George Scott	8	67, 68, 71-76	410
Steve Garvey	4	74–77	399
Don Mattingly	9	85–89, 91-94	398
Bill White	7	60–66	394
Wes Parker	6	67–72	378
		Avg. =	422

Catcher

	GG	Years Won	HEQ
Gary Carter	3	80–82	499
Tony Pena	4	83–85, 91	484
Johnny Bench	10	68–77	481
Jim Sundberg	6	76–81	478
Bob Boone	7	78, 79, 82, 86–89	460
Bill Freehan	5	65–69	444
Ivan Rodriquez	5	92–96	442
Benito Santiago	3	88–90	438
Del Crandall	4	58–60, 62	420
		Avg. =	461

Outfielders

	GG	Years Won	HEQ
Richie Ashburn	0		582
Kirby Puckett	6	86–89, 91, 92	516
Dwayne Murphy	6	80–85	507
Willie Mays	12	57–68	501
Devon White	7	88, 89, 91-95	475
Andre Dawson	8	80–85, 87, 88	459
Gary Maddox	8	75–82	458
Paul Blair	8	67, 69–75	449
Willie Wilson	1	80	441
Curt Flood	7	63–69	439
Cesar Cedeno	5	72–76	428
Andy Van Slyke	5	88–92	423
Gary Pettis	5	85, 86, 88–90	421
Jim Landis	5	60–64	420
Kenny Lofton	4	93–96	417

Dale Murphy	5	82–86	417
Marquis Grissom	4	93–96	414
Al Kaline	10	57–59, 61-67	410
Ken Griffey Jr	7	90–96	404
Tony Gwynn	5	86, 87, 89–91	401
Carl Yastrzemski	7	63, 65, 67–69, 71, 77	400
Barry Bonds	6	90–94, 96	392
Dave Winfield	7	79, 80, 82–85, 87	391
Dwight Evans	8	76, 78, 79, 81-85	379
Roberto Clemente	12	61-72	369
		Avg. =	437

Some Observations:

1. A HEQ defensive score of 400 for a season defines a great defensive season. Therefore, any player above who has a score greater than 400 for his four best seasons can be considered a great defensive player (at least over the short haul).

Since the vast majority of the players above have scores over 400 (59 out of 69 = 86%), it means that the GG awards have proven to be quite accurate *for the players who have won four awards or more.*

2. Keep in mind that to be considered a great fielder for a career, a player must average over 400 for his *ten* best seasons. If you examine the numbers in Appendix A and B (as mentioned above), you will find those players who were able to sustain this level of fielding excellence over ten seasons.

3. It is certainly accurate to say that the offensive efforts of some of these players helped them to win multiple GG awards. Among the outfielders, Bonds, Winfield, Evans and Clemente are certainly examples of this. Another interesting example would be Steve Garvey at first base. When we choose his four best defensive seasons (as above), his HEQ average is 399 — very respectable. But if we take the average for the four seasons for which he actually won the GG (1974–77), we find that his HEQ average is only 353. And if you check Appendix B, you will find that his career defensive HEQ (ten best years) is 371— OK, but not great. In fact, some of his most effective fielding seasons came *after* he won his four GG. This appears to be an obvious case of a player's offensive efforts and reputation swaying the voters.

4. Perhaps the best example of offensive skills and reputation influencing the voters is that of Roberto Clemente. Clemente won twelve GG — more than any other outfielder except Willie Mays who also won twelve. As you can see above, for his four best seasons he averaged just 369 — the lowest of any of the outfielders listed here (compared to Mays' 501 for four years). If you look at Appendix A, you will see that for his ten best seasons he averaged only 339 compared to Mays' 456. Babe Ruth, not known as a particularly good right fielder, had a better career fielding HEQ of 343. In fact, in an eighteen year

career Clemente never had 400 putouts in a season — the most he ever had was 318. Ruth had more putouts than that in four different seasons.

Then how did Clemente win twelve GG? Two reasons: He had one of the best arms ever, and throwing runners out from right field certainly looks impressive (he led the league five different times in assists)— and he was a really good hitter. In fact, he was probably the best all-around right fielder in the National League during his playing days and he certainly deserves to be in the HOF. But his numbers do not justify ranking him as a *great fielder* and his twelve GG probably represents the best example of reputation and hitting skill influencing the voters in the selection process.

5. It appears that at the present time a similar situation has developed with Barry Bonds. By the end of the 1996 season, Bonds had won six GG and yet his HEQ score for his four best seasons was not over the 400 mark. If you check Appendix B, you will find that his defensive HEQ for his best ten seasons is only 348. But, of course, his offensive HEQ is the best in Appendix B. Once again, the voters appear to believe that the GG election is for the All Star team instead of for the *best fielder*.

A Few Serious Omissions

We have stated above that the GG awards have been quite accurate when we consider the cases of the players who have won the award four or more times. And, of course, if you look at the lists above, you will find a few players who have not won four awards but who are truly great defensive players. Rafael Palmeiro, who had no GG by the end of 1996, and Cal Ripken and Graig Nettles, who won two each, would be three such players. We will now consider a few cases where the GG awards apparently were not presented to the best fielder.

We mentioned at the beginning of the chapter the case of Richie Ashburn in 1957 — particularly significant because Ashburn was the greatest defensive outfielder of all time. We also mentioned above a scenario involving Don Mattingly. We will elaborate on Mattingly's case here because it illustrates a number of lessons.

As stated above, Mattingly had his most effective defensive season in 1984 with a HEQ of 441. He did not win the GG that year, Eddie Murray did with a HEQ of 479 (the last of Murray's three GG). Mattingly then won nine GG in ten years, missing out only in 1990 when Mark McGwire won. Mattingly was a good defensive first baseman with a four-year HEQ of 398 and a ten-year HEQ of 364. (Mattingly's biggest problem with the HEQ rating is that he just did not play enough. During his ten best seasons, Mattingly averaged 141 games at first base compared to, for example, Eddie Murray who averaged 155 games per season.) During the nine seasons in which he won the GG, there were at least six seasons when he did not come close to being the most effective fielding first baseman in the American League. But it is very difficult to dislodge a popular player from the minds of the people who select the GG recipients.

In 1985, Mattingly's first GG season, at least two players had better defensive seasons at first base. Eddie Murray had won three GG in a row from 1982 to 1984. In 1985, he had a 462 defensive HEQ compared to Mattingly's 367. Murray would seem to have been the obvious choice for a fourth GG. However, in 1985 Mattingly had a sensational all-around season (a total HEQ of 1019) and he was voted the MVP in the American League. And so, as often happens, the voters confused "all-star first baseman" with "best fielding first baseman."

But, believe it or not, Eddie Murray was not the player who was "robbed" of the GG in 1985. As fate would have it, another first baseman in the American League was having a fabulous season. In that year Bill Buckner set the all-time season record for assists by a first baseman at 184 and registered the highest defensive HEQ ever at first base of 517. Buckner never won a GG despite the fact that he had five outstanding defensive seasons — of which the 1985 season was clearly the best. In 1983, while playing in the National League, he had a HEQ of 475 at first base while Keith Hernandez (the most effective fielding first baseman ever) won the GG with a score of 468. It appears that Buckner's timing was unfortunate — to say the least. (There are those who have suggested that Buckner's assists were indirectly related to his bad ankles. It seems to me, however, that his numbers speak for themselves.)

As if 1985 was not bad enough, Mattingly won the GG in four other years when other first basemen had more effective seasons. Take a look at these numbers:

1987	Mattingly 354	Murray	461
1989	Mattingly 361	Murray	434
1992	Mattingly 393	Palmeiro	436
1993	Mattingly 349	Palmeiro	460

As we stated above, Don Mattingly was a fine defensive first baseman and a great all-around player — a good bet for the Hall of Fame. He was one of the most popular and respected players of his time. But he was not the most effective defensive first baseman in the American League during all of the nine seasons that he was awarded the GG.

Graig Nettles won two GG in 1977 and 1978. Nettles was the second most effective defensive third baseman of all time. His ten-year defensive HEQ of 437 is second only to Brooks Robinson at 451. Unfortunately for Nettles, his early seasons were played during the years when Robinson was on his sixteen-years-in-a-row domination of the GG at third base in the American League from 1960 to 1975. However, there was at least one of those years when Nettles should have won over Robinson. In 1971 Graig Nettles had the *most effective defensive season of any player in history at third base* when he registered a defensive HEQ of 527 and set the assist record for third basemen at 412. (Robinson's best defensive HEQ was 503 in 1967.) In 1971, Brooks Robinson had a HEQ of 433 (one of the fourteen seasons when he had a defensive HEQ of 400 or better). There is no doubt that Brooks Robinson is the most effective defensive third baseman of all time, but in 1971 Graig Nettles should have won the GG.

Ozzie Smith won thirteen GG from 1980 to 1992 and was the most effective fielding shortstop since the GG were introduced. His ten-year defensive HEQ is 465.4. It is probably fair to say that most observers of the game suspected this for years. But it probably is not as well known that Cal Ripken was the second most effective defensive shortstop during this period with a ten-year defensive HEQ of 464.5 — only nine-tenths of a point behind Smith. Ozzie had eleven 400 defensive seasons while Cal had thirteen. Yet, Ripken won only two GG — in 1991 and 1992. There were probably a number of years from 1983 to 1990 when Ripken should have won the GG, but we will mention only two—1984 and 1989.

In 1984 Cal Ripken posted the third most effective defensive season in history by a shortstop with a HEQ score of 521 (Ozzie had a 534 in 1980, Dave Bancroft a 531 in 1921 and Lou Boudreau also a 521 in 1944). Meanwhile, Alan Trammell won his fourth GG at shortstop in the American League with a HEQ score of 299! Does baseball need an objective defensive rating system or what?

What happened in 1989 is a little more understandable. Tony Fernandez won his fourth GG at shortstop with a great 447 season. However, in 1989 Ripken had his second best defensive season with a HEQ score of 499.

Cal Ripken's career viv-à-vis the GG awards closely resembles Graig Nettles' mentioned above. That is, both players were the second most effective fielders at their respective positions during the past forty years — yet each player won the GG on only two occasions.

Kirby Puckett was treated more fairly by the voters for the GG awards. Based on his ten-year HEQ score, Kirby was the third most effective defensive outfielder since the GG awards began — behind only Ashburn and Mays. He won the award six times between 1986 and 1992. What is odd is that he did not win a GG in his best defensive season ever. In 1985 Puckett had a defensive HEQ of 545 — one of the most effective defensive years ever by an outfielder and better than any defensive season that Mays ever had. That year the following outfielders were awarded the GG in the American League: Gary Pettis (432), Dave Winfield (374), Dwight Evans (325) and Dwayne Murphy (450) — the last two tied for third place. Clearly, Pettis and Murphy had great defensive years but would you not have voted for Kirby Puckett for a GG award if you had this analysis available?

Benito Santiago's case is somewhat similar to Puckett's but even stranger.

He won GG as a catcher in 1988, 1989 and 1990. Given this fact he should have been the favorite in 1991— assuming that he had a very good year. In fact he had his most effective defensive year ever in 1991 with a defensive HEQ of 488. So, how is it possible that Tom Pagnozzi won the GG as the catcher in the National League with a HEQ score of 409? Granted that Pagnozzi had a very good defensive season, but not nearly as good as Santiago who was the "incumbent." And the history of the GG award shows that it is usually difficult to unseat an incumbent if he has a good year.

These are just a few examples of where the fielder who had the most effective defensive season did not win the GG. I am sure that many fans have their own examples of great defensive seasons being overlooked by the voters. But, to be fair (as we have noted above), the Gold Glove awards have been quite accurate over the years — in the sense that 86% of those who have won four or more awards have indeed been very effective fielders. And, given the nature of the selection process, we probably cannot hope for much better than that.

Chapter 17

The Most Effective Players
of the 20th Century

Appendix A contains the HEQ rankings for the 105 position players in the Hall of Fame who have played in this century. Appendix B contains a similar ranking for 52 players who are or were considered candidates for selection to the Hall. In this chapter we will merge the two lists and give the ranking for those players from either list who are Group A, B or C players. The players from Appendix B will appear in italics to distinguish them from the players in the HOF.

You will recall from chapter nine that we defined these groups as follows:

Group A — The player's career HEQ is 920 or above. These are the truly great effective players.

Group B — The player's career HEQ is between 860 and 919. These are the very effective players who clearly have HOF numbers.

Group C — The player's career HEQ is between 820 and 859. These players have numbers that may be considered HOF numbers.

The list that follows contains the rankings of the 112 players who have a career HEQ score greater than 820. As in Appendix A, the columns headed Def, Off, and Total represent the average defense, offense and total HEQ scores for a player's ten best seasons — where 400 and 600 are great defensive and offensive scores, respectively, and 1000 is an outstanding overall season.

The columns headed 400, 600, and 1000 represent the number of such seasons a player had. So, for example, Mike Schmidt over his ten best seasons averaged 415 defensively and 578 offensively for a career HEQ of 993 — 13th place on the list. He had six 400 defensive seasons, two 600 offensive seasons, and six 1000 seasons.

The Group A Players

		Def		Off		Total	400	600	1000
1. Babe Ruth	RF	343	+	767	=	1110	3	10	9
2. Willie Mays	CF	456	+	645	=	1101	9	9	10
3. Lou Gehrig	1B	340	+	750	=	1090	0	10	9
4. Jimmie Foxx	1B	366	+	686	=	1052	1	9	7
5. Joe DiMaggio	CF	423	+	613	=	1036	6	5	6
6. Tris Speaker	CF	484	+	542	=	1026	10	3	4
7. Charlie Gehringer	2B	432	+	592	=	1024	10	4	7
8. Ty Cobb	CF	411	+	608	=	1019	4	5	4
9. Stan Musial	LF	387	+	630	=	1017	4	6	5
10. Rogers Hornsby	2B	388	+	625	=	1013	5	6	6
11. Hank Aaron	RF	367	+	628	=	995	2	8	4
12. Cal Ripken	SS	*465*	+	*529*	=	*994*	*10*	*1*	*4*
13. Mike Schmidt	3B	415	+	578	=	993	6	2	6
14. Ted Williams	LF	338	+	655	=	993	0	9	5
15. Earl Averill	CF	408	+	582	=	990	4	6	4
16. Mel Ott	RF	379	+	604	=	983	4	7	4
17. Mickey Mantle	CF	382	+	589	=	971	5	5	3
18. Max Carey*	CF	490	+	480	=	970	10	0	3
19. Ernie Banks	SS	423	+	545	=	968	8	4	5
20. Richie Ashburn*	CF	529	+	434	=	963	10	0	3
21. Al Simmons	LF	366	+	596	=	962	3	4	4
22. Kirby Puckett	CF	*453*	+	*503*	=	*956*	*7*	*2*	*4*
23. Barry Bonds	LF	*348*	+	*606*	=	*954*	*1*	*6*	*3*
24. Joe Cronin	SS	424	+	530	=	954	8	1	2
25. Eddie Murray	1B	*416*	+	*538*	=	*954*	*7*	*0*	*2*
26. Paul Waner	RF	402	+	551	=	953	5	3	2
27. Ron Santo	3B	*431*	+	*520*	=	*951*	*6*	*0*	*3*
28. Goose Goslin	LF	380	+	570	=	950	3	4	3
29. Honus Wagner	SS	408	+	534	=	942	6	0	2
30. Eddie Mathews	3B	373	+	565	=	938	0	2	2
31. Rickey Henderson	LF	*379*	+	*551*	=	*930*	*3*	*2*	*3*
32. Duke Snider	CF	368	+	562	=	930	3	4	4
33. Johnny Bench	C	436	+	493	=	929	8	1	2
34. Robin Yount	SS	*416*	+	*512*	=	*928*	*6*	*1*	*2*
35. Keith Hernandez	1B	*440*	+	*485*	=	*925*	*9*	*0*	*2*
36. Frank Robinson	RF	341	+	584	=	925	1	3	1
37. Gary Carter *	C	*474*	+	*450*	=	*924*	*10*	*0*	*1*
38. Ryne Sandberg	2B	*407*	+	*517*	=	*924*	*6*	*1*	*2*
39. Rafael Palmeiro	1B	*394*	+	*529*	=	*923*	*4*	*4*	*3*
40. Bill Terry	1B	393	+	528	=	921	5	2	3

The Group B Players

		Def		Off		Total	400	600	1000
41. Dale Murphy	CF	*382*	+	*534*	=	*916*	*5*	*3*	*2*
42. Frankie Frisch	2B	409	+	506	=	915	6	0	2
43. Brooks Robinson	3B	451	+	462	=	913	10	0	0
44. George Sisler	1B	387	+	525	=	912	3	3	2
45. Vada Pinson	CF	*387*	+	*524*	=	*911*	*3*	*0*	*2*
46. Joe Morgan	2B	382	+	527	=	909	3	2	1

			Def		Off	Total	400	600	1000
47.	Bobby Doerr	2B	425	+	482 =	907	8	0	1
48.	Hank Greenberg	1B	328	+	579 =	907	1	5	5
49.	Joe Medwick	LF	358	+	549 =	907	1	3	3
50.	Eddie Collins	2B	384	+	521 =	905	4	0	0
51.	Sam Rice	RF	413	+	492 =	905	6	0	1
52.	Arky Vaughan	SS	417	+	485 =	902	6	0	1
53.	Carl Yastrzemski	LF	364	+	533 =	897	1	2	0
54.	*Pete Rose*	*LF*	*390*	+	*507 =*	*897*	*4*	*0*	*0*
55.	Kiki Cuyler	RF	373	+	524 =	897	3	2	3
56.	Joe Sewell	SS	437	+	460 =	897	9	0	0
57.	*Andre Dawson*	*LF*	*387*	+	*508 =*	*895*	*5*	*2*	*1*
58.	*Gil Hodges*	*1B*	*376*	+	*519 =*	*895*	*3*	*1*	*2*
59.	Luke Appling	SS	442	+	450 =	892	10	0	1
60.	*George Brett*	*3B*	*364*	+	*528 =*	*892*	*3*	*2*	*2*
61.	*Ken Boyer*	*3B*	*387*	+	*504 =*	*891*	*2*	*0*	*0*
62.	Chuck Klein	RF	337	+	552 =	889	3	5	4
63.	*Dave Winfield*	*RF*	*350*	+	*538 =*	*888*	*2*	*1*	*1*
64.	Johnny Mize	1B	333	+	549 =	882	1	4	2
65.	*Joe Torre*	*C*	*408*	+	*460 =*	*868*	*6*	*1*	*0*
66.	Pie Traynor	3B	392	+	484 =	876	4	0	1
67.	Nap Lajoie	2B	372	+	503 =	875	3	1	1
68.	*Steve Garvey*	*1B*	*371*	+	*500 =*	*871*	*2*	*0*	*0*
69.	*Orlando Cepeda*	*1B*	*337*	+	*533 =*	*870*	*0*	*1*	*0*
70.	Yogi Berra	C	399	+	469 =	868	8	0	1
71.	*Graig Nettles*	*3B*	*437*	+	*441 =*	*878*	*7*	*0*	*0*
72.	Billy Williams	LF	301	+	566 =	867	0	2	0
73.	*Tony Perez*	*1B*	*361*	+	*504 =*	*865*	*1*	*1*	*0*
74.	PeeWee Reese	SS	420	+	445 =	865	7	0	0
75.	Al Kaline	RF	357	+	507 =	864	3	0	1
76.	Harmon Killebrew	1B	303	+	561 =	864	0	1	1
77.	*Don Mattingly*	*1B*	*364*	+	*500 =*	*864*	*1*	*2*	*2*
78.	George Davis	SS	388	+	474 =	862	4	0	0
79.	Rabbit Maranville	SS	471	+	391 =	862	10	0	0
80.	*Dave Parker*	*RF*	*344*	+	*518 =*	*862*	*1*	*1*	*1*
81.	Billy Herman	2B	427	+	434 =	861	7	0	0

The Group C Players

			Def		Off	Total	400	600	1000
82.	Ralph Kiner	LF	321	+	537 =	858	1	4	2
83.	Nellie Fox	2B	433	+	424 =	857	10	0	0
84.	*Minnie Minoso*	*LF*	*349*	+	*507 =*	*856*	*1*	*0*	*1*
85.	Frank Baker	3B	402	+	451 =	853	6	1	1
86.	Harry Heilmann	RF	305	+	548 =	853	1	2	0
87.	*Wade Boggs*	*3B*	*357*	+	*493 =*	*850*	*3*	*0*	*0*
88.	Larry Doby	CF	373	+	475 =	848	2	0	1
89.	Lou Boudreau	SS	435	+	408 =	843	8	0	1
90.	Rod Carew	2B	364	+	470 =	843	2	1	1
91.	*Jim Rice*	*LF*	*282*	+	*561 =*	*843*	*3*	*1*	*1*
92.	*Ozzie Smith*	*SS*	*465*	+	*378 =*	*843*	*10*	*0*	*0*
93.	Luis Aparicio	SS	442	+	400 =	842	10	0	0

94. Red Schoendienst	2B	419 + 423 =	842	8	0	0
95. Tony Lazzeri	2B	361 + 479 =	840	2	0	0
96. Lloyd Waner	CF	429 + 410 =	839	7	0	2
97. Zack Wheat	LF	371 + 466 =	837	3	0	0
98. Jim Bottomley	1B	317 + 517 =	834	0	3	0
99. Dwight Evans	*RF*	*342 + 491 =*	*833*	*0*	*2*	*0*
100. Jimmy Collins	3B	395 + 437 =	832	5	0	0
101. Carlton Fisk	*C*	*403 + 426 =*	*829*	*4*	*0*	*0*
102. Heinie Manush	LF	326 + 501 =	827	0	1	0
103. Roberto Clemente	RF	339 + 486 =	825	1	0	0
104. Al Oliver	*CF*	*353 + 471 =*	*824*	*1*	*0*	*0*
105. Bobby Wallace	SS	422 + 401 =	823	8	0	0
106. Tony Gwynn	*RF*	*347 + 474 =*	*821*	*1*	*0*	*0*
107. Reggie Jackson	RF	288 + 533 =	821	0	1	0
108. Enos Slaughter	RF	338 + 483 =	821	1	0	0
109. Lou Brock	LF	286 + 534 =	820	0	0	0
110. Travis Jackson	SS	420 + 400 =	820	6	0	1
111. Edd Roush	CF	389 + 431 =	820	4	0	0
112. Willie Wilson	*CF*	*396 + 424 =*	*820*	*4*	*0*	*1*

Note that among the candidates for the HOF there are eleven in Group A, fourteen in Group B and ten in Group C.

The asterisk (*) next to the names of a few of the players in Group A identifies those players whose defensive HEQ is greater than their offensive HEQ. There are only three such players. Two are presently in the HOF: Max Carey and Richie Ashburn. And one (Gary Carter) awaits induction.

A word of caution about a "too strict" interpretation of the rankings. Earl Averill emerges as #15 on our list because he had at least ten very impressive seasons. Does that mean that he was a "better player" than Mickey Mantle who is #17? The answer is no because we have not defined "better player." What it does mean is that Averill posted more effective numbers in his ten best seasons than Mantle did in his ten best.

There are players who are presently in the Hall of Fame whose career HEQ score is below 820 and who, therefore, are not on the list above (see Appendix A). Their exclusion from this list is not meant to imply that these players should not be in the HOF. We all know that there are players in the HOF whose numbers alone may not justify their induction, but who presumably have made other substantial contributions to the game. Two such players whom we have discussed earlier are Jackie Robinson and Roy Campanella. Both of these players were denied access to the major leagues during their early twenties because of the color barrier. It is obvious from their subsequent performances in the majors that had they been allowed to play during what would have been some of their most productive years, they certainly would have had the numbers to be in Group A or B.

The following is a list of the twenty-five most effective offensive players of this century based on their ten best seasons. Note that all but two of these players (Barry Bonds and Jim Rice) are in the Hall of Fame.

The Most Effective Offensive Players

1.	Babe Ruth	RF	767
2.	Lou Gehrig	1B	750
3.	Jimmie Foxx	1B	686
4.	Ted Williams	LF	655
5.	Willie Mays	CF	645
6.	Stan Musial	LF	630
7.	Hank Aaron	RF	628
8.	Rogers Hornsby	2B	625
9.	Joe DiMaggio	CF	613
10.	Ty Cobb	CF	608
11.	*Barry Bonds*	*LF*	*606*
12.	Mel Ott	RF	604
13.	Al Simmons	LF	596
14.	Charlie Gehringer	2B	592
15.	Mickey Mantle	CF	589
16.	Frank Robinson	RF	584
17.	Earl Averill	CF	582
18.	Hank Greenberg	1B	579
19.	Mike Schmidt	3B	578
20.	Goose Goslin	LF	570
21.	Billy Williams	LF	566
22.	Eddie Mathews	3B	565
23.	Duke Snider	CF	562
24.	Harmon Killebrew	1B	561
25.	*Jim Rice*	*LF*	*561*

Here are the players who were the most effective fielders at their respective positions. Once again, the rankings are based on the ten best seasons that each player recorded. Note that a number of these players are not in the HOF (italics) and some are not on our list above of Group A, B and C players because their HEQ total was less than 820.

The Most Effective Defensive Players

Catchers		*First Basemen*	
Gary Carter	474	*Keith Hernandez*	440
Ray Schalk	457	*Eddie Murray*	416
Johnny Bench	436	*Rafael Palmeiro*	394
Bob Boone	419	Bill Terry	393
Joe Torre	408	George Sisler	387
Carlton Fisk	403	Gil Hodges	376
Avg. =	433	Avg. =	401

Shortstops

Rabbit Maranville	471
Ozzie Smith	465
Cal Ripken Jr	465
Dave Bancroft	445
Luis Aparicio	442
Luke Appling	442
Avg. =	455

Second Basemen

Bill Mazeroski	444
Nellie Fox	433
Charlie Gehringer	432
Billy Herman	427
Bobby Doerr	425
Red Schoendienst	419
Avg. =	430

Third Basemen

Brooks Robinson	451
Graig Nettles	437
Ron Santo	431
Mike Schmidt	415
Frank Baker	402
Jimmy Collins	395
Avg. =	422

Outfielders

Richie Ashburn	529	*Curt Flood*	402
Max Carey	490	Paul Waner	402
Tris Speaker	484	*Willie Wilson*	396
Willie Mays	456	*Pete Rose*	390
Kirby Puckett	453	Edd Roush	389
Lloyd Waner	429	Stan Musial	387
Joe DiMaggio	423	*Andre Dawson*	387
Sam Rice	413	*Vada Pinson*	387
Ty Cobb	411	Mickey Mantle	382
Earl Averill	408	*Dale Murphy*	382
		Avg. =	420

Of these twenty most effective outfielders, all but five were primarily center fielders. The exceptions were Sam Rice, Paul Waner, Pete Rose, Stan Musial and Andre Dawson.

These then are the most effective players of the twentieth century as compiled from our lists in Appendix A and B — the players in the Hall of Fame and the candidates for that honor. It is my hope that baseball fans may find the HEQ system useful in attempting to come to an understanding as to who were the greatest players to play baseball in the twentieth century.

Chapter 18

1997 — The Year That the Ultimate Complete Player Returned to Baseball

After an absence of thirty-five years, the "ultimate complete player" returned to baseball during the 1997 season. The ultimate complete player is the player who is able to combine in the same season a super hitting effort (an offensive HEQ of 700 or more) with a great defensive year (a defensive HEQ of 400 or more).

In 1997 Ken Griffey Jr. of the Seattle Mariners became only the twelfth player in major league history (and the first since Willie Mays in 1962) to achieve this rare double. He posted an offensive score of 718 and a defensive score of 424 for a total HEQ score of 1142. In doing so he joined some of the biggest names in baseball history who have also accomplished the feat: Babe Ruth, Ty Cobb, Rogers Hornsby, George Sisler, Chuck Klein, Kiki Cuyler, Hank Greenberg, Jimmie Foxx, Joe DiMaggio, Mickey Mantle and Willie Mays. Such great sluggers as Lou Gehrig, Ted Williams, Stan Musial and Hank Aaron never managed to do it.

Here are the twelve players who have accomplished this feat and the sixteen seasons in which they did it:

Ty Cobb	1911	746 + 476 =	1222
George Sisler	1920	723 + 431 =	1154
Babe Ruth	1921	894 + 414 =	1308
Rogers Hornsby	1922	793 + 410 =	1203
Babe Ruth	1923	782 + 446 =	1228
Babe Ruth	1924	735 + 400 =	1135
Rogers Hornsby	1929	760 + 411 =	1171
Chuck Klein	1930	804 + 544 =	1348
Kiki Cuyler	1930	713 + 473 =	1186
Chuck Klein	1932	759 + 429 =	1188
Joe DiMaggio	1937	771 + 486 =	1257

Jimmie Foxx	1938	777 + 400 =	1177
Hank Greenberg	1938	737 + 433 =	1170
Mickey Mantle	1956	704 + 414 =	1118
Willie Mays	1962	710 + 449 =	1159
Ken Griffey Jr.	1997	718 + 424 =	1142

As you can see, only three players accomplished this feat more than once. Babe Ruth did it three times and Rogers Hornsby and Chuck Klein did it twice. It may come as a surprise to some fans to see how good a defensive outfielder Babe Ruth really was in his prime.

Larry Walker of the Colorado Rockies also had a fantastic offensive season in 1997. In fact, he had the best offensive season in forty-eight years. His HEQ offensive score of 754 was the best in the major leagues since Ted Williams had a score of 759 in 1949. Walker's was the 23rd best offensive season in history.

There have only been nine 700 offensive seasons since Williams' 1949 season. Here they are:

Mickey Mantle	1956	704
Willie Mays	1962	710
Frank Robinson	1962	706
Jim Rice	1978	702
Barry Bonds	1993	709
Albert Belle	1996	708
Ellis Burks	1996	725
Ken Griffey Jr.	1997	718
Larry Walker	1997	754

Only seventeen Hall of Famers have ever had a HEQ offensive season of 700 or better. These seventeen players had forty-two such seasons among them. Those who had multiple 700 seasons are Babe Ruth (9), Lou Gehrig (7), Jimmie Foxx (4), Hank Greenberg (4), Rogers Hornsby (3) and Chuck Klein (3).

Here are the top 25 offensive seasons in major league history (by the end of the 1997 season):

1. Babe Ruth	1921	894
2. Lou Gehrig	1927	836
3. Lou Gehrig	1931	833
4. Jimmie Foxx	1932	819
5. Babe Ruth	1927	815
6. Hack Wilson	1930	815
7. Chuck Klein	1930	804
8. Lou Gehrig	1930	799
9. Rogers Hornsby	1922	793
10. Lou Gehrig	1936	790
11. Babe Ruth	1923	782
12. Jimmie Foxx	1938	777

13. Lou Gehrig	1936	776
14. Hank Greenberg	1937	776
15. Joe DiMaggio	1937	771
16. Babe Ruth	1920	771
17. Rogers Hornsby	1929	760
18. Babe Ruth	1930	760
19. Chuck Klein	1932	759
20. Ted Williams	1949	759
21. Babe Ruth	1928	757
22. Babe Ruth	1931	755
23. *Larry Walker*	*1997*	*754*
24. Ty Cobb	1911	746
25. Stan Musial	1948	742

Note that Walker's 1997 season would rank as #23 on the list. That is, the 23rd best offensive season in history and the best in 48 years. Only nine players ever had a better offensive season.

However, Walker was not able to join Griffey in the exclusive ultimate complete player's club because his defensive HEQ was only 305. You may wonder how Larry Walker could have won his third Gold Glove if he had a defensive HEQ of 305 when seven other outfielders had defensive scores of 400 or better. Obviously the voters are allowing the offensive numbers to sway their judgment when they are supposed to be voting for the best fielders. Unfortunately, this is often the case where the Gold Glove awards are concerned.

Ken Griffey and Larry Walker were the Most Valuable Players for 1997 in the American and National Leagues respectively, and most fans would agree that they deserved the awards. But were there any other players who had truly outstanding years in 1997?

And, given the fact that of the eight 700 offensive seasons since 1950 — four of them were in 1996 or 1997 — can we say that baseball has entered into a "golden age" just prior to the millennium? The answer appears to be a resounding "yes."

Perhaps a better indication of how the players' numbers have improved dramatically in 1996 and 1997 is to examine how many players had HEQ seasons of 1000 or more in these years. Recall that a HEQ season of 1000 or more signifies that a player had a super season. For example, Mickey Mantle, in an eighteen year career, only had three 1000 seasons (of which one was an 1100 season in 1956). Hank Aaron had four 1000 seasons but never had an 1100 season. And Reggie Jackson never had even one 1000 season. In fact, of the 105 position players in the Hall of Fame in this century, forty-six of them (44%) never had a 1000 season and nineteen others (18%) only had one. So you can appreciate that a 1000 season is not exactly a common event.

Now, if a HEQ season of 1000 is special, an 1100 season is even more so. To put this achievement into some sort of perspective, consider the following. There have been only two 1300 HEQ seasons and six 1200 seasons in major league history — Willie Mays' 1955 score of 1211 being the only one of these after 1950. From 1950 to 1997, only eight players had an 1100 season. Here are those twelve seasons:

			Off		*Def*		*HEQ*
Willie Mays	CF	1954	647	+	522	=	1169
Willie Mays	CF	1955	696	+	515	=	1211
Mickey Mantle	CF	1956	704	+	414	=	1118
Willie Mays	CF	1957	651	+	480	=	1131
Willie Mays	CF	1958	637	+	487	=	1124
Willie Mays	CF	1962	710	+	449	=	1159
Johnny Bench	C	1970	632	+	473	=	1105
Kirby Puckett	CF	1988	606	+	508	=	1114
Cal Ripken Jr.	SS	1991	614	+	486	=	1100
Andres Galarraga	1B	1996	683	+	434	=	1117
Jeff Bagwell	1B	1997	674	+	448	=	1122
Ken Griffey Jr.	CF	1997	718	+	424	=	1142

You will note that Willie Mays' 1955 HEQ score of 1211 is the highest on this list but does not qualify for the 700/400 ultimate complete player category. Only three seasons on this list qualify for that honor: Mickey Mantle in 1956, Mays in 1962 and Ken Griffey in 1997.

Perhaps the most significant fact to note is that between 1996 and 1997 three different players had an 1100 season. Whereas, in the previous thirty years a total of only three players had such a season.

And add to these scores the other players who had 1000 seasons in 1996 and 1997 and we have an explosion of numbers that has not occurred since the 1930s.

1996

Ken Griffey Jr.	662	+ 428	=	1090
Rafael Palmeiro	650	+ 426	=	1076
Alex Rodriquez	688	+ 385	=	1073
Jeff Bagwell	644	+ 421	=	1065
Albert Belle	708	+ 333	=	1041
Brady Anderson	655	+ 379	=	1034
Ellis Burks	725	+ 301	=	1026
Steve Finley	619	+ 407	=	1026
Kenny Lofton	600	+ 420	=	1020
Barry Bonds	685	+ 318	=	1003

1997

Andres Galarraga	653	+ 441	=	1094
Mike Piazza	623	+ 450	=	1073
Larry Walker	754	+ 305	=	1059
Nomar Garciaparra	625	+ 422	=	1047
Craig Biggio	626	+ 420	=	1046
Tino Martinez	621	+ 382	=	1003

At least eleven players in 1996 and eight in 1997 had seasons of 1000 or better. One conclusion that we can certainly draw from these extraordinary numbers is that we are seeing more *complete players* (players who are both very effective hitters and fielders). Whether this is attributable to a livelier ball or more diluted pitching due to expansion or some compact ballfields or any other reason, it seems very clear that the 1996 and 1997 seasons have produced the most impressive numbers in at least the last thirty years.

What is really impressive for me from the lists above is that three players had 1100 seasons in 1996 or 1997: Jeff Bagwell, Andres Galarraga and Ken Griffey Jr. As we will see in a subsequent chapter, four players had such a season in 1998: Griffey, Sammy Sosa, Mark McGwire and Alex Rodriguez. This means that Griffey had *two 700/400 seasons in a row.* The only other player in major league history to accomplish this feat was Babe Ruth in 1923 and 1924 — 74 years between these amazing seasons!

Whether these players can put together ten truly outstanding seasons is yet to be seen. Keep Chuck Klein in mind when considering the question of longevity. As you can see above, Klein had the single greatest season in baseball history in 1930 when he had an offensive HEQ score of 804 and a defensive score of 544 for a total HEQ of 1348. (He set the record for assists by an outfielder at 44 that season.) He had four other outstanding seasons but was then traded by the Philadelphia Phillies and left the friendly confines of Baker Bowl — and was never as productive again. He is in the Hall of Fame and ranks 44th among the Hall of Famers and 62nd among the most effective players of the 20th century (his career HEQ is 889).

Obviously, having a few very productive seasons is quite different from having ten or more solid seasons (the career HEQ is based on a player's ten best seasons). To illustrate this, let us examine the *tentative* career HEQ scores of two players who are still active. By the end of the 1998 season, Rafael Palmeiro and Barry Bonds had each played in the majors for thirteen seasons. This is how their career HEQ scores looked at that time. Keep in mind that since they are still active, each of these players can improve on these scores.

| Barry Bonds | 606 + 348 | = | 954 |
| Rafael Palmeiro | 529 + 394 | = | 923 |

Barry Bond's career HEQ score ranks him as the 23rd most effective player of the twentieth century. Perhaps even more impressive is the fact that his offensive score of 606 establishes him as the eleventh most effective hitter of the century. He is, of course, a Group A candidate for the Hall of Fame (there are only forty group A players who have played the game in this century.)

Rafael Palmeiro's numbers are almost as impressive. His 923 career HEQ ranks him as the 39th most effective player of the century and the fifth most effective first basemen — just ahead of Bill Terry. He would also be a Group A candidate for the Hall of Fame.

The 1997 season was one of the most productive in many years. In chapter 19 we will demonstrate the use of the HEQ system as we determine who were the top ten performers at each of the positions during the season.

The 1997 Season —
Rating the Position Players

The 1997 baseball season produced some extraordinary performances by a number of players. As mentioned in the previous chapter, we saw the most effective hitting season in forty-eight years by Larry Walker and the best all-around season in thirty-five years by Ken Griffey Jr. Every position saw a player have an historically significant year except third base and left field.

In the following pages we will examine each of the eight positions (excluding pitcher) and indicate for each position who were the ten most effective all-around players, the ten most effective hitters and the ten most effective fielders. We will also put these performances into an historical context by indicating some of the best seasons ever at that position.

The choice of Larry Walker and Ken Griffey Jr. as the Most Valuable Players in their leagues for 1997 was right on the money. Both players had fabulous seasons. However, the choice of certain players for a Gold Glove award was very questionable — as we will see. The only choices that were clearly indisputable were: Rafael Palmeiro and J.T. Snow at first, Craig Biggio at second, Omar Vizquel at short, Ken Griffey in the outfield and Ivan Rodriquez and Charles Johnson at catcher. Each of these players had a defensive HEQ greater than 400.

You will recall that under the HEQ rating system, the offensive score (for all positions) =

Total bases + R + RBI + SB + .5BB (where total bases = S + 2D + 3T + 4HR)

The most effective offensive players for 1997 were:

	Games	*HEQ Offensive Score*
1. Larry Walker	153	754
2. Ken Griffey Jr.	157	718
3. Jeff Bagwell	162	674

	Games	HEQ Offensive Score
4. Andres Galarraga	154	653
5. Barry Bonds	159	645
6. Craig Biggio	162	626
7. Nomar Garciaparra	153	625
8. Mike Piazza	152	623
9. Tino Martinez	158	621
10. Frank Thomas	146	615
11. Mark McGwire	156	612
12. Tim Salmon	157	582

As you can see from this list, only eleven major leaguers managed to produce a 600 hitting season in 1997 — a super effective offensive season.

The Center Fielders

The defensive score for outfielders = PO + 4A + 4DP − 2E

In order to put the 1997 scores into some sort of context, here are the best single seasons enjoyed by the following center fielders (the H denotes that the player is in the Hall of Fame):

		Games	Off.	Def.		HEQ
Joe DiMaggio (H)	1937	151	771 +	486	=	1257
Ty Cobb (H)	1911	146	746 +	476	=	1222
Willie Mays (H)	1955	152	696 +	515	=	1211
Hack Wilson (H)	1930	155	815 +	363	=	1178
Tris Speaker (H)	1912	153	648 +	512	=	1160
Mickey Mantle (H)	1956	150	714 +	414	=	1118
Kirby Puckett	1988	158	606 +	508	=	1114
Earl Averill (H)	1931	155	687 +	426	=	1113
Max Carey (H)	1922	155	590 +	523	=	1113
Richie Ashburn (H)	1951	154	483 +	608	=	1091
Ken Griffey Jr	1996	140	662 +	428	=	1090
Dale Murphy	1983	160	645 +	401	=	1046

Willie Mays ranks as the most effective center fielder in history with an average HEQ score of 1101 for his ten best seasons — second only to Babe Ruth's 1110. Joe DiMaggio is the second most effective center fielder at 1036, followed by Tris Speaker (1026), Ty Cobb (1019), Earl Averill (990) and Mickey Mantle (971). Only ten players in history (at any position) have a career HEQ greater than 1000 and these four top center fielders are among them. In fact, Mays, DiMaggio and Cobb are the only players who have averaged over 600 offensively *and* over 400 defensively for their ten best seasons making them the best all-around players to ever play the game.

Here are the HEQ rankings for the most effective center fielders for the

1997 season. Note that Ken Griffey Jr. had one of the best all-around seasons ever enjoyed by a center fielder. From the list above you can see that only five other players ever had a better all-around season in center field. In fact, his season was truly remarkable in another aspect. Only twelve players in history (at any position) have ever combined a 700 offensive score with a 400 defensive score. And no one has done it in thirty-five years — since Willie Mays in 1962.

The 10 Most Effective Center Fielders — 1997

	Games	Off		Def		HEQ
Ken Griffey Jr	157	718	+	424	=	1142
Brian Hunter	162	496	+	432	=	928
Rondell White	151	481	+	405	=	886
Steve Finley	143	496	+	382	=	878
Ray Lankford	133	533	+	298	=	831
Jim Edmonds	133	448	+	377	=	825
Bernie Williams	129	536	+	277	=	813
Marquis Grissom	144	405	+	391	=	796
Tom Goodwin	150	394	+	388	=	782
Brady Anderson	151	507	+	274	=	781

Ken Griffey had an extraordinary all-around season while Brian Hunter had a great season. White, Finley, Lankford, Edmonds and Bernie Williams all had very good all-around seasons.

The 10 Most Effective Hitters

Ken Griffey	718
Bernie Williams	536
Ray Lankford	533
Brady Anderson	507
Brian Hunter	496
Steve Finley	496
Rondell White	481
Jim Edmonds	448
Ellis Burks	446
Kenny Lofton	408

The 10 Most Effective Fielders

Brian Hunter	432
Ken Griffey	424
Darren Bragg	411
Gerald Williams	410
Rondell White	405
Marguis Grissom	391
Tom Goodwin	388
Steve Finley	382
Jim Edmonds	377
Otis Nixon	355

Obviously, Griffey had the best offensive year among the center fielders. Bernie Williams, Ray Lankford and Brady Anderson also had very productive seasons at bat with offensive scores better than 500.

Five center fielders had great fielding seasons with defensive HEQ scores over 400: Brian Hunter, Ken Griffey, Darren Bragg, Gerald Williams and

Rondell White. To get some idea of how these scores compare with the best, here are the career defensive HEQ scores for the six most effective defensive center fielders from Appendices A and B (based on the average of their ten best seasons).

Richie Ashburn	529	Willie Mays	456
Max Carey	490	Kirby Puckett	453
Tris Speaker	484	Lloyd Waner	429

All of these players except Kirby Puckett are in the Hall of Fame. Other center fielders with a career defensive HEQ greater than 400 are Joe DiMaggio (423), Ty Cobb (411), Earl Averill (408) and Curt Flood (402).

The Right Fielders

The defensive score for outfielders = PO + 4A + 4DP − 2E

In order to put the 1997 scores into some sort of context, here are the best single seasons enjoyed by the following right fielders (the H denotes that the player is in the Hall of Fame):

		Games	*Off.*	*Def.*	*HEQ*
Chuck Klein (H)	1930	156	804 + 544 =		1348
Babe Ruth (H)	1921	152	894 + 414 =		1308
Kiki Cuyler (H)	1930	156	713 + 473 =		1186
Mel Ott (H)	1929	149	698 + 470 =		1168
Dave Parker	1977	159	579 + 499 =		1078
Hank Aaron (H)	1961	155	642 + 431 =		1073
Frank Robinson (H)	1962	161	706 + 359 =		1065
Paul Waner (H)	1927	143	622 + 423 =		1045
Sam Rice (H)	1920	153	513 + 530 =		1043
Al Kaline (H)	1956	153	593 + 419 =		1012
Dave Winfield	1979	159	606 + 402 =		1008
Roberto Clemente (H)	1966	154	596 + 374 =		970

Chuck Klein's 1930 season and Babe Ruth's 1921 season are the only 1300 seasons in baseball history. Babe Ruth ranks as the number one right fielder of all time (and the number one player) with an average HEQ score for his ten best seasons of 1110. Hank Aaron is the second ranking right fielder with 995 followed by Mel Ott (983), Paul Waner (953), Frank Robinson (925) and Sam Rice (905).

Here are the HEQ rankings for the most effective right fielders for the 1997 season. Note that Larry Walker had one of the best hitting seasons ever enjoyed by a right fielder. From the list above you can see that only two of these players ever had a better offensive season in right field.

The 10 Most Effective Right Fielders — 1997

	Games	Off	Def	HEQ
Larry Walker	153	754 + 305 =		1059
Tim Salmon	157	582 + 414 =		996
Raul Mondesi	159	569 + 374 =		943
Sammy Sosa	162	562 + 376 =		938
Jay Buhner	157	546 + 328 =		874
Paul O'Neill	149	538 + 316 =		854
Tony Gwynn	149	574 + 258 =		832
Manny Ramirez	150	531 + 292 =		823
Jeromy Burnitz	153	501 + 307 =		808
Dave Martinez	145	381 + 336 =		717

Larry Walker had a super all-around season while Tim Salmon, Raul Mondesi and Sammy Sosa had great seasons. Jay Buhner, Paul O'Neill, Tony Gwynn, Manny Ramirez and Jeromy Burnitz all had very good all-around seasons in right field.

The 10 Most Effective Hitters

Larry Walker	754
Tim Salmon	582
Tony Gwynn	574
Raul Mondesi	569
Sammy Sosa	562
Jay Buhner	546
Paul O'Neill	538
Manny Ramirez	531
Jeromy Burnitz	501
Geronimo Berroa	482

The 10 Most Effective Fielders

Tim Salmon	414
Sammy Sosa	376
Raul Mondesi	374
Andruw Jones	342
Dave Martinez	336
Jay Buhner	328
Paul O'Neill	316
Matt Lawton	314
Jeromy Burnitz	307
Larry Walker	305

Larry Walker's offensive season was truly remarkable. Only nine players in history (at any position) have ever had an offensive HEQ score greater than his 754. It represented the greatest hitting season in forty-eight years — since Ted Williams had a score of 759 in 1949.

As you can see from the list, eight other right fielders had very productive years at bat with HEQ offensive scores better than 500.

Only Tim Salmon among the right fielders can be said to have had a great defensive season since he is the only one with a HEQ defensive score greater than 400. When you look at Larry Walker's defensive score of 305, you have to wonder how he ever was awarded the Gold Glove for fielding. Obviously, as is often the case, a player's offensive numbers influence the voting even though they are not supposed to count.

To get some idea of how these defensive scores compare to the best, here are the career defensive HEQ scores for the six most effective defensive right fielders from appendices A and B (the average of their ten best seasons):

Sam Rice	413		Kiki Cuyler	373
Paul Waner	402		Hank Aaron	367
Mel Ott	379		Al Kaline	357

All of these players are in the Hall of Fame. Note that only two right fielders in history had a career defensive HEQ over 400, despite the fact that on our list of best seasons there were a number of players who had great defensive seasons. This shows that it is possible for a player of moderate fielding skills to have one or two outstanding years in right field, but it is something quite different to average 400 over ten seasons. For example, as you can see above, Dave Parker in 1977 had a defensive score of 499. That was the only season that he was over 400 and his career defensive HEQ is 344.

Roberto Clemente, who is generally thought to have had one of the best arms from right field and won twelve Gold Gloves, has a career defensive HEQ score of only 339. His putouts each season were simply below par partly because of playing time.

The Left Fielders

The defensive score for outfielders = PO + 4A + 4DP − 2E

In order to put the 1997 scores into some sort of context here are the best single seasons enjoyed by the following left fielders (the H denotes that the player is in the Hall of Fame):

		Games	*Off.*	*Def.*		*HEQ*
Ted Williams (H)	1949	155	759 +	385 =		1144
Stan Musial (H)	1948	155	742 +	388 =		1130
Al Simmons (H)	1925	153	668 +	455 =		1123
Rickey Henderson	1985	143	630 +	461 =		1091
Joe Medwick (H)	1936	155	640 +	435 =		1075
Goose Goslin (H)	1925	150	611 +	461 =		1072
Ralph Kiner (H)	1947	152	656 +	412 =		1068
Andre Dawson	1983	159	602 +	449 =		1051
Albert Belle	1996	158	708 +	333 =		1041
Barry Bonds	1993	159	709 +	328 =		1037
Jim Rice	1983	155	586 +	431 =		1017
Carl Yastrzemski (H)	1967	161	649 +	339 =		988

Stan Musial ranks as the number one left fielder of all time with an average HEQ score for his ten best seasons of 1017. Only ten players (at any position) have produced a career HEQ over 1000. Ted Williams is the second ranking left fielder with 993 followed by Al Simmons (962), Barry Bonds (954), Goose Goslin (950) and Rickey Henderson (930). (Williams is the fourth best hitter of all time, behind only Ruth, Gehrig and Foxx.)

Here are the HEQ rankings for the most effective left fielders for the 1997 season. Note that Barry Bonds had the best all-around season. As mentioned above, after thirteen seasons, Bonds has already established himself as the fourth most effective left fielder in history — with a chance to move even higher since he is still in his prime.

The 10 Most Effective Left Fielders — 1997

	Games	Off	Def		HEQ
Barry Bonds	159	645 + 324	=	969
Rusty Greer	157	569 + 330	=	899
Bob Higginson	146	526 + 373	=	899
Albert Belle	161	548 + 334	=	882
Garret Anderson	154	448 + 400	=	848
Moises Alou	150	512 + 263	=	775
B.J. Surhoff	147	436 + 314	=	750
Dante Bichette	151	506 + 239	=	745
Bernard Gilkey	145	421 + 321	=	742
Jason Giambi	142	432 + 276	=	708

Barry Bonds had a great all-around season in left field while Rusty Greer, Bob Higginson, Albert Belle and Garret Anderson had very good seasons.

The 10 Most Effective Hitters

Barry Bonds	645
Rusty Greer	569
Albert Belle	548
Bob Higginson	526
David Justice	523
Moises Alou	512
Dante Bichette	506
Garret Amderson	448
B.J. Surhoff	436
Jason Giambi	432

The 10 Most Effective Fielders

Garret Anderson	400
Bob Higginson	373
Albert Belle	334
Rusty Greer	330
Barry Bonds	324
Bernard Gilkey	321
B.J. Surhoff	314
Luis Gonzalez	304
Doug Glanville	301
Wil Cordero	277

Barry Bonds had another great offensive season with a HEQ score of 645. This was the fifth best offensive performance in 1997. Six other left fielders had very productive years at bat with HEQ offensive scores better than 500: Greer, Belle, Higginson, Justice, Alou and Bichette.

Only Garret Anderson, with a defensive score of 400, can be said to have had a great defensive season in left field. In fact, except for Anderson and Bob

Higginson, no other left fielder even had a good defensive season since no one else is above 350. How could Barry Bonds at 324 have ever won a Gold Glove? Once again, good offense is influencing the vote for the best fielders.

To get some idea of how these defensive scores compare to the best, here are the career defensive HEQ scores for the six most effective defensive left fielders from appendices A and B (the average of their ten best seasons):

Stan Musial	387	Rickey Henderson	379
Andre Dawson	387	Zach Wheat	371
Goose Goslin	380	Carl Yastrzemski	370

Musial, Goslin, Wheat and Yastrzemski are in the Hall of Fame. Note that no left fielder has a career defensive HEQ score over 400 despite the fact that on our list of best seasons some of the left fielders had a great defensive season. Jim Rice, for example, in 1983 had a defensive HEQ of 431 which was his only defensive season over 400. His career defensive score is only 282. Al Simmons' 455 in 1925 and Ralph Kiner's 412 in 1947 are also significant departures from their normal defensive scores.

The Second Basemen

The defensive formula for second basemen = .460(PO + A + DP − 2E)

In order to put the following scores into some sort of context consider the following: Prior to 1997 only eight second basemen had ever had a 600 hitting season — Rogers Hornsby had six such seasons, Charlie Gehringer had four, Joe Morgan had two and Ryne Sandberg, Jackie Robinson, Rod Carew, Nap Lajoie and Chuck Knoblauch had one each. Only four second basemen have ever had more than one 1000 season: Gehringer had seven (only Willie Mays and Babe Ruth had more than seven), Hornsby had six, and Sandberg and Frankie Frisch had two each. Here are the best single seasons enjoyed by the following second basemen (the H denotes that the player is in the Hall of Fame):

		Games	*Off.*	*Def.*		*HEQ*
Rogers Hornsby (H)	1922	154	793 +	410 =		1203
Charlie Gehringer (H)	1936	154	662 +	454 =		1116
Frankie Frisch (H)	1927	153	551 +	506 =		1057
Nap Lajoie (H)	1901	131	659 +	397 =		1056
Jackie Robinson (H)	1949	156	639 +	415 =		1054
Joe Morgan (H)	1973	157	605 +	435 =		1040
Ryne Sandberg	1984	156	587 +	439 =		1026
Bobby Doerr (H)	1950	149	564 +	452 =		1016
Billy Herman (H)	1935	154	540 +	448 =		988

		Games	Off.	Def.		HEQ
Carlos Baerga	1992	161	524 +	448	=	972
Roberto Alomar	1996	153	598 +	372	=	970
Nellie Fox (H)	1957	155	471 +	469	=	940

Only ten players in history have achieved a career HEQ score of 1000 or better (over their ten best seasons). Charlie Gehringer at 1024 and Rogers Hornsby at 1013 are two of them. Ryne Sandberg at 924 is the third most effective second baseman in history followed by Frankie Frisch at 915 and Joe Morgan at 909.

Here are the HEQ rankings for the most effective second basemen for the 1997 season. Note that Craig Biggio had one of the best hitting seasons and one of the best all-around seasons ever enjoyed by a second baseman. The list above indicates that only five second basemen ever had a season better than his 1997 season.

The 10 Most Effective Second Basemen — 1997

	Games	Off		Def		HEQ
Craig Biggio	162	626 +	420	=		1046
Jeff Kent	155	520 +	395	=		915
Chuck Knoblauch	156	540 +	364	=		904
Eric Young	155	495 +	408	=		903
Tony Womack	155	457 +	372	=		829
Delino DeShields	150	489 +	332	=		821
John Valentin	143	495 +	319	=		814
Mike Lansing	144	460 +	347	=		807
Damion Easley	151	479 +	325	=		804
Ray Durham	155	465 +	325	=		790

Craig Biggio had a super all-around season in 1997 while Jeff Kent, Chuck Knoblauch, and Eric Young had great years. Tony Womack, Delino DeShields, John Valentin, Mike Lansing and Damion Easley had very good seasons at second base.

The 10 Most Effective Hitters

Craig Biggio	626
Chuck Knoblauch	540
Jeff Kent	520
Eric Young	495
John Valentin	495
Delino DeShields	489
Damion Easley	479
Ray Durham	465
Mike Lansing	460
Tony Womack	457

The 10 Most Effective Fielders

Craig Biggio	420
Eric Young	408
Jeff Kent	395
Tony Womack	372
Chuck Knoblauch	364
Scott Spiezio	357
Mike Lansing	347
Quilvio Veras	336
Delino DeShields	332
Ray Durham	325

Craig Biggio had a fabulous hitting season with an offensive score of 625. Chuck Knoblauch at 540 and Jeff Kent at 520 also had very productive seasons at bat.

Only two second basemen had great fielding seasons in 1997 with defensive HEQ scores over 400. To get some idea of how these scores compare with the best, here are the career defensive HEQ scores for the six most effective defensive second basemen from Appendices A and B (based on the average of their ten best seasons).

Bill Mazeroski	444	Billy Herman	427
Nellie Fox	433	Bobby Doerr	425
Charlie Gehringer	432	Red Schoendienst	419

All of these players except Mazeroski are in the Hall of Fame. However, we must keep in mind that Mazeroski also has the lowest offensive HEQ score (356) compared to the others — Schoendienst at 423 is the next lowest.

Other second basemen who have career defensive HEQ scores over 400 and who were great defensive players are Bobby Grich (411), Frankie Frisch (409) and Ryne Sandberg (407).

The Shortstops

The defensive formula for shortstops = .548(PO + A + DP − 2E)

In order to put the following scores into some sort of context consider the following: prior to 1997 only five shortstops had ever had a 600 hitting season — Ernie Banks had four such seasons while Joe Cronin, Robin Yount, Cal Ripken Jr. and Alex Rodriquez had one each. Only five shortstops have ever had more than two 1000 seasons: Banks had five, Ripken had four and Cronin, Yount and Honus Wagner had two each. Here are the best single seasons enjoyed by the following shortstops (the H denotes that the player is in the Hall of Fame):

		Games	*Off.*		*Def.*		*HEQ*
Cal Ripken Jr.	1991	162	614	+	486	=	1100
Ernie Banks (H)	1958	154	657	+	436	=	1093
Joe Cronin (H)	1930	154	607	+	477	=	1084
Robin Yount	1982	156	651	+	432	=	1083
Alex Rodriquez	1996	146	688	+	385	=	1073
Lou Boudreau (H)	1948	152	573	+	471	=	1044
Dave Bancroft (H)	1921	153	505	+	531	=	1036
Honus Wagner (H)	1905	147	576	+	456	=	1032
Luke Appling (H)	1936	138	559	+	454	=	1013
Rabbit Maranville (H)	1922	155	487	+	510	=	997

	Games	Off.	Def.	HEQ
Pee Wee Reese (H)	1949	155	542 + 453 =	995
Ozzie Smith	1987	158	497 + 467 =	964

Cal Ripken Jr. ranks as the most effective shortstop in history with an average HEQ score of 993 for his ten best seasons. Ernie Banks is second at 968, Joe Cronin is third at 954, Honus Wagner is fourth at 942 and Robin Yount fifth at 928.

Here are the HEQ rankings for the most effective shortstops for the 1997 season. Note that Nomar Garciaparra, in his first full season, had one of the best hitting seasons and one of the best all-around seasons ever enjoyed by a shortstop. From the list above, you can see that only five other players ever had a better all-around season at short.

The 10 Most Effective Shortstops — 1997

	Games	Off	Def	HEQ
Nomar Garciaparra	153	625 + 422 =	1047
Derek Jeter	159	511 + 412 =	923
Jay Bell	153	491 + 423 =	914
Alex Rodriquez	141	525 + 351 =	876
Omar Vizquel	153	418 + 414 =	832
Royce Clayton	154	412 + 403 =	815
Mark Grudzielanek	156	413 + 393 =	806
Edgar Renteria	154	407 + 394 =	801
Jeff Blauser	151	450 + 344 =	794
Jose Vizcaino	151	358 + 394 =	752

Nomar Garciaparra had a super season in 1997 while Derek Jeter and Jay Bell had great years. Alex Rodriquez, Omar Vizquel, Royce Clayton, Marl Grudzielanek and Edgar Renteria had very good seasons at shortstop.

The 10 Most Effective Hitters

Nomar Garciaparra	625
Alex Rodriquez	525
Derek Jeter	511
Jay Bell	491
Jeff Blauser	450
Omar Vizquel	418
Mark Grudzielanek	413
Royce Clayton	412
Edgar Renteria	407
Shawon Dunston	385

The 10 Most Effective Fielders

Jay Bell	423
Nomar Garciaparra	422
Omar Vizquel	414
Derek Jeter	412
Royce Clayton	403
Mike Bordick	394
Edgar Renteria	394
Jose Vizcaino	394
Mark Grudzielanek	393
Chris Gomez	389

Nomar Garciaparra had a fabulous hitting season with an offensive score of 625. Alex Rodriquez at 525 and Derek Jeter at 511 also had very productive seasons at bat.

Five shortstops had great fielding seasons with defensive HEQ scores over 400. And the other five on the list above were not far behind. To get some idea of how these scores compare with the best, here are the career defensive HEQ scores for the six most effective defensive shortstops in appendices A and B (based on the average of their ten best seasons).

Rabbit Maranville	471	Dave Bancroft	445
Ozzie Smith	465.4	Luis Aparicio	441.7
Cal Ripken Jr.	464.5	Luke Appling	441.6

Maranville, Bancroft, Aparicio and Appling are all in the Hall of Fame.

It is not uncommon for a good defensive shortstop to play regularly even though he may not hit very well. Dave Bancroft was a great defensive shortstop whose career offensive HEQ score was only 362 — compared to 545 for Ernie Banks.

Prior to 1998 every shortstop in the Hall of Fame who played in the twentieth century had a career defensive HEQ of 400 or better — meaning that they were all great fielders. Not too surprising since most of the shortstops were known for their glove and not their bat. George Davis, selected by the Veteran's committee in 1998, has a career defensive HEQ of 388.

A word about the Gold Glove for shortstop in 1997. Omar Vizquel was awarded the GG in the American League and it would be hard to argue with this choice since he had a defensive HEQ of 414. But Rey Ordonez, the winner in the National League, is another matter. Ordonez played shortstop in only 118 games in 1997 (his defensive HEQ was 317). It seems to me that there is no way that a shortstop who plays that few games can be the "best fielding shortstop" in the league — no matter how good a fielder he is.

The Third Basemen

The defensive formula for third basemen = .888(PO + A + DP − 2E)

In order to put the following scores into some sort of context consider the following: only seven third basemen have ever had a 600 hitting season — Mike Schmidt, Eddie Mathews and George Brett have had two such seasons each while Paul Molitor, Frank Baker, Freddy Lindstrom and Ken Caminiti had one each. Only four third basemen have ever had more than one 1000 season: Schmidt had six 1000 seasons, Ron Santo had three and Mathews and Brett had two each. Here are the best single seasons enjoyed by the following third basemen (the H denotes that the player is in the Hall of Fame):

	Games	Off.		Def.	HEQ
		Off.		*Def.*	*HEQ*
Mike Schmidt (H)	1974	162	610 + 467 =		1077
George Brett	1979	154	632 + 435 =		1067
Frank Baker (H)	1912	149	623 + 440 =		1063
Ron Santo	1967	161	554 + 498 =		1052
Eddie Mathews (H)	1953	157	659 + 389 =		1048
George Kell (H)	1950	157	561 + 455 =		1016
Pie Traynor (H)	1925	150	535 + 467 =		1002
Graig Nettles	1971	158	472 + 527 =		999
Paul Molitor	1982	150	583 + 413 =		996
Fred Lindstrom (H)	1928	153	564 + 424 =		988
Ken Caminiti	1996	146	628 + 356 =		984
Brooks Robinson (H)	1964	163	546 + 437 =		982

Mike Schmidt ranks as the most effective third baseman in history with an average HEQ score of 993 for his ten best seasons (#12 of all players in the Hall of Fame). Ron Santo is second at 951 followed by Eddie Mathews (938), Brooks Robinson (913) and George Brett (892).

Here are the HEQ rankings for the most effective third basemen for the 1997 season. Unlike many of the other positions, no third baseman had the sort of year in 1997 that would rank with the outstanding years above.

The 10 Most Effective Third Basemen — 1997

	Games	Off		Def	HEQ
Vinny Castilla	159	566 + 385 =			951
Travis Fryman	154	493 + 392 =			885
Scott Rolen	156	502 + 369 =			871
Matt Williams	151	500 + 341 =			841
Chipper Jones	157	555 + 277 =			832
Jeff Cirillo	154	437 + 390 =			827
Ken Caminiti	137	480 + 314 =			794
Cal Ripken Jr.	162	439 + 348 =			787
Todd Zeile	160	494 + 290 =			784
Dave Hollins	149	479 + 302 =			781

Vinnie Castilla had a great all-around year at third base while Travis Fryman, Scott Rolen, Matt Williams, Chipper Jones and Jeff Cirillo all had very good seasons.

The 10 Most Effective Hitters

Vinny Castilla	566
Chipper Jones	555
Scott Rolen	502

The 10 Most Effective Fielders

Travis Fryman	392
Jeff Cirillo	390
Vinny Castilla	385

The 10 Most Effective Hitters   The 10 Most Effective Fielders
(continued)

Matt Williams	500	Scott Rolen	369
Todd Zeile	494	Cal Ripken	348
Travis Fryman	493	Matt Williams	341
Ken Caminiti	480	Scott Brosius	340
Dave Hollins	479	Edgardo Alfonzo	336
Bobby Bonilla	479	Ken Caminiti	314
Cal Ripken	439	Dave Hollins	302

Vinny Castilla at 566 and Chipper Jones at 555 had very productive offensive seasons while Scott Rolen and Matt Williams also had effective seasons of 500 or more.

No third baseman had a great season in the field since none had a 400 defensive HEQ, but Fryman, Cirillo and Castilla had very good defensive seasons.

To get some idea of how these scores compare with the best, here are the career defensive HEQ scores for the six most effective defensive third basemen from Appendices A and B (based on the average of their ten best seasons).

Brooks Robinson	451	Mike Schmidt	415
Graig Nettles	437	Frank Baker	402
Ron Santo	431	Jimmy Collins	395

Clete Boyer at 420 and Buddy Bell at 416 are two other third basemen with a HEQ career defensive score over 400. Mike Schmidt, Brooks Robinson, Frank Baker and Jimmy Collins are all in the Hall of Fame. Ron Santo, the second most effective third baseman of all time (after Schmidt), remains the most qualified player (at any position) who is *not* in the Hall of Fame.

If you examine the players who played in this century and are in the Hall of Fame, there are fewer third basemen than any other position.

The First Basemen

The defensive formula for first basemen = .510(.25PO + 3A + DP − 2E)

In order to put the following scores into some sort of context consider the following. It is generally safe to say that more offensive production is expected of a first baseman than of any other infield position. And the greatest range of defensive skills exists here — from the brilliance of a Keith Hernandez (career defensive HEQ = 440) to the efforts of a Frank Chance (career defensive HEQ = 245).

In 1997 Jeff Bagwell joined a number of other first basemen who have had 1100 seasons — a truly spectacular all-around season. Here are the best single seasons enjoyed by the following first basemen (the H denotes that the player is in the Hall of Fame):

		Games	Off.	Def.	HEQ
Lou Gehrig (H)	1927	155	836 + 386 =		1222
Jimmie Foxx (H)	1932	141	819 + 365 =		1184
Hank Greenberg (H)	1937	154	776 + 399 =		1175
George Sisler (H)	1920	154	723 + 431 =		1154
Bill Terry (H)	1930	154	697 + 440 =		1137
Andres Galarraga	1996	159	683 + 434 =		1117
Johnny Mize (H)	1947	154	674 + 412 =		1086
Rafael Palmeiro	1993	160	619 + 460 =		1079
Keith Hernandez	1979	161	585 + 479 =		1064
Eddie Murray	1985	154	587 + 462 =		1049
Gil Hodges	1954	154	611 + 437 =		1048
Don Mattingly	1986	162	645 + 390 =		1035
Willie McCovey (H)	1970	152	596 + 405 =		1001

Lou Gehrig, the second greatest hitter in history after Babe Ruth, ranks as the most effective first baseman with an average HEQ score of 1090 for his ten best seasons. Jimmie Foxx is second at 1052 followed by Eddie Murray (954), Keith Hernandez (925), Rafael Palmeiro (923), Bill Terry (921) and George Sisler (912).

Here are the HEQ rankings for the most effective first basemen for the 1997 season. Note that Jeff Bagwell had a season that would place him just behind Bill Terry on the list above — meaning that only five first basemen in history had a better all-around season than Bagwell.

The 10 Most Effective First Basemen — 1997

	Games	Off.	Def	HEQ
Jeff Bagwell	162	674 + 448 =		1122
Andres Galarraga	154	653 + 441 =		1094
Tino Martinez	158	621 + 382 =		1003
Mark McGwire	156	612 + 372 =		984
Tony Clark	159	560 + 390 =		950
Jeff King	155	502 + 443 =		945
Rafael Palmeiro	158	542 + 393 =		935
Jim Thome	147	554 + 356 =		910
J.T. Snow	157	510 + 391 =		901
John Olerud	154	491 + 404 =		895

Besides Bagwell, Andres Galarraga and Tino Martinez also had super all-around seasons. McGwire, Clark, King, Palmeiro, Thome and Snow also had very effective years.

The 10 Most Effective Hitters

Jeff Bagwell	674
Andres Galarraga	653
Tino Martinez	621
Frank Thomas	615
Mark McGwire	612
Tony Clark	560
Jim Thome	554
Rafael Palmeiro	542
Eric Karros	524
J.T. Snow	510

The 10 Most Effective Fielders

Jeff Bagwell	448
Jeff King	443
Andres Galarraga	441
John Olerud	404
Rafael Palmeiro	393
J.T. Snow	391
Tony Clark	390
Eric Karros	386
Tino Martinez	382
Mark Grace	379

Bagwell, Galarraga, Martinez, Thomas and McGwire all had terrific offensive seasons with a HEQ greater than 600. In fact, the second five on our offensive list also had very productive seasons at bat with a HEQ greater than 500.

Jeff Bagwell heads a group of four first basemen who all had great defensive seasons with a HEQ defensive score over 400. Keep in mind that it is one thing to have one or two great defensive seasons but something very different to average 400 over ten seasons.

To get some idea of how these scores compare with the best, here are the career defensive HEQ scores for the six most effective defensive first basemen in appendices A and B (based on the average of their ten best seasons).

Keith Hernandez	440	Bill Terry	393
Eddie Murray	416	George Sisler	390
Rafael Palmeiro	394	Gil Hodges	376

Of the group above only Bill Terry and George Sisler are in the Hall of Fame. This means, of course, that no first baseman in the Hall has a career defensive HEQ over 400. First basemen are not usually noted for their fielding skills — so this result is not too surprising. Besides Hernandez and Murray, Mark Grace at 409 has a career defensive HEQ over 400.

A word should be said about some of the defensive scores in the list of the best seasons above lest the impression is left that most of the players on that list were good fielders. In fact, some were not good fielders at all. Here is a list of those players showing their HEQ defensive score for the year on the list above and their career HEQ defensive score (the average of their ten best seasons).

		Career HEQ
Hank Greenberg	399	328
Lou Gehrig	386	340
Johnny Mize	412	333
Willie McCovey	405	312

It becomes obvious that their best season is not indicative of their long-term fielding ability. It does show, however, that at first base even an average fielder can have one or two very effective defensive seasons.

The Catchers

The defensive formula for catchers = .445(PO + 3A + 2DP — 2E) where 800 is the maximum number of putouts allowed in the formula. This is necessary in order to correct for the effect that an excessive number of strikeouts in a given season can have on the score.

In order to put the 1997 scores into some sort of context, consider the following: prior to 1997 Johnny Bench, Roy Campanella and Joe Torre were the only catchers to ever have a 600 hitting season (they each had one such season in their careers). Before Mike Piazza, Bench was the only catcher in history to have more than one 1000 season — he had two. Here are the best single seasons enjoyed by the following catchers (the H denotes that the player is in the Hall of Fame):

		Games	Off.	Def.	HEQ
Johnny Bench (H)	1970	158	632 + 473 =		1105
Roy Campanella (H)	1953	144	600 + 431 =		1031
Yogi Berra (H)	1950	151	590 + 434 =		1024
Mike Piazza	1993	149	526 + 489 =		1015
Gary Carter	1982	154	513 + 491 =		1004
Joe Torre	1970	161	537 + 459 =		996
Ivan Rodriquez	1996	153	528 + 464 =		992
Todd Hundley	1996	153	535 + 451 =		986
Bill Dickey (H)	1937	140	562 + 418 =		980
Mickey Cochrane (H)	1932	139	544 + 425 =		969
Carlton Fisk	1977	152	532 + 435 =		967
Gabby Hartnett (H)	1930	141	554 + 381 =		935

Here are the HEQ rankings for the catchers for the 1997 season. Note that Mike Piazza in 1997 had a HEQ score of 1073 — meaning that only Johnny Bench ever had a more effective season as a catcher. It marked the second season in which he had a HEQ score greater than 1000 — tying Bench in this regard (Bench had a score of 1099 in 1974). If Piazza can play at this level for another number of years, he has a chance to challenge Bench as the most effective catcher in history.

The 10 Most Effective Catchers — 1997

	Games	Off	Def	HEQ
Mike Piazza	152	623 + 450 =		1073
Ivan Rodriquez	150	490 + 458 =		948

	Games	Off	Def	HEQ
Jason Kendall	144	362 + 499 =		861
Dan Wilson	146	382 + 459 =		841
Mike Lieberthal	134	362 + 451 =		813
Todd Hundley	132	437 + 371 =		808
Javy Lopez	123	362 + 431 =		793
Sandy Alomar	125	402 + 384 =		786
Charles Johnson	124	325 + 461 =		786
Brad Ausmus	130	274 + 463 =		737

Besides Piazza's impressive season, Ivan Rodriquez also had a great all-around year. You will note that besides these two outstanding players, no other catcher had a 900 season — demonstrating how infrequently a catcher combines a solid hitting effort with an effective fielding season. As examples of this fact, consider the following. Roy Campanella only had two seasons with a HEQ greater than 900: 942 in 1951 and the 1953 season mentioned above. The 1937 season above is the only one where Bill Dickey had a 900 HEQ score. And, Mickey Cochrane's 1932 season above was the only one where he had a score greater than 900.

The 10 Most Effective Hitters

Mike Piazza	623
Ivan Rodriquez	490
Todd Hundley	437
Sandy Alomar	402
Dan Wilson	382
Jason Kendall	362
Mike Lieberthal	362
Javy Lopez	362
Charles Johnson	325
Terry Steinbach	314

The 10 Most Effective Fielders

Jason Kendall	499
Brad Ausmus	463
Charles Johnson	461
Dan Wilson	459
Ivan Rodriquez	458
Mike Lieberthal	451
Mike Piazza	450
Joe Girardi	434
Javy Lopez	431
Scott Servais	426

Mike Piazza, with an offensive HEQ of 623 had an outstanding year at bat. As you can see, no other catcher had even a 500 season.

All ten of the catchers above had very effective defensive seasons. How to explain this when we have already seen that there are very few catchers in baseball history with a career defensive score greater than 400? Here are the six most effective defensive catchers in appendices A and B (the score is the *average* of their ten best seasons):

Gary Carter	474	Bob Boone	419
Ray Schalk	457	Joe Torre	408
Johnny Bench	442	Carlton Fisk	403

Ray Schalk and Johnny Bench are both in the Hall of Fame and they are the only catchers in the Hall with a career defensive HEQ greater than 400.

Other catchers with a career defensive HEQ over 400 are Tony Pena (457), Jim Sundberg (432) and Bill Freehan (417). Yogi Berra came close at 399.

Two factors seem to be working in favor of some of the more recent catchers which influence their HEQ defensive score. First of all, many seem to be benefiting from the increased number of strikeouts being recorded (this is one reason why the putouts are capped at 800 in the formula). But, more importantly, more of today's catchers are catching 130 or more games per season — presumably because of their better physical conditioning. Catching that many games well pretty much assures a HEQ defensive score over 400.

Look at the list of the most effective seasons by a catcher above and note that in every one of those seasons the player played in more than 130 games. Now consider that the following catchers caught in more than 130 games in this many seasons: Bench (7), Berra (7), Campanella (2), Cochrane (3), Dickey (1), Hartnett (2), Carter (9) and Fisk (7). Both Pena and Sundberg caught in more than 130 games in ten different seasons.

A catcher can have a few good defensive seasons if his skills are outstanding. But it takes a special kind of athlete to be able to catch more than 130 games at the major league level for seven or more seasons. And, since the HEQ career defensive score is based on the ten best seasons, this explains why such Hall of Famers as Bill Dickey (career defensive HEQ of 354) and Mickey Cochrane (348) did not achieve higher scores. With catchers in particular the number of games played each season is the key because the position takes such a heavy physical toll.

It is not uncommon for a good defensive catcher to play regularly even though he may not hit very well. Probably the best example of this in baseball history is Ray Schalk. Schalk has the highest career defensive HEQ score (457) of the ten Hall of Fame catchers who have played in this century (Bench is second with 436). Yet Schalk's career offensive HEQ score (264) is the *lowest* of the 105 twentieth century position players in the Hall of Fame. Bob Boone has similar numbers with a 419 career defensive HEQ but an offensive HEQ of only 283.

This concludes our analysis of the results of the 1997 season for the position players. This analysis illustrates the use of the HEQ system in determining which players had the *most effective all-around seasons*. I hope it also demonstrates the value of a *total-season statistic* in helping us make some sense of the jumble of statistics that face us as baseball fans.

Chapter 20

1998 —
A Memorable Season

In 1998 the home run race between Mark McGwire and Sammy Sosa rejuvenated major league baseball in the eyes of the country in a manner that had not been seen in many years. McGwire wound up with the new home run record of 70 while Sosa finished with 66. An interesting question arises as to just how good a season McGwire and Sammy Sosa had in 1998 when compared to the great players of the past. That is, how does a home run record-breaking season compare statistically to some of the other great individual seasons of the century?

The HEQ rating system now gives us the ability to answer this question in a surprisingly straightforward manner. While the sports world marvels at the remarkable achievement of the two players, we can now step back and put the accomplishments of the 1998 season into their proper historical context.

Clearly, the feat of shattering the home run record that had stood for thirty-seven years places each player's season in a unique position among the great seasons of the game. But, as we all know, home runs alone do not define a player's offensive contribution, nor his overall contributions to his team. It is very interesting to compare the 1998 numbers with those of other outstanding seasons.

Recall that the offensive HEQ season score is obtained by adding together a player's total bases, runs scored, runs batted in, stolen bases and half of the walks:

Offensive HEQ for the season: S + 2D + 3T + 4HR + R + RBI + SB + .5BB

You can see from the formula that home run production has a big impact on the HEQ offensive score for the season and so we would expect that McGwire and Sosa would each have compiled an impressive offensive score for 1998. And this is indeed the case.

Before we examine the numbers produced in 1998, let us recall the two very special seasons enjoyed by Larry Walker and Ken Griffey Jr. in 1997.

The Two Extraordinary Seasons in 1997

To create some sort of perspective for the 1998 numbers, consider the seasons that the following two players enjoyed in 1997:

Larry Walker	754 + 305 =	1059
Ken Griffey Jr.	718 + 424 =	1142

Each of these 1997 seasons, in its own way, was one of the most extraordinary in the second half of the 20th century — even though neither received (understandably) one iota of the attention heaped upon the home run race in 1998.

Larry Walker's 754 offensive score in 1997 was the highest offensive season total since Ted Williams' had 759 in 1949 (a period of forty-eight years). In fact, at the time, Walker's score was the 23rd best offensive season in baseball history. As we will point out below, Sammy Sosa surpassed this offensive total in 1998.

Perhaps even more impressive than Walker's offensive score was Ken Griffey's achievement in 1997. His total season score of 1142 made him only the third player since 1950 to combine a 700 hitting season with a 400 fielding season — the ultimate all-around season. The other two players to do it were Mickey Mantle and Willie Mays (not bad company to keep). Griffey's 1997 season was the *greatest all-around season in thirty-five years*!

Mickey Mantle	1956	704 + 414 =	1118
Willie Mays	1962	710 + 44 =	1159
Ken Griffey	1997	718 + 424 =	1142

How good is a 700 offensive season? Prior to the 1998 season, there had only been nine 700 seasons since 1950:

Mickey Mantle	1956	704	Albert Belle	1996	708
Willie Mays	1962	710	Ellis Burks	1996	725
Frank Robinson	1962	706	Larry Walker	1997	754
Jim Rice	1978	702	Ken Griffey	1997	718
Barry Bonds	1993	709			

Amazingly, five players had 700 seasons in 1998: Sammy Sosa, Mark McGwire, Ken Griffey, Albert Belle and Alex Rodriguez.

Besides Walker and Griffey, nine other players had 600 offensive seasons in 1997. They were:

Jeff Bagwell	674	Mike Piazza	623
Andres Galarraga	653	Tino Martinez	621

Barry Bonds	645	Frank Thomas	615
Craig Biggio	626	Mark McGwire	612
Nomar Garciaparra	625		

Now, how good exactly were the seasons enjoyed by Mark McGuire and Sammy Sosa in 1998 when compared to the other players who had great seasons at bat? In the chart below we give the HEQ scores for these two players as well as for the other players who also had outstanding offensive seasons in 1998 — that is, a score of 600 or better.

The 1998 Season — The Most Effective Offensive Players

		Off.		*Def.*		*Total*
Sammy Sosa	RF	763	+	380	=	1143
Mark McGwire	1B	742	+	369	=	1111
Ken Griffey	CF	711	+	450	=	1161
Albert Belle	LF	711	+	355	=	1066
Alex Rodriquez	SS	700	+	423	=	1123
Juan Gonzalez	RF	674	+	244	=	918
Barry Bonds	LF	671	+	295	=	966
Vinny Castilla	3B	657	+	389	=	1046
Manny Ramirez	RF	638	+	322	=	960
Greg Vaughn	LF	624	+	286	=	910
Moises Alou	LF	621	+	274	=	895
Rafael Palmeiro	1B	620	+	430	=	1050
Craig Biggio	2B	618	+	372	=	990
Vladimir Guerrerro	RF	616	+	339	=	955
Nomar Garciaparra	SS	615	+	354	=	969
Mo Vaughn	1B	613	+	317	=	930
Jeff Bagwell	1B	610	+	406	=	1016

Note that there are a number of players who had outstanding batting averages in 1998 but who did not attain a 600 offensive score: Larry Walker (554), John Olerud (541), Bernie Williams (537) and Derek Jeter (571)—to name a few. This illustrates the value of the HEQ system — measuring *offensive effectiveness* and not just hits compared to times-at-bat.

The HEQ system demonstrates that both Mark McGwire and Sammy Sosa not only had extraordinary offensive seasons in 1998 (an offensive score over 700) but also decent defensive seasons. This indicates that both players were not only outstanding hitters but complete players as well. This is in contrast to Juan Gonzalez, for example, who had an impressive offensive score (674) but whose defensive score reflects the fact that he did not play regularly in the field (244).

Sammy Sosa's awesome offensive score of 763 in 1998 is, of course, better than Larry Walker's 1997 total of 754. This means that Sosa's offensive production was the most effective in baseball since Jimmie Foxx's 777 in 1938 — 60 years before! Sosa's season was the 17th most effective offensive season total in baseball history — better than any offensive season enjoyed by such superstars as Ted Williams, Stan Musial, Mickey Mantle, Willie Mays or Hank Aaron.

Eleven players had a 600 or better offensive season in 1997 while seventeen had such a season in 1998. But note that of those seventeen players only four had great defensive seasons as well (400 or better): Ken Griffey (450), Alex Rodriguez (423), Rafael Palmeiro (430) and Jeff Bagwell (406). Incredibly, two of these players, Griffey and Rodriguez, had 700/400 seasons — ultimate all-around seasons.

It is interesting to note that the only players to have a 600 or better offensive season for *both* 1997 and 1998 were Ken Griffey, Mark McGwire, Barry Bonds, Craig Biggio, Nomar Garciaparra and Jeff Bagwell. Albert Belle had 700 seasons in 1996 and 1998.

Of the seventeen players who had a 600+ offensive season in 1998, only eight managed a 1000+ overall season — giving you some idea of just how special a 1000 HEQ season is.

Ken Griffey's Accomplishment

The comparison above shows that despite not staying in the race to break the home run record, Ken Griffey had the best all-around season in 1998 — just as he did in 1997. This is primarily because Griffey is not only an outstanding offensive player but a truly great defensive player as well.

In 1998 Griffey did something of monumental significance — he had two 700/400 seasons in succession. In the long history of baseball, only one other player has ever accomplished the feat of having back-to-back 700/400 seasons: Babe Ruth in 1923 and 1924. Even at this stage of his career, Griffey deserves comparison with the three greatest all-around players of all time: Willie Mays, Joe DiMaggio and Ty Cobb — each of whom had just one 700/400 season. However, these are the only three players to average 600/400 over ten seasons.

Griffey's numbers in 1998 just surpass those of Mays in 1962 (1161 versus 1159) — meaning that Junior's 700/400 season in 1998 is *the greatest all-around season since 1938, a period of sixty years!* (See Jimmie Foxx's 1938 numbers in the list below.)

Griffey's accomplishment is so extraordinary that it almost compares to the setting of the new home run record for those baseball fans who are serious analysts of the statistics of the game.

Alex Rodriguez's Accomplishment

In 1998 Alex Rodriguez enjoyed *the greatest all-around season at short-stop in baseball history*. Now that is quite an accomplishment! No other short-stop has ever had a 700 offensive season. And Alex combined that hitting season with a great defensive season of 423.

In order to appreciate the magnitude of this incredible achievement, consider the fact that the only other infielder (non–first baseman) to ever have a 700/400 season was second baseman Rogers Hornsby in 1922 (as indicated in the list below).

Rodriguez joins Griffey, Mickey Mantle and Willie Mays as the only players in the second half of the twentieth century to have a 700/400 season.

By all means let us celebrate Mark McGwire's monumental new home run record. But at the same time, as serious followers of the game, let us also single out for extreme praise the once-in-a-generation performances by Sammy Sosa, Ken Griffey and Alex Rodriguez. Only a comprehensive comparative system like the HEQ enables us to identify such special achievements.

Barry Bonds' Accomplishment

Prior to the 1998 season only eleven players in baseball history had achieved a HEQ career offensive score of 600 or better: Babe Ruth (767), Lou Gehrig (750), Jimmie Foxx (686), Ted Williams (655), Willie Mays (645), Stan Musial (630), Hank Aaron (628), Rogers Hornsby (625), Joe DiMaggio (613), Ty Cobb (608) and Mel Ott (604). Hank Aaron was the last player to accomplish this and he retired after the 1976 season — 22 years before.

Barry Bonds' 1998 offensive HEQ of 671 now gives him a career offensive score of 606 — making him only the twelfth player to achieve this plateau. Bonds now ranks as the eleventh most effective hitter in baseball history — just behind Ty Cobb and just ahead of Mel Ott. And he still has time to improve on his score.

Mike Piazza's Accomplishment

Mike Piazza did not manage to produce a 600 offensive season in 1998 (as he did in 1997). His 1998 HEQ score was 549 + 466 = 1015. But this means that Piazza became the first catcher in baseball history to have three 1000 HEQ seasons in his career (he had 1015 in 1993 and 1073 in 1997). In fact, only one other catcher had as many as two such seasons. That was Johnny Bench who had 1105 in 1970 and 1099 in 1974 (Bench also had 999 in 1972). If Piazza can keep up this sort of performance for a few more years, he may eventually move ahead of Bench as the most effective catcher of all time.

How Do They Compare to the Best?

Perhaps a better basis for comparison for these 1998 seasons is to take a look at the best season enjoyed by each of the sixteen superstars at the top of the HEQ career rankings.

Babe Ruth	1921	894 + 414 =	1308
Willie Mays	1955	696 + 515 =	1211
Lou Gehrig	1927	836 + 386 =	1222
Jimmie Foxx	1938	777 + 400 =	1177
Joe DiMaggio	1937	771 + 486 =	1257
Tris Speaker	1912	648 + 512 =	1160
Charlie Gehringer	1936	662 + 454 =	1116
Stan Musial	1948	742 + 390 =	1132
Ty Cobb	1911	746 + 476 =	1222
Rogers Hornsby	1922	793 + 410 =	1203
Mike Schmidt	1974	610 + 467 =	1077
Ted Williams	1949	759 + 385 =	1144
Hank Aaron	1961	642 + 431 =	1073
Earl Averill	1931	687 + 426 =	1113
Mel Ott	1929	698 + 470 =	1168
Mickey Mantle	1956	704 + 414 =	1118

In the history of baseball, there have only been two 1300 seasons and six 1200 seasons. Chuck Klein had the other 1300 season in 1930 and Babe Ruth the other 1200 season (that is not on the list above) in 1923. Mays' 1200 season in 1955 was the last one ever recorded.

Ruth's offensive score of 894 in 1921 represents the most effective hitting season ever. Note that his defensive score that year was an excellent 414 — meaning that the young Ruth was quite a good defensive outfielder. This was a 700/400 season for Ruth (an ultimate all-around season). You will note that there are only five other such seasons on our list: Jimmie Foxx, Joe DiMaggio, Ty Cobb, Rogers Hornsby, and Mickey Mantle. This is the sort of company that Ken Griffey joined in 1997. And Griffey and Rodriguez matched in 1998.

Only two players on this list never had an 1100 season: Mike Schmidt and Hank Aaron. This means that these two players had to be models of consistency over a long period of time in order to wind up in the top-sixteen category without such a season.

Finally, one last note of comparison. How do the 1998 seasons of McGwire and Sosa compare to the seasons of Babe Ruth (1927) and Roger Maris (1961) when each passed the sixty home run barrier?

Babe Ruth	1927	815 + 374 =	1189
Sammy Sosa	1998	763 + 380 =	1143
Mark McGwire	1998	742 + 369 =	1111
Roger Maris	1961	687 + 288 =	975

Babe Ruth had his second 800 offensive season in 1927 and he also had a good fielding year. So, his numbers are clearly the best. Sosa and McGwire come in second and third respectively. Note that Roger Maris' offensive score fell short of the 700 mark. In fact, his defensive score in 1961 was so poor that, surprisingly, he did not even make the special 1000 total for the season.

Mark McGwire and Sammy Sosa each had monumental seasons in 1998. And it is interesting and valuable to see how their complete seasons compare to those of some of the other great players. Both had spectacular 700 offensive seasons and good defensive seasons.

But as all true believers of the game know, the real significance of their exciting 1998 home run race was in its broader contribution to baseball. No other sporting event in a generation has galvanized the American public like the race for the home run record put on by Mark McGwire and Sammy Sosa. I don't know about you — but I have the feeling that baseball is definitely still the National Pastime!

Epilogue:
The Longevity Factor —
The 100 Outstanding Players

As noted earlier in this book, the essential purpose of the HEQ rating system is to establish a fair, unbiased and relatively simple method for comparing the seasons of position players in baseball — using the actual numbers that the players have put into the record books. We do not use percentages (like the batting average), estimates (like runs created), adjustments (like adjusting for era) or opinions of various people because these tend to distort the actual accomplishments of the players. Our position is that the fairest way to compare the players is by looking, in a reasonable and logical manner, at the "pure" numbers that they recorded.

We have also made the point that one can get a very good idea of how good a "career" a player had by examining his ten best seasons. The HEQ ratings in Appendix A and B and elsewhere in the book reflect this concept. And so, the HEQ ratings are essentially rankings based on a player's *peak performance*— where the peak is defined to be his ten best seasons. But, no matter how close the ten best seasons may come to defining a player's place in the list of great players, there is no denying that this process does not take a player's longevity into account. Common sense would appear to dictate that there should be another element involved in order to make a distinction between, for example, the thirteen seasons that Joe DiMaggio played and the twenty-three seasons that Hank Aaron enjoyed.

Of course, as we all know, the word *career* is usually understood to mean the totality of a player's accomplishments over his entire playing time. The difficulty in attempting to account for longevity is to decide what elements should be included and what weight should be given to these elements when compared to the player's HEQ score (his ten best seasons). Keep in mind that the HEQ score already takes into account virtually all of the offensive and defensive numbers for those ten best seasons, so we want to account for those career numbers that separate the truly great long-playing players from their shorter-playing colleagues.

In deciding which numbers to include for longevity purposes, we decided to opt for simplicity rather than to attempt to include "everything." So, for example, if we attempted to include the number of home runs hit during a career, then we would have to also include the number of triples, doubles, etc. We ultimately decided to include only three elements in our longevity factor — the three offensive categories that we believe (when taken with the ten best seasons) truly separate the great players from the greatest players — and, at the same time, do not unfairly favor the slugger over the hitter. These three elements are hits, runs scored and runs batted in.

In listing the leaders in each offensive category, the official website of Major League Baseball (www.majorleaguebaseball.com) lists the following (March 1998):

1. The 107 players who have had more than 2300 hits during their careers.
2. The 129 players who have scored more than 1200 runs during their careers.
3. The 97 players who have knocked in more than 1200 runs during their careers.

We will use these numbers to award longevity points in the three categories listed. So, we will add to the HEQ scores:

1. One point for every twenty hits over 2300.
2. One point for every ten runs scored over 1200.
3. One point for every ten runs batted in over 1200.

Remember that we are using these categories because we wish to award longevity points only to those players who have truly distinguished themselves over a long period of time and we do not wish to favor the slugger over the hitter. We are using these cut-off points because we believe that the scores chosen by MLB are appropriate for our purpose.

The Player Career Total (PCT) is the sum of the accomplishments of the player's ten best seasons (the HEQ offensive and defensive scores) together with the longevity components (number of hits, runs and RBIs above the criteria above). As you can see from the table below, Babe Ruth ranks highest on the PCT with a score of 1337. His PCT is composed of the following: a defensive HEQ of 343, an offensive HEQ of 767, 29 points for hits (2873), 97 points for runs scored (2174) and 101 points for runs batted in (2210).

$$\text{Babe Ruth: } 343 + 767 + 29 + 97 + 101 = 1337$$

We believe that the PCT ranking reflects the outstanding position players of the twentieth century.

Here are the rankings of the 100 outstanding position players according to the PCT. The number in parentheses next to the player's name indicates the HEQ rating (peak performance based on only the ten best seasons). This is followed by the position usually associated with the player, the HEQ defensive score, the HEQ offensive score, the longevity points accumulated from hits, runs scored and runs-batted-in and the PCT score. Note that based on peak performance alone, Joe DiMaggio, for example, would rank fifth while Pete Rose would rank fifty-fourth.

The Player Career Total —
The Outstanding Players of the Twentieth Century

			Def	Off	Hits	Runs	RBIs	PCT
1.	Babe Ruth	(1) RF	343	767	29	97	101	1337
2.	Willie Mays	(2) CF	456	645	49	86	70	1306
3.	Ty Cobb	(8) CF	411	608	95	105	74	1293
4.	Hank Aaron	(11) RF	367	628	74	97	110	1276
5.	Lou Gehrig	(3) 1B	340	750	21	69	79	1259
6.	Stan Musial	(9) LF	387	630	67	75	75	1234
7.	Jimmie Foxx	(4) 1B	366	686	17	55	72	1196
8.	Tris Speaker	(6) CF	484	542	61	68	33	1188
9.	Mel Ott	(16) RF	379	604	29	66	66	1144
10.	Ted Williams	(14) LF	338	655	18	60	64	1135
11.	Charlie Gehringer	(7) 2B	432	592	27	57	23	1131
12.	Rogers Hornsby	(10) 2B	388	625	32	38	38	1121
13.	Eddie Murray	(25) 1B	416	538	46	41	40	1111
14.	Honus Wagner	(29) SS	408	534	56	54	53	1105
15.	Pete Rose	(54) LF	390	507	98	97	11	1103
16.	Al Simmons	(21) LF	366	596	31	31	63	1087
17.	Cal Ripken Jr	(12) SS	465	529	29	31	31	1085
18.	Frank Robinson	(36) RF	341	584	32	63	61	1081
19.	Joe DiMaggio	(5) CF	423	613	–	19	34	1079
20.	Carl Yastrzemski	(53) LF	364	533	56	62	64	1079
21.	Mike Schmidt	(13) 3B	415	578	–	31	40	1064
22.	Mickey Mantle	(17) CF	382	589	6	48	31	1056
23.	Paul Waner	(26) RF	402	551	43	43	11	1050
24.	Goose Goslin	(28) LF	380	570	22	28	41	1041
25.	Dave Winfield	(63) RF	350	538	41	47	63	1039
26.	Ernie Banks	(19) SS	423	545	14	11	44	1037
27.	Rickey Henderson	(31) LF	379	551	19	81	–	1030
28.	Robin Yount	(34) SS	416	512	42	43	21	1034
29.	Eddie Collins	(50) 2B	384	521	51	62	10	1028
30.	Max Carey	(18) CF	490	480	18	35	–	1023
31.	George Brett	(60) 3B	364	528	43	38	40	1013
32.	Eddie Mathews	(30) 3B	373	565	1	31	25	995
33.	Nap Lajoie	(68) 2B	372	503	47	31	40	993

		Def	*Off*	*Hits*	*Runs*	*RBIs*	*PCT*
34. Earl Averill	(15) CF	408	582	–	2	–	992
35. Richie Ashburn	(20) CF	529	434	14	12	–	989
36. Frankie Frisch	(42) 2B	409	506	29	33	4	981
37. Joe Cronin	(24) SS	424	530	–	3	22	979
38. Al Kaline	(75) RF	357	507	35	42	38	979
39. Andre Dawson	(57) LF	387	508	24	17	39	975
40. Barry Bonds	(23) LF	348	606	–	16	2	972
41. Sam Rice	(51) RF	413	492	34	31	–	970
42. Joe Morgan	(46) 2B	382	527	11	45	–	965
43. Ron Santo	(27) 3B	431	520	–	–	13	964
44. Brooks Robinson	(43) 3B	451	462	27	3	16	959
45. Kirby Puckett	(22) CF	453	503	–	–	–	956
46. Vada Pinson	(45) CF	387	524	23	17	–	951
47. Duke Snider	(32) CF	368	562	–	6	13	949
48. Johnny Bench	(33) C	436	493	–	–	18	947
49. George Sisler	(44) 1B	387	525	26	8	–	946
50. Ryne Sandberg	(38) 2B	407	517	4	12	–	940
51. Tony Perez	(73) 1B	361	504	22	7	45	939
52. George Davis	(78) SS	388	474	18	34	24	938
53. Billy Williams	(72) LF	301	566	21	21	28	937
54. Joe Medwick	(49) LF	358	549	9	–	18	934
55. Gary Carter	(37) C	474	450	–	–	3	927
56. Luke Appling	(59) SS	442	450	22	12	–	926
57. Keith Hernandez	(35) 1B	440	485	–	–	–	925
58. Dale Murphy	(41) CF	382	534	–	–	7	923
59. Rafael Palmeiro	(39) 1B	394	529	–	–	–	923
60. Bill Terry	(40) 1B	393	528	–	–	–	921
61. Reggie Jackson	(107) RF	288	533	14	35	50	920
62. Dave Parker	(80) RF	344	518	21	7	29	919
63. Hank Greenberg	(48) 1B	328	579	–	–	8	915
64. Harry Heilmann	(86) RF	305	548	18	9	34	914
65. Bobby Doerr	(47) 2B	425	482	–	–	5	912
66. Joe Carter	LF	357	528	–	–	25	910
67. Harmon Killebrew	(76) 1B	303	561	–	8	38	910
68. Wade Boggs	(87) 3B	357	493	31	27	–	908
69. Kiki Cuyler	(55) RF	373	524	–	11	–	908
70. Gil Hodges	(58) 1B	376	519	–	–	7	902
71. Arky Vaughan	(52) SS	417	485	–	–	–	902
72. Lou Brock	(109) LF	286	534	36	41	–	897
73. Steve Garvey	(69) 1B	371	500	15	–	11	897
74. Joe Sewell	(56) SS	437	460	–	–	–	897
75. Johnny Mize	(66) 1B	333	549	–	–	14	896
76. Rod Carew	(90) 2B	364	470	38	22	–	893
77. Roberto Clemente	(103) RF	339	486	35	22	11	893
78. Yogi Berra	(71) C	399	469	–	–	23	891
79. Ken Boyer	(61) 3B	387	504	–	–	–	891
80. Orlando Cepeda	(70) 1B	337	533	3	–	17	890
81. Sam Crawford	RF	298	507	33	19	33	890

		Def	*Off*	*Hits*	*Runs*	*RBIs*	*PCT*
82.	Dom DiMaggio	CF	440	450	–	–	–	890
83.	Chuck Klein	(62) RF	337	552	–	–	–	889
84.	Graig Nettles	(65) 3B	437	441	–	–	11	889
85.	Pie Traynor	(67) 3B	392	484	6	–	7	889
86.	Dwight Evans	(99) RF	342	491	7	27	18	885
87.	Nellie Fox	(83) 2B	433	424	18	8	–	883
88.	Rabbit Maranville	(79) SS	471	391	15	6	–	883
89.	Jim Rice	(91) LF	282	561	8	5	25	881
90.	Zack Wheat	(97) LF	371	466	29	9	6	881
91.	Fred Clarke	LF	356	462	19	42	–	879
92.	PeeWee Reese	(74) SS	420	445	–	14	–	879
93.	Luis Aparicio	(93) SS	442	400	19	14	–	875
94.	Willie Keeler	RF	285	505	32	52	–	874
95.	Paul Molitor	3B	217	536	51	58	11	873
96.	Joe Torre	(64) C	408	460	2	–	–	870
97.	Al Oliver	(104) CF	353	471	22	23	–	869
98.	Don Mattingly	(77) 1B	364	500	–	–	–	864
99.	Billy Herman	(81) 2B	427	434	3	–	–	864
100.	Tony Gwynn	(106) RF	347	474	31	10	–	862

Honorable Mention

101.	Ralph Kiner	(82) LF	321	537	–	–	–	858
102.	Jim Bottomley	(98) 1B	317	517	1	–	22	857
103.	Ozzie Smith	(92) SS	465	378	8	6	–	857
104.	Minnie Minoso	(84) LF	349	507	–	–	–	856
105.	Joe Gordon	2B	377	478	–	–	–	855
106.	Frank Baker	(85) 3B	402	451	–	–	–	853
107.	Carlton Fisk	(101) C	403	426	3	8	13	853
108.	Red Schoendienst	(94) 2B	419	423	7	2	–	851
109.	Larry Doby	(88) CF	373	475	–	–	–	848
110.	Heinie Manush	(102) LF	326	501	11	9	–	847
111.	Lloyd Waner	(96) CF	429	410	8	–	–	847
112.	Lou Boudreau	(89) SS	435	408	–	–	–	843
113.	Tony Lazzeri	(95) 2B	361	479	–	–	–	840
114.	Enos Slaughter	(108) RF	338	483	4	5	10	840
115.	Willie McCovey	1B	312	488	–	3	36	839
116.	Jimmy Collins	(100) 3B	395	437	–	–	–	832

Note that, according to the PCT ranking, there have been only two *1300 players*, four *1200 players*, nine *1100 players* and a total of thirty-one *1000 players* who have played the game in this century. There are forty-seven players on the lists above who have achieved points in all three of the longevity categories.

The PCT lists above represent the twentieth century players whom we have found who have a score greater than 830 — the score that represents "Hall of Fame numbers." You will note that there are a number of Hall of Fame players who are not on this list such as Jackie Robinson (796), Bill Dickey (780) and Willie Stargell (782). This is solely because these players simply did not post adequate numbers during their playing days.

The exclusion of such players from this list is not meant to imply that these players should not be in the HOF. We all know that there are players in the HOF whose numbers alone may not justify their induction — but who presumably have made other substantial contributions to the game. Two such players are Jackie Robinson and Roy Campanella. Both of these players were denied access to the major leagues during their early twenties because of the color barrier. It is obvious from their subsequent performances in the majors that had they been allowed to play during what would have been some of their most productive years — they certainly would have had substantially higher numbers.

Here are the first, second and third team PCT All Stars taken from the list above.

PCT All Stars — First Team

		Def	Off	Hits	Runs	RBIs	PCT
Babe Ruth	RF	343	767	29	97	101	1337
Willie Mays	CF	456	645	49	86	70	1306
Lou Gehrig	1B	340	750	21	69	79	1259
Stan Musial	LF	387	630	67	75	75	1234
Charlie Gehringer	2B	432	592	27	57	23	1131
Honus Wagner	SS	408	534	56	54	53	1105
Mike Schmidt	3B	415	578	–	31	40	1064
Johnny Bench	C	436	493	–	–	18	947

PCT All Stars — Second Team

		Def	Off	Hits	Runs	RBIs	PCT
Ty Cobb	CF	411	608	95	105	74	1293
Hank Aaron	RF	367	628	74	97	110	1276
Jimmie Foxx	1B	366	686	17	55	72	1196
Ted Williams	LF	338	655	18	60	64	1135
Rogers Hornsby	2B	388	625	32	38	38	1121
Cal Ripken Jr	SS	465	529	29	31	31	1085
George Brett	3B	364	528	43	38	40	1013
Gary Carter	C	474	450	–	–	3	927

PCT All Stars — Third Team

		Def	Off	Hits	Runs	RBIs	PCT
Tris Speaker	CF	484	542	61	68	33	1188
Mel Ott	RF	379	604	29	66	66	1144

		Def	*Off*	*Hits*	*Runs*	*RBIs*	*PCT*
Eddie Murray	1B	416	538	46	41	40	1111
Pete Rose	LF	390	507	98	97	11	1103
Ernie Banks	SS	423	545	14	11	44	1037
Eddie Collins	2B	384	521	51	62	10	1028
Eddie Mathews	3B	373	565	1	31	25	995
Yogi Berra	C	399	469	–	–	23	891

Only four players on these teams are not in the Hall of Fame: Cal Ripken Jr., Gary Carter, Eddie Murray and Pete Rose. Carter is currently eligible for induction but Ripken, Murray and Rose are not yet eligible.

These PCT rankings as well as the HEQ ratings are based exclusively on a combination of the actual numbers that the players produced during their playing days (both offensive and defensive). Obviously, many other combinations of these numbers are possible. This is but one attempt to put the numbers together in a relatively simple, yet objective and valid, manner.

The significance of the rankings being based solely on the numbers is that it will make it easier for those fans who enjoy adjusting the actual numbers of the players to account for such things as the era in which the player performed or the ballpark in which he played. In a similar manner, a fan can increase or decrease a particular component of the PCT (or add other components) to determine what effect such an adjustment would have on the total score.

Comparing the careers of baseball players to determine who were the greatest players is an exercise that many of us enjoy. This book has attempted to introduce yet another such process in the hope that it may add to the baseball fan's enjoyment of the game.

Appendix A:
Career HEQ Score for Players
in the Hall of Fame (1998)

This list shows the ranking for all the Hall of Famers of the twentieth century (position players) based on their 10 best seasons — 105 players.

The columns headed Def, Off, and Total represent the average defense, offense, and total HEQ scores for a player's ten best seasons — where 400 and 600 are great defensive and offensive scores, respectively, and 1000 is an outstanding overall season.

The columns headed 400, 600, and 1000 represent the number of such seasons a player had. So, for example, Mike Schmidt over his ten best seasons averaged 415 defensively and 578 offensively for a career HEQ of 993 — 12th place on the list. He had six 400 defensive seasons, two 600 offensive seasons, and six 1000 seasons.

			Def	*Off*	*Total*	*400*	*600*	*1000*
Group A								
1.	Babe Ruth	RF	343 +	767 =	1110	3	10	9
2.	Willie Mays	CF	456 +	645 =	1101	9	9	10
3.	Lou Gehrig	1B	340 +	750 =	1090	0	10	9
4.	Jimmie Foxx	1B	366 +	686 =	1052	1	9	7
5.	Joe DiMaggio	CF	423 +	613 =	1036	6	5	6
6.	Tris Speaker	CF	484 +	542 =	1026	10	3	4
7.	Charlie Gehringer	2B	432 +	592 =	1024	10	4	7
8.	Ty Cobb	CF	411 +	608 =	1019	4	5	4
9.	Stan Musial	LF	387 +	630 =	1017	4	6	5
10.	Rogers Hornsby	2B	388 +	625 =	1013	5	6	6
11.	Hank Aaron	RF	367 +	628 =	995	2	8	4
12.	Mike Schmidt	3B	415 +	578 =	993	6	2	6
13.	Ted Williams	LF	338 +	655 =	993	0	9	5
14.	Earl Averill	CF	408 +	582 =	990	4	6	4

		Def	*Off*	*Total*	*400*	*600*	*1000*
15. Mel Ott	RF	379 + 604	=	983	4	7	4
16. Mickey Mantle	CF	382 + 589	=	971	5	5	3
17. Max Carey	CF	490 + 480	=	970	10	0	3
18. Ernie Banks	SS	423 + 545	=	968	8	4	5
19. Richie Ashburn	CF	529 + 434	=	963	10	0	3
20. Al Simmons	LF	366 + 596	=	962	3	4	4
21. Joe Cronin	SS	424 + 530	=	954	8	1	2
22. Paul Waner	RF	402 + 551	=	953	5	3	2
23. Goose Goslin	LF	380 + 570	=	950	3	4	3
24. Honus Wagner	SS	408 + 534	=	942	6	0	2
25. Eddie Mathews	3B	373 + 565	=	938	0	2	2
26. Duke Snider	CF	368 + 562	=	930	3	4	4
27. Johnny Bench	C	436 + 493	=	929	8	1	2
28. Frank Robinson	RF	341 + 584	=	925	1	3	1
29. Bill Terry	1B	393 + 528	=	921	5	2	3

Group B

30. Frankie Frisch	2B	409 + 506	=	915	6	0	2
31. Brooks Robinson	3B	451 + 462	=	913	10	0	0
32. George Sisler	1B	387 + 525	=	912	3	3	2
33. Joe Morgan	2B	382 + 527	=	909	3	2	1
34. Bobby Doerr	2B	425 + 482	=	907	8	0	1
35. Hank Greenberg	1B	328 + 579	=	907	1	5	5
36. Joe Medwick	LF	358 + 549	=	907	1	3	3
37. Eddie Collins	2B	384 + 521	=	905	4	0	0
38. Sam Rice	RF	413 + 492	=	905	6	0	1
39. Arky Vaughan	SS	417 + 485	=	902	6	0	1
40. Carl Yastrzemski	LF	364 + 533	=	897	1	2	0
41. Kiki Cuyler	RF	373 + 524	=	897	3	2	3
42. Joe Sewell	SS	437 + 460	=	897	9	0	0
43. Luke Appling	SS	442 + 450	=	892	10	0	1
44. Chuck Klein	RF	337 + 552	=	889	3	5	4
45. Johnny Mize	1B	333 + 549	=	882	1	4	2
46. Pie Traynor	3B	392 + 484	=	876	4	0	1
47. Nap Lajoie	2B	372 + 503	=	875	3	1	1
48. Yogi Berra	C	399 + 469	=	868	8	0	1
49. Billy Williams	LF	301 + 566	=	867	0	2	0
50. PeeWee Reese	SS	420 + 445	=	865	7	0	0
51. Al Kaline	RF	357 + 507	=	864	3	0	1
52. Harmon Killebrew	1B	303 + 561	=	864	0	1	1
53. George Davis	SS	388 + 474	=	862	4	0	0
54. Rabbit Maranville	SS	471 + 391	=	862	10	0	0
55. Billy Herman	2B	427 + 434	=	861	7	0	0

Group C

56. Ralph Kiner	LF	321 + 537	=	858	1	4	2
57. Nellie Fox	2B	433 + 424	=	857	10	0	0
58. Frank Baker	3B	402 + 451	=	853	6	1	1
59. Harry Heilmann	RF	305 + 548	=	853	1	2	0

		Def	Off	Total	400	600	1000
60.	Larry Doby	CF	373 + 475 = 848		2	0	1
61.	Lou Boudreau	SS	435 + 408 = 843		8	0	1
62.	Luis Aparicio	SS	442 + 400 = 842		10	0	0
63.	Red Schoendienst	2B	419 + 423 = 842		8	0	0
64.	Tony Lazzeri	2B	361 + 479 = 840		2	0	0
65.	Lloyd Waner	CF	429 + 410 = 839		7	0	2
66.	Zack Wheat	LF	371 + 466 = 837		3	0	0
67.	Jim Bottomley	1B	317 + 517 = 834		0	3	0
68.	Rod Carew	2B	364 + 470 = 834		2	1	1
69.	Jimmy Collins	3B	395 + 437 = 832		5	0	0
70.	Heinie Manush	LF	326 + 501 = 827		0	1	0
71.	Roberto Clemente	RF	339 + 486 = 825		1	0	0
72.	Bobby Wallace	SS	422 + 401 = 823		8	0	0
73.	Reggie Jackson	RF	288 + 533 = 821		0	1	0
74.	Enos Slaughter	RF	338 + 483 = 821		1	0	0
75.	Lou Brock	LF	286 + 534 = 820		0	0	0
76.	Travis Jackson	SS	420 + 400 = 820		6	0	1
77.	Edd Roush	CF	389 + 431 = 820		4	0	0

Group D

		Def	Off	Total	400	600	1000
78.	Fred Clarke	LF	356 + 462 = 818		1	0	0
79.	Earle Combs	CF	347 + 467 = 814		3	0	0
80.	Dave Bancroft	SS	445 + 362 = 807		9	0	2
81.	George Kelly	1B	363 + 442 = 805		4	0	0
82.	Sam Crawford	RF	298 + 507 = 805		0	0	0
83.	Willie McCovey	1B	312 + 488 = 800		1	1	1
84.	Jackie Robinson	2B	340 + 456 = 796		2	1	1
85.	Willie Keeler	RF	285 + 505 = 790		0	2	0
86.	Mickey Cochrane	C	348 + 435 = 783		1	0	0
87.	Phil Rizzuto	SS	423 + 360 = 783		6	0	0
88.	Bill Dickey	C	354 + 426 = 780		3	0	0
89.	Hack Wilson	CF	302 + 478 = 780		2	3	3
90.	Harry Hooper	RF	344 + 422 = 766		0	0	0
91.	Elmer Flick	RF	297 + 463 = 760		0	0	0
92.	George Kell	3B	366 + 391 = 757		4	0	1
93.	Joe Tinker	SS	400 + 353 = 753		4	0	0
94.	Willie Stargell	RF	258 + 490 = 748		0	1	0
95.	Roy Campanella	C	363 + 384 = 747		2	1	1
96.	Freddy Lindstrom	3B	327 + 420 = 747		3	1	0
97.	Ray Schalk	C	457 + 264 = 721		8	0	0
98.	Gabby Hartnett	C	336 + 377 = 713		0	0	0
99.	Chick Hafey	LF	267 + 400 = 667		1	0	0
100.	Ross Youngs	RF	280 + 387 = 667		0	0	0
101.	Johnny Evers	2B	322 + 337 = 659		0	0	0
102.	Roger Bresnahan	C	330 + 280 = 610		2	0	0
103.	Rick Ferrell	C	310 + 297 = 607		0	0	0
104.	Ernie Lombardi	C	258 + 320 = 578		0	0	0
105.	Frank Chance	1B	245 + 327 = 572		0	0	0

Average HEQ Score — by Position

HEQ		Defense		Offense	
CF (14)	937	SS	426	1B	541
LF (13)	878	CF	415	LF	538
1B (11)	876	2B	390	RF	528
2B (14)	874	3B	390	CF	522
3B (8)	864	C	359	2B	484
SS (16)	863	LF	340	3B	474
RF (19)	862	1B	335	SS	437
C (10)	734	RF	334	C	375

Here are the most effective hitters and the most effective fielders in the Hall of Fame.

The Most Effective Hitters

			Off. HEQ	# of 600 seasons
1.	Babe Ruth	RF	767	10
2.	Lou Gehrig	1B	750	10
3.	Jimmie Foxx	1B	686	9
4.	Ted Williams	LF	655	9
5.	Willie Mays	CF	645	9
6.	Stan Musial	LF	630	6
7.	Hank Aaron	RF	628	8
8.	Rogers Hornsby	2B	625	6
9.	Joe DiMaggio	CF	613	5
10.	Ty Cobb	CF	608	5
11.	Mel Ott	RF	604	7
12.	Al Simmons	LF	596	4
13.	Charlie Gehringer	2B	592	4
14.	Mickey Mantle	CF	589	5
15.	Frank Robinson	RF	584	3

The Most Effective Fielders

			Def. HEQ	# of 400 seasons
1.	Richie Ashburn	CF	529	10
2.	Max Carey	CF	490	10
3.	Tris Speaker	CF	484	10
4.	Rabbit Maranville	SS	471	10
5.	Ray Schalk	C	457	8
6.	Willie Mays	CF	456	9
7.	Brooks Robinson	3B	451	10
8.	Dave Bancroft	SS	445	9

		Def. HEQ	# of 400 seasons
9. Luis Aparicio	SS	442	10
10. Luke Appling	SS	442	10
11. Joe Sewell	SS	437	9
12. Johnny Bench	C	436	8
13. Lou Boudreau	SS	435	8
14. Nellie Fox	2B	433	10
15. Charlie Gehringer	2B	432	10

Appendix B:
Career HEQ Score for
HOF Candidates (1998)

This list shows the ranking for fifty-two candidates (or former candidates) for the HOF based on their ten best seasons.

The columns headed Def, Off, and Total represent the average defense, offense, and total HEQ scores for a player's ten best seasons — where 400 and 600 are great defensive and offensive seasons respectively, and 1000 is an outstanding overall season.

The columns headed 400, 600, and 1000 represent the number of such seasons a player had. So, for example, Robin Yount over his ten best seasons averaged 416 defensively and 512 offensively for a career HEQ of 928 — 7th place on this list. He had six 400 defensive seasons, one 600 offensive season, and two 1000 seasons.

		Def	Off	Total	400	600	1000
Group A							
1. Cal Ripken	SS	465 + 529 =		994	10	1	4
2. Kirby Puckett	CF	453 + 503 =		956	7	2	4
3. Barry Bonds	LF	348 + 606 =		954	1	6	3
4. Eddie Murray	1B	416 + 538 =		954	7	0	2
5. Ron Santo	3B	431 + 520 =		951	6	0	3
6. Rickey Henderson	LF	379 + 551 =		930	3	2	3
7. Robin Yount	SS	416 + 512 =		928	6	1	2
8. Keith Hernandez	1B	440 + 485 =		925	9	0	2
9. Gary Carter	C	474 + 450 =		924	10	0	1
10. Ryne Sandberg	2B	407 + 517 =		924	6	1	2
11. Rafael Palmeiro	1B	394 + 529 =		923	4	3	3

		Def		Off		Total	400	600	1000

Group B

12.	Dale Murphy	CF	382	+	534	=	916	5	3	2
13.	Vada Pinson	CF	387	+	524	=	911	3	0	2
14.	Pete Rose	LF	390	+	507	=	897	4	0	0
15.	Andre Dawson	LF	387	+	508	=	895	5	2	1
16.	Gil Hodges	1B	376	+	519	=	895	3	1	2
17.	George Brett	3B	364	+	528	=	892	3	2	2
18.	Ken Boyer	3B	387	+	504	=	891	2	0	0
19.	Dave Winfield	RF	350	+	538	=	888	2	1	1
20.	Graig Nettles	3B	437	+	441	=	878	7	0	0
21.	Steve Garvey	1B	371	+	500	=	871	2	0	0
22.	Orlando Cepeda	1B	337	+	533	=	870	0	1	0
23.	Joe Torre	C	408	+	460	=	868	6	1	0
24.	Tony Perez	1B	361	+	504	=	865	1	1	0
25.	Don Mattingly	1B	364	+	500	=	864	1	2	2
26.	Dave Parker	RF	344	+	518	=	862	1	1	1

Group C

27.	Minnie Minoso	LF	349	+	507	=	856	1	0	1
28.	Wade Boggs	3B	357	+	493	=	850	3	0	0
29.	Jim Rice	LF	282	+	561	=	843	3	1	1
30.	Ozzie Smith	SS	465	+	378	=	843	10	0	0
31.	Dwight Evans	RF	342	+	491	=	833	0	2	0
32.	Carlton Fisk	C	403	+	426	=	829	4	0	0
33.	Al Oliver	CF	353	+	471	=	824	1	0	0
34.	Tony Gwynn	RF	347	+	474	=	821	1	0	0
35.	Willie Wilson	CF	396	+	424	=	820	4	0	1

Group D

36.	Bobby Grich	2B	411	+	403	=	814	5	0	0
37.	Dick Allen	1B	292	+	519	=	811	0	1	0
38.	Alan Trammell	SS	372	+	439	=	811	2	0	0
39.	Dave Concepcion	SS	418	+	390	=	808	8	0	0
40.	Lou Whitaker	2B	362	+	439	=	801	1	0	0
41.	Bill Mazeroski	2B	444	+	356	=	800	8	0	0
42.	Steve Sax	2B	371	+	420	=	791	1	0	0
43.	Curt Flood	CF	402	+	387	=	789	7	0	0
44.	Joe Jackson	RF	292	+	461	=	753	0	2	0
45.	Paul Molitor	3B	217	+	536	=	753	2	1	0
46.	Willie Randolph	2B	370	+	382	=	752	2	0	0
47.	Jack Clark	LF	304	+	442	=	746	0	0	0
48.	Tony Oliva	LF	256	+	476	=	732	0	1	0
49.	Carney Lansford	3B	303	+	414	=	717	0	0	0
50.	Pedro Guerrero	1B	283	+	428	=	711	0	0	0
51.	Bob Boone	C	419	+	283	=	702	7	0	0
52.	Kirk Gibson	LF	214	+	394	=	608	0	0	0

There are fifty-two players on this list of HOF candidates. They are distributed by position as follows: ten first basemen, six second basemen, five shortstops, seven third basemen, six center fielders, seven right fielders, seven left fielders and four catchers.

Here are the ten most effective hitters and the ten most effective fielders from the list of candidates:

The Ten Most Effective Hitters

	Off. HEQ	# of 600 seasons
Barry Bonds	606	6
Jim Rice	561	1
Rickey Henderson	551	2
Eddie Murray	538	0
Dave Winfield	538	1
Paul Molitor	536	1
Dale Murphy	534	3
Orlando Cepeda	533	1
Rafael Palmeiro	529	3
Cal Ripken	529	1

The Ten Most Effective Fielders

		Def. HEQ	# of 400 seasons
Gary Carter	C	474	10
Ozzie Smith	SS	465	10
Cal Ripken	SS	465	10
Kirby Puckett	CF	453	7
Bill Mazeroski	2B	444	8
Keith Hernandez	1B	440	9
Graig Nettles	3B	437	7
Ron Santo	3B	431	6
Bob Boone	C	419	7
Dave Concepcion	SS	418	8

Appendix C:
The HEQ Formulas —
Offensive and Defensive

The HEQ Offensive Formula

The offensive formula uses the following categories: Single (S), Double (D), Triple (T), Home run (HR), Run scored (R), Run batted in (RBI), Stolen base (SB), and Walk (BB).

Start with the concept of TOTAL BASES (S + 2D + 3T + 4HR) and add to it (R + RBI + SB + .5BB) creating a sum of the player's offensive output for the year.

Therefore, a player's HEQ offensive score for the year would be:

$$R + S + 2D + 3T + 4HR + RBI + .5BB + SB$$

An offensive HEQ score of 600 means that a particular player had an outstanding year at bat. Babe Ruth had the greatest HEQ offensive score of all the Hall of Famers in 1921 with a score of 894.

1. Babe Ruth and Lou Gehrig were the only players to have ten seasons with a HEQ offensive score over 600 each season.

2. There have been only 11 Hall of Famers who have averaged better than 600 offensively over ten seasons: Babe Ruth (767), Lou Gehrig (750), Jimmie Foxx (686), Ted Williams (655), Willie Mays (645), Hank Aaron (632), Stan Musial (630), Rogers Hornsby (625), Joe DiMaggio (613), Ty Cobb (608) and Mel Ott (604).

The HEQ Defensive Formulas

An assist or a double play by an outfielder requires more skill than a simple putout. The same is true for a catcher. Whereas, a putout by a first baseman generally requires very little skill. The maximum number of putouts that can be used in the formula for a catcher is 800. A weight of (-2) is assigned for an error at any position.

The defensive formulas use only the following categories: Putouts (P), Assists (A), Errors (E), and Double plays (DP).

The HEQ defensive formulas are as follows:

		MF
For outfielders:	PO + 4A - 2E + 4DP	1.00
For catchers:	PO + 3A - 2E + 2DP	.445
For second basemen:	PO + A - 2E + DP	.460
For third basemen:	PO + A - 2E + DP	.888
For shortstops:	PO + A - 2E + DP	.548
For first basemen:	.25PO + 3A - 2E + DP	.510

The position multiplication factor (MF) indicated is the number by which each sum is multiplied in order to make the different positions equivalent. It is based on a defensive benchmark of 400 for an outstanding season. The benchmark of 400 and the appropriate MFs were derived from a careful analysis of Gold Glove winners together with a comparison of outstanding defensive seasons at each position.

Only nine Hall of Famers had ten 400 defensive seasons: three center fielders, three shortstops, two second basemen, and one third baseman. They were Richie Ashburn, Max Carey, Tris Speaker, Rabbit Maranville, Luis Aparicio, Luke Appling, Nellie Fox, Charlie Gehringer, and Brooks Robinson.

Appendix D:
The Hall of Famers —
Their Ten Best Seasons

HANK AARON — RIGHT FIELD

	Games	Def.		Off.		HEQ
1957	151	370	+	649	=	1019
1958	153	343	+	566	=	909
1959	154	322	+	673	=	995
1960	153	384	+	608	=	992
1961	155	431	+	642	=	1073
1962	156	374	+	669	=	1043
1963	161	299	+	691	=	990
1966	158	375	+	628	=	1003
1967	155	367	+	615	=	982
1968	160	408	+	532	=	940
HEQ		367		628		995

LUKE APPLING — SHORTSTOP

	Games	Def.		Off.		HEQ
1933	151	463	+	480	=	943
1935	153	496	+	442	=	938
1936	138	454	+	559	=	1013
1937	154	457	+	488	=	945
1939	148	411	+	397	=	808
1940	150	412	+	463	=	875
1941	154	426	+	440	=	866
1943	155	462	+	453	=	915
1946	149	426	+	376	=	802
1949	142	409	+	402	=	811
HEQ		442		450		892

LUIS APARICIO — SHORTSTOP

	Games	Def.		Off.		HEQ
1958	145	438	+	355	=	793
1959	152	429	+	435	=	864
1960	153	513	+	426	=	939
1961	156	426	+	427	=	853
1962	153	435	+	353	=	788
1963	146	400	+	375	=	775
1964	146	419	+	422	=	841
1966	151	446	+	421	=	867
1969	156	474	+	402	=	876
1970	146	437	+	387	=	824
HEQ		442		400		842

RICHIE ASHBURN — CENTER FIELD

	Games	Def.		Off.		HEQ
1949	154	556	+	372	=	928
1950	151	435	+	410	=	845
1951	154	608	+	483	=	1091
1952	154	522	+	408	=	930
1953	156	574	+	466	=	1040
1954	153	523	+	436	=	959
1955	140	425	+	437	=	862
1956	154	541	+	435	=	976
1957	156	588	+	414	=	1002
1958	152	519	+	481	=	1000
HEQ		529		434		963

EARL AVERILL — CENTER FIELD

	Games	Def.		Off.		HEQ
1929	151	424	+	572	=	996
1930	139	371	+	546	=	917
1931	155	426	+	687	=	1113
1932	153	440	+	642	=	1082
1933	151	410	+	489	=	899
1934	154	444	+	636	=	1080
1935	140	389	+	510	=	899
1936	152	397	+	681	=	1078
1937	156	400	+	562	=	962
1938	134	377	+	498	=	875
HEQ		408		582		990

FRANK BAKER — THIRD BASE

	Games	Def.		Off.		HEQ
1909	148	371	+	433	=	804
1910	146	413	+	415	=	828
1911	148	406	+	570	=	976
1912	149	440	+	623	=	1063
1913	149	394	+	577	=	971
1914	150	431	+	471	=	902
1916	100	280	+	285	=	565
1917	146	475	+	372	=	847
1918	126	409	+	360	=	769
1919	141	396	+	408	=	804
HEQ		402		451		853

DAVE BANCROFT — SHORTSTOP

	Games	Def.		Off.		HEQ
1915	153	416	+	355	=	771
1916	142	427	+	248	=	675
1918	125	415	+	292	=	707
1920	150	529	+	404	=	933
1921	153	531	+	505	=	1036
1922	156	522	+	505	=	1027
1923	107	359	+	327	=	686
1925	128	412	+	367	=	779
1926	127	400	+	323	=	723
1928	149	443	+	291	=	734
HEQ		445		362		807

ERNIE BANKS — SHORTSTOP

	Games	Def.		Off.		HEQ
1955	154	455	+	602	=	1057
1956	139	372	+	484	=	856

ERNIE BANKS — SHORTSTOP (cont.)

	Games	Def.		Off.		HEQ
1957	156	402	+	602	=	1004
1958	154	436	+	657	=	1093
1959	155	472	+	625	=	1097
1960	156	454	+	579	=	1033
1962	154	410	+	518	=	928
1964	157	454	+	447	=	901
1965	163	414	+	493	=	907
1967	151	362	+	440	=	802
HEQ		423		545		968

JOHNNY BENCH — CATCHER

	Games	Def.		Off.		HEQ
1968	154	493	+	410	=	903
1969	148	457	+	463	=	920
1970	158	473	+	632	=	1105
1971	149	416	+	406	=	822
1972	147	440	+	559	=	999
1973	152	429	+	472	=	901
1974	160	502	+	597	=	1099
1975	142	360	+	512	=	872
1977	142	417	+	474	=	891
1979	130	371	+	404	=	775
HEQ		436		493		929

YOGI BERRA — CATCHER

	Games	Def.		Off.		HEQ
1950	151	434	+	590	=	1024
1951	141	428	+	476	=	904
1952	142	413	+	485	=	898
1953	137	337	+	476	=	813
1954	151	411	+	526	=	937
1955	147	402	+	477	=	879
1956	140	412	+	512	=	924
1957	134	405	+	397	=	802
1958	122	337	+	375	=	712
1959	131	406	+	374	=	780
HEQ		399		469		868

JIM BOTTOMLEY — FIRST BASE

	Games	Def.		Off.		HEQ
1924	137	270	+	493	=	763
1925	153	347	+	605	=	952
1926	154	328	+	556	=	884
1927	152	374	+	556	=	930
1928	149	302	+	667	=	969

JIM BOTTOMLEY— FIRST BASE (cont.)

	Games	Def.		Off.		HEQ
1929	146	335	+	601	=	936
1930	131	267	+	456	=	723
1933	145	345	+	381	=	726
1934	142	323	+	412	=	735
1936	140	274	+	448	=	722
HEQ		317		517		834

LOU BOUDREAU — SHORTSTOP

	Games	Def.		Off.		HEQ
1940	155	438	+	519	=	957
1941	148	430	+	443	=	873
1942	147	418	+	347	=	765
1943	152	487	+	394	=	881
1944	150	521	+	461	=	982
1945	97	307	+	257	=	564
1946	140	422	+	350	=	772
1947	150	478	+	409	=	887
1948	152	471	+	573	=	1044
1949	134	381	+	321	=	702
HEQ		435		408		843

ROGER BRESNAHAN — CATCHER

	Games	Def.		Off.		HEQ
1902	116	273	+	304	=	577
1903	113	268	+	407	=	675
1904	109	255	+	321	=	576
1905	104	375	+	264	=	642
1906	124	438	+	322	=	760
1907	110	356	+	259	=	615
1908	140	479	+	341	=	820
1910	88	261	+	189	=	450
1911	81	276	+	195	=	471
1914	101	317	+	192	=	509
HEQ		330		280		610

LOU BROCK — LEFT FIELD

	Games	Def.		Off.		HEQ
1964	155	302	+	526	=	828
1965	155	296	+	543	=	839
1966	156	271	+	506	=	777
1967	159	298	+	578	=	876
1968	159	281	+	504	=	785
1969	157	263	+	506	=	769
1970	155	271	+	532	=	803
1971	157	274	+	561	=	835

LOU BROCK — LEFT FIELD (cont.)

	Games	Def.		Off.		HEQ
1973	160	302	+	538	=	840
1974	153	303	+	544	=	847
HEQ		286		534		820

ROY CAMPANELLA — CATCHER

1948	83	247	+	214	=	461
1949	130	372	+	364	=	736
1950	126	379	+	429	=	808
1951	143	418	+	524	=	942
1952	128	371	+	419	=	790
1953	144	431	+	600	=	1031
1954	111	344	+	275	=	619
1955	123	373	+	478	=	851
1956	124	352	+	299	=	651
1957	103	343	+	239	=	582
HEQ		384		363		747

ROD CAREW — SECOND BASE

1971	147	323	+	384	=	707
1972	142	351	+	349	=	700
1973	149	398	+	505	=	903
1974	153	386	+	483	=	869
1975	143	351	+	510	=	861
1976	156	406	+	550	=	956
1977	155	446	+	637	=	1083
1978	152	387	+	470	=	857
1980	144	237	+	422	=	659
1982	138	361	+	387	=	748
HEQ		364		470		834

MAX CAREY— CENTER FIELD

1912	150	459	+	487	=	946
1913	154	467	+	467	=	934
1916	154	571	+	449	=	1020
1917	155	524	+	455	=	979
1918	126	461	+	370	=	831
1921	140	475	+	437	=	912
1922	155	523	+	590	=	1113
1923	153	540	+	547	=	1087
1924	149	472	+	496	=	968

MAX CAREY —
CENTER FIELD (cont.)

	Games	Def.		Off.		HEQ
1925	133	411	+	498	=	909
HEQ		490		480		970

FRANK CHANCE —
FIRST BASE

1901	69	135	+	203	=	338
1902	75	167	+	204	=	371
1903	125	249	+	464	=	713
1904	124	332	+	392	=	724
1905	118	278	+	409	=	687
1906	136	321	+	470	=	791
1907	111	289	+	306	=	595
1908	129	309	+	330	=	639
1909	93	192	+	255	=	447
1910	88	178	+	241	=	419
HEQ		245		327		572

FRED CLARKE —
LEFT FIELD

1895	132	342	+	469	=	811
1896	131	297	+	477	=	774
1897	128	306	+	543	=	849
1898	149	386	+	467	=	853
1899	148	393	+	528	=	921
1901	129	316	+	470	=	786
1905	141	336	+	409	=	745
1907	148	358	+	422	=	780
1908	151	398	+	393	=	791
1909	152	428	+	441	=	869
HEQ		356		462		818

ROBERTO CLEMENTE —
RIGHT FIELD

1958	140	400	+	355	=	755
1960	144	314	+	468	=	782
1961	146	366	+	531	=	897
1962	144	333	+	437	=	770
1964	155	329	+	514	=	843
1965	152	336	+	459	=	795
1966	154	374	+	596	=	970
1967	147	339	+	567	=	906
1969	138	276	+	486	=	762
1971	132	323	+	444	=	767
HEQ		339		486		825

TY COBB — CENTER FIELD

	Games	Def.		Off.		HEQ
1907	150	384	+	560	=	944
1909	156	318	+	616	=	934
1910	140	365	+	573	=	938
1911	146	476	+	746	=	1222
1912	140	384	+	609	=	993
1915	156	408	+	674	=	1082
1916	145	399	+	555	=	954
1917	152	495	+	630	=	1125
1921	128	397	+	577	=	974
1924	155	485	+	540	=	1025
HEQ		411		608		1019

MICKEY COCHRANE —
CATCHER

1925	134	293	+	341	=	634
1927	126	364	+	409	=	773
1928	131	367	+	411	=	778
1929	135	392	+	494	=	886
1930	130	388	+	484	=	872
1931	122	333	+	460	=	793
1932	139	425	+	544	=	969
1933	130	303	+	446	=	749
1934	129	322	+	377	=	699
1935	115	291	+	378	=	669
HEQ		348		435		783

EDDIE COLLINS —
SECOND BASE

1909	153	362	+	515	=	877
1910	153	400	+	511	=	911
1912	153	368	+	551	=	919
1913	148	350	+	538	=	888
1914	152	345	+	552	=	897
1915	155	387	+	528	=	915
1920	153	437	+	545	=	982
1922	154	408	+	459	=	867
1923	145	374	+	475	=	849
1924	152	407	+	534	=	941
HEQ		384		521		905

JIMMY COLLINS —
THIRD BASE

1895	107	309	+	292	=	601
1897	134	393	+	525	=	918

JIMMY COLLINS — THIRD BASE (cont.)

	Games	Def.	Off.		HEQ
1898	152	454	+ 536	=	990
1899	151	483	+ 453	=	936
1900	142	465	+ 470	=	935
1901	138	404	+ 517	=	921
1902	108	332	+ 359	=	691
1903	130	367	+ 437	=	804
1904	156	414	+ 424	=	838
1905	131	330	+ 356	=	686
HEQ		395	+ 437		832

EARLE COMBS — CENTER FIELD

1925	150	439	+ 497	=	936
1926	145	391	+ 461	=	852
1927	152	407	+ 578	=	985
1928	149	478	+ 513	=	991
1929	142	392	+ 504	=	896
1930	137	281	+ 542	=	823
1931	138	345	+ 474	=	819
1932	144	355	+ 521	=	876
1933	122	231	+ 374	=	605
1935	89	149	+ 209	=	358
HEQ		347	467		814

SAM CRAWFORD — RIGHT FIELD

1901	131	275	+ 497	=	772
1905	154	356	+ 442	=	798
1907	144	383	+ 488	=	871
1908	152	322	+ 486	=	808
1909	156	345	+ 500	=	845
1911	146	247	+ 594	=	841
1912	149	247	+ 525	=	772
1913	153	289	+ 498	=	787
1914	157	271	+ 519	=	790
1915	156	243	+ 514	=	757
HEQ		298	507		805

JOE CRONIN — SHORTSTOP

1930	154	477	+ 607	=	1084
1931	156	449	+ 573	=	1022
1932	143	430	+ 525	=	955
1933	152	467	+ 524	=	991

JOE CRONIN — SHORTSTOP (cont.)

	Games	Def.	Off.		HEQ
1935	144	401	+ 456	=	857
1937	148	406	+ 536	=	942
1938	143	433	+ 529	=	962
1939	143	423	+ 515	=	938
1940	149	391	+ 541	=	932
1941	143	361	+ 498	=	859
HEQ		424	530		954

KIKI CUYLER — RIGHT FIELD

1924	117	306	+ 477	=	783
1925	153	436	+ 685	=	1121
1926	157	469	+ 547	=	1016
1928	133	331	+ 470	=	801
1929	139	356	+ 560	=	916
1930	156	473	+ 713	=	1186
1931	154	385	+ 527	=	912
1932	110	255	+ 356	=	611
1934	142	367	+ 445	=	812
1936	144	352	+ 457	=	809
HEQ		373	524		897

GEORGE DAVIS — SHORTSTOP

1890	136	427	+ 417	=	844
1891	136	385	+ 506	=	891
1893	133	342	+ 593	=	935
1894	122	297	+ 540	=	837
1896	124	348	+ 495	=	843
1897	130	391	+ 598	=	989
1901	130	413	+ 390	=	803
1902	132	396	+ 428	=	824
1904	152	442	+ 400	=	842
1905	151	436	+ 377	=	813
HEQ		388	474		862

BILL DICKEY — CATCHER

1929	130	340	+ 349	=	689
1931	130	405	+ 376	=	781
1932	108	352	+ 373	=	725
1933	130	438	+ 416	=	854
1934	104	303	+ 342	=	645
1935	120	325	+ 359	=	684

BILL DICKEY — CATCHER
(cont.)

	Games	Def.		Off.		HEQ
1936	112	300	+	490	=	790
1937	140	418	+	562	=	980
1938	132	328	+	498	=	826
1939	128	331	+	493	=	824
HEQ		354		426		780

JOE DIMAGGIO — CENTER FIELD

1936	138	423	+	640	=	1063
1937	151	486	+	771	=	1257
1938	145	439	+	653	=	1092
1939	120	379	+	573	=	952
1940	132	375	+	576	=	951
1941	139	450	+	637	=	1087
1942	154	447	+	579	=	1026
1946	132	374	+	464	=	838
1948	153	462	+	655	=	1117
1950	139	392	+	583	=	975
HEQ		423		613		1036

LARRY DOBY — CENTER FIELD

1948	121	319	+	400	=	719
1949	147	373	+	503	=	876
1950	142	369	+	543	=	912
1951	134	365	+	437	=	802
1952	140	442	+	539	=	981
1953	149	394	+	495	=	889
1954	153	487	+	545	=	1032
1955	131	337	+	447	=	784
1956	140	385	+	477	=	862
1957	119	259	+	359	=	618
HEQ		373		475		848

BOBBY DOERR — SECOND BASE

1938	145	395	+	387	=	782
1940	151	440	+	527	=	967
1942	144	410	+	459	=	869
1943	155	469	+	441	=	910
1944	125	352	+	457	=	809
1946	151	463	+	513	=	976
1947	146	427	+	446	=	873

BOBBY DOERR — SECOND BASE (cont.)

	Games	Def.		Off.		HEQ
1948	140	415	+	516	=	931
1949	139	430	+	509	=	939
1950	149	452	+	564	=	1016
HEQ		425		482		907

JOHNNY EVERS — SECOND BASE

1903	124	252	+	334	=	586
1904	152	388	+	305	=	693
1906	154	344	+	351	=	695
1907	151	386	+	341	=	727
1908	126	270	+	345	=	615
1909	127	262	+	333	=	595
1910	125	284	+	336	=	620
1912	143	352	+	400	=	752
1913	136	340	+	332	=	672
1914	139	339	+	299	=	638
HEQ		322		337		659

RICK FERRELL — CATCHER

1930	101	236	+	221	=	457
1931	117	295	+	299	=	594
1932	126	321	+	354	=	675
1933	140	388	+	358	=	746
1934	132	333	+	301	=	634
1935	133	336	+	342	=	678
1936	121	318	+	336	=	654
1937	104	263	+	207	=	470
1938	135	324	+	309	=	633
1941	121	282	+	241	=	523
HEQ		310		297		607

ELMER FLICK — RIGHT FIELD

1898	134	299	+	434	=	733
1899	127	320	+	464	=	784
1900	138	300	+	576	=	876
1901	138	374	+	526	=	900
1902	121	209	+	388	=	597
1903	140	269	+	398	=	667
1904	150	323	+	477	=	800
1905	132	241	+	429	=	670
1906	157	324	+	501	=	825
1907	147	313	+	437	=	750
HEQ		297		463		760

NELLIE FOX — SECOND BASE

	Games	Def.		Off.		HEQ
1951	147	432	+	436	=	868
1952	152	425	+	374	=	799
1953	154	436	+	427	=	863
1954	155	403	+	447	=	850
1955	154	434	+	443	=	877
1956	154	448	+	431	=	879
1957	155	469	+	471	=	940
1958	155	430	+	380	=	810
1959	156	409	+	438	=	847
1960	150	441	+	396	=	837
HEQ		433		424		857

JIMMIE FOXX — FIRST BASE

	Games	Def.		Off.		HEQ
1929	149	338	+	625	=	963
1930	153	332	+	695	=	1027
1932	154	365	+	819	=	1184
1933	149	356	+	741	=	1097
1934	150	393	+	677	=	1068
1935	147	385	+	636	=	1021
1936	155	342	+	708	=	1050
1937	150	380	+	604	=	984
1938	149	400	+	777	=	1177
1940	144	372	+	579	=	951
HEQ		366		686		1052

FRANKIE FRISCH — SECOND BASE

	Games	Def.		Off.		HEQ
1921	153	400	+	591	=	991
1922	132	365	+	432	=	797
1923	151	422	+	590	=	1012
1924	145	477	+	522	=	999
1927	153	506	+	551	=	1057
1928	141	412	+	495	=	907
1929	138	355	+	473	=	828
1930	133	403	+	559	=	962
1931	131	354	+	434	=	788
1933	147	395	+	415	=	810
HEQ		409		506		915

LOU GEHRIG — FIRST BASE

	Games	Def.		Off.		HEQ
1927	155	386	+	836	=	1222
1928	154	349	+	697	=	1046

LOU GEHRIG — FIRST BASE (cont.)

	Games	Def.		Off.		HEQ
1929	154	371	+	641	=	1012
1930	154	342	+	799	=	1141
1931	155	309	+	833	=	1142
1932	156	313	+	718	=	1031
1933	152	305	+	691	=	996
1934	154	342	+	766	=	1108
1936	155	357	+	790	=	1147
1937	157	329	+	731	=	1060
HEQ		340		750		1090

CHARLIE GEHRINGER — SECOND BASE

	Games	Def.		Off.		HEQ
1928	154	421	+	504	=	925
1929	155	438	+	633	=	1071
1930	154	441	+	622	=	1063
1932	152	433	+	569	=	1002
1933	155	449	+	545	=	994
1934	154	431	+	635	=	1066
1935	150	419	+	588	=	1007
1936	154	454	+	662	=	1116
1937	144	411	+	578	=	989
1938	152	424	+	587	=	1011
HEQ		432		592		1024

GOOSE GOSLIN — LEFT FIELD

	Games	Def.		Off.		HEQ
1923	150	404	+	484	=	888
1924	154	401	+	578	=	979
1925	150	461	+	611	=	1072
1926	147	475	+	561	=	1036
1927	148	366	+	562	=	928
1930	148	347	+	655	=	1002
1931	151	351	+	596	=	947
1932	150	382	+	518	=	900
1934	151	328	+	522	=	850
1936	147	288	+	605	=	893
HEQ		380		570		950

HANK GREENBERG — FIRST BASE

	Games	Def.		Off.		HEQ
1933	117	283	+	385	=	668
1934	153	361	+	654	=	1015
1935	152	394	+	728	=	1122

HANK GREENBERG —
FIRST BASE (cont.)

	Games	Def.		Off.		HEQ
1937	154	399	+	776	=	1175
1938	155	433	+	737	=	1170
1939	138	314	+	589	=	903
1940	148	328	+	716	=	1044
1945	78	141	+	278	=	419
1946	142	345	+	536	=	881
1947	125	280	+	389	=	669
HEQ		328		579		907

CHICK HAFEY —
LEFT FIELD

	Games	Def.		Off.		HEQ
1925	93	206	+	250	=	456
1927	103	275	+	359	=	634
1928	138	329	+	554	=	883
1929	134	294	+	583	=	877
1930	120	227	+	541	=	768
1931	122	238	+	476	=	714
1932	83	141	+	203	=	344
1933	144	438	+	401	=	839
1934	140	386	+	424	=	810
1937	89	140	+	209	=	349
HEQ		267		400		667

GABBY HARTNETT —
CATCHER

	Games	Def.		Off.		HEQ
1924	111	288	+	338	=	626
1925	117	327	+	368	=	695
1927	127	350	+	364	=	714
1928	120	347	+	348	=	695
1930	141	381	+	554	=	935
1933	140	348	+	375	=	723
1934	130	391	+	390	=	781
1935	116	317	+	405	=	722
1936	121	327	+	316	=	643
1937	110	285	+	346	=	631
HEQ		336		377		713

HARRY HEILMANN —
RIGHT FIELD

	Games	Def.		Off.		HEQ
1921	149	271	+	647	=	918
1922	118	200	+	493	=	693
1923	144	353	+	612	=	965
1924	153	406	+	577	=	983

HARRY HEILMANN —
RIGHT FIELD (cont.)

	Games	Def.		Off.		HEQ
1925	150	300	+	597	=	897
1926	141	302	+	501	=	803
1927	141	266	+	584	=	850
1928	151	344	+	509	=	853
1929	125	223	+	492	=	715
1930	142	380	+	469	=	849
HEQ		305		548		853

BILLY HERMAN —
SECOND BASE

	Games	Def.		Off.		HEQ
1932	154	439	+	452	=	891
1933	153	461	+	366	=	827
1935	154	448	+	540	=	988
1936	153	465	+	526	=	991
1937	138	399	+	471	=	870
1938	152	458	+	399	=	857
1939	156	414	+	386	=	800
1940	135	397	+	369	=	766
1942	155	390	+	373	=	763
1943	153	402	+	457	=	859
HEQ		427		434		861

HARRY HOOPER —
RIGHT FIELD

	Games	Def.		Off.		HEQ
1910	155	353	+	370	=	723
1912	147	314	+	406	=	720
1913	148	358	+	430	=	788
1915	149	359	+	393	=	752
1916	151	342	+	380	=	722
1917	151	321	+	390	=	711
1920	139	337	+	456	=	793
1922	152	368	+	508	=	876
1923	145	320	+	440	=	760
1924	130	363	+	447	=	810
HEQ		344		422		766

ROGERS HORNSBY —
SECOND BASE

	Games	Def.		Off.		HEQ
1917	145	424	+	445	=	869
1920	149	403	+	561	=	964
1921	154	391	+	678	=	1069
1922	154	410	+	793	=	1203
1924	143	396	+	638	=	1034

ROGERS HORNSBY— SECOND BASE (cont.)

	Games	Def.		Off.		HEQ
1925	138	336	+	704	=	1040
1926	134	321	+	467	=	788
1927	155	427	+	643	=	1070
1928	140	362	+	559	=	921
1929	156	411	+	760	=	1171
HEQ		388		625		1013

REGGIE JACKSON— RIGHT FIELD

	Games	Def.		Off.		HEQ
1969	152	320	+	645	=	965
1971	150	343	+	503	=	846
1973	151	300	+	562	=	862
1974	148	316	+	511	=	827
1975	157	363	+	549	=	912
1976	134	306	+	480	=	786
1977	146	238	+	546	=	784
1979	131	302	+	462	=	764
1980	143	172	+	555	=	727
1982	153	216	+	522	=	738
HEQ		288		533		821

TRAVIS JACKSON— SHORTSTOP

	Games	Def.		Off.		HEQ
1924	151	466	+	429	=	895
1925	112	344	+	293	=	637
1926	111	345	+	317	=	662
1927	127	407	+	417	=	824
1928	150	506	+	420	=	926
1929	149	512	+	496	=	1008
1930	116	368	+	402	=	770
1931	145	454	+	400	=	854
1934	137	391	+	424	=	815
1935	128	408	+	397	=	805
HEQ		420		400		820

AL KALINE — RIGHT FIELD

	Games	Def.		Off.		HEQ
1955	152	364	+	591	=	955
1956	153	419	+	593	=	1012
1957	149	369	+	482	=	851
1958	146	420	+	469	=	889
1959	136	372	+	497	=	869
1960	147	381	+	432	=	813
1961	153	418	+	547	=	965
1963	145	263	+	506	=	769

AL KALINE — RIGHT FIELD (cont.)

	Games	Def.		Off.		HEQ
1966	142	293	+	485	=	778
1967	131	273	+	469	=	742
HEQ		357		507		864

WILLIE KEELER— RIGHT FIELD

	Games	Def.		Off.		HEQ
1894	129	300	+	616	=	916
1895	131	328	+	585	=	913
1896	126	315	+	591	=	906
1897	129	259	+	605	=	864
1898	129	256	+	444	=	700
1899	141	298	+	522	=	820
1900	136	299	+	483	=	782
1901	136	273	+	450	=	723
1902	133	274	+	370	=	644
1904	143	250	+	379	=	629
HEQ		285		505		790

GEORGE KELL— THIRD BASE

	Games	Def.		Off.		HEQ
1945	147	464	+	324	=	788
1946	131	374	+	370	=	744
1947	152	431	+	450	=	881
1949	134	378	+	443	=	821
1950	157	455	+	561	=	1016
1951	147	425	+	431	=	856
1952	114	286	+	313	=	599
1953	134	313	+	394	=	707
1955	128	243	+	337	=	580
1956	123	292	+	285	=	577
HEQ		366		391		757

GEORGE KELLY— FIRST BASE

	Games	Def.		Off.		HEQ
1920	155	429	+	424	=	853
1921	149	424	+	551	=	975
1922	151	416	+	524	=	940
1923	145	339	+	476	=	815
1924	144	356	+	566	=	922
1925	147	388	+	485	=	873
1926	136	357	+	394	=	751
1928	116	261	+	295	=	556
1929	147	407	+	447	=	854

GEORGE KELLY —
FIRST BASE (cont.)

	Games	Def.		Off.		HEQ
1930	90	253	+	255	=	508
HEQ		363		442		805

HARMON KILLEBREW —
FIRST BASE

	Games	Def.		Off.		HEQ
1959	153	372	+	533	=	905
1961	150	343	+	599	=	942
1962	155	234	+	567	=	801
1963	142	241	+	506	=	747
1964	158	222	+	569	=	791
1966	162	325	+	557	=	882
1967	163	338	+	590	=	928
1969	162	357	+	651	=	1008
1970	157	302	+	561	=	863
1971	147	297	+	472	=	769
HEQ		303		561		864

RALPH KINER —
LEFT FIELD

	Games	Def.		Off.		HEQ
1946	144	349	+	400	=	749
1947	152	412	+	656	=	1068
1948	156	390	+	580	=	970
1949	152	357	+	669	=	1026
1950	150	325	+	616	=	941
1951	151	336	+	637	=	973
1952	149	270	+	493	=	763
1953	158	322	+	556	=	878
1954	147	308	+	472	=	780
1955	113	145	+	288	=	433
HEQ		321		537		858

CHUCK KLEIN —
RIGHT FIELD

	Games	Def.		Off.		HEQ
1929	149	381	+	708	=	1089
1930	156	544	+	804	=	1348
1931	148	326	+	626	=	952
1932	154	429	+	759	=	1188
1933	152	433	+	629	=	1062
1934	115	236	+	407	=	643
1935	119	267	+	381	=	648
1936	146	302	+	545	=	847
1937	115	211	+	355	=	566
1938	129	245	+	303	=	548
HEQ		337		552		889

NAP LAJOIE —
SECOND BASE

	Games	Def.		Off.		HEQ
1897	127	259	+	572	=	831
1898	147	379	+	556	=	935
1900	102	293	+	444	=	737
1901	131	397	+	659	=	1056
1903	125	353	+	467	=	820
1904	140	347	+	542	=	889
1906	152	436	+	494	=	930
1907	137	400	+	355	=	755
1908	157	469	+	408	=	877
1910	159	392	+	530	=	922
HEQ		372		503		875

TONY LAZZERI —
SECOND BASE

	Games	Def.		Off.		HEQ
1926	155	364	+	508	=	872
1927	153	402	+	526	=	928
1929	147	406	+	556	=	962
1930	143	398	+	528	=	926
1931	135	314	+	402	=	716
1932	142	377	+	502	=	879
1933	139	352	+	504	=	856
1934	123	308	+	368	=	676
1935	130	320	+	397	=	717
1936	150	370	+	495	=	865
HEQ		361		479		840

FRED LINDSTROM —
THIRD BASE

	Games	Def.		Off.		HEQ
1925	104	230	+	245	=	475
1926	140	350	+	425	=	775
1927	138	330	+	440	=	770
1928	153	424	+	564	=	988
1929	130	345	+	470	=	815
1930	148	360	+	622	=	982
1932	144	400	+	437	=	837
1933	138	414	+	438	=	852
1934	97	213	+	308	=	521
1935	90	208	+	250	=	458
HEQ		327		420		747

ERNIE LOMBARDI —
CATCHER

	Games	Def.		Off.		HEQ
1932	118	223	+	330	=	553
1934	132	255	+	293	=	548

ERNIE LOMBARDI —
CATCHER

	Games	Def.		Off.		HEQ
1936	121	214	+	313	=	527
1937	120	218	+	282	=	500
1938	129	324	+	431	=	755
1939	130	320	+	365	=	685
1940	109	238	+	324	=	562
1941	117	313	+	261	=	574
1944	117	217	+	250	=	467
1945	115	255	+	317	=	572
HEQ		258		320		578

MICKEY MANTLE —
CENTER FIELD

	Games	Def.		Off.		HEQ
1952	142	403	+	514	=	917
1953	127	358	+	474	=	832
1954	146	416	+	572	=	988
1955	147	422	+	601	=	1023
1956	150	414	+	704	=	1118
1957	144	338	+	619	=	957
1958	150	343	+	614	=	957
1959	144	402	+	525	=	927
1960	153	360	+	577	=	937
1961	153	363	+	688	=	1051
HEQ		382		589		971

HEINIE MANUSH —
LEFT FIELD

	Games	Def.		Off.		HEQ
1926	136	303	+	489	=	792
1927	151	387	+	490	=	877
1928	154	381	+	616	=	997
1929	142	341	+	484	=	825
1930	137	289	+	511	=	800
1931	146	257	+	471	=	728
1932	149	346	+	587	=	933
1933	153	357	+	536	=	893
1934	137	309	+	493	=	802
1935	119	295	+	331	=	626
HEQ		326		501		827

RABBIT MARANVILLE —
SHORTSTOP

	Games	Def.		Off.		HEQ
1913	143	414	+	351	=	765
1914	156	517	+	394	=	911
1916	155	482	+	370	=	852
1917	142	433	+	359	=	792

RABBIT MARANVILLE —
SHORTSTOP (cont.)

	Games	Def.		Off.		HEQ
1921	153	470	+	441	=	911
1922	155	510	+	487	=	997
1923	141	477	+	355	=	832
1924	152	455	+	406	=	861
1929	146	487	+	384	=	871
1930	142	465	+	366	=	831
HEQ		471		391		862

EDDIE MATHEWS —
THIRD BASE

	Games	Def.		Off.		HEQ
1953	157	389	+	659	=	1048
1954	138	344	+	553	=	897
1955	141	356	+	567	=	923
1956	151	348	+	536	=	884
1957	148	377	+	560	=	937
1959	148	385	+	626	=	1011
1960	153	355	+	597	=	952
1961	152	393	+	559	=	952
1962	152	382	+	517	=	899
1963	158	398	+	479	=	877
HEQ		373		565		938

WILLIE MAYS —
CENTER FIELD

	Games	Def.		Off.		HEQ
1954	151	522	+	647	=	1169
1955	152	515	+	696	=	1211
1956	152	477	+	581	=	1058
1957	152	480	+	651	=	1131
1958	152	487	+	637	=	1124
1961	154	409	+	645	=	1054
1962	162	449	+	710	=	1159
1963	157	413	+	606	=	1019
1964	157	414	+	645	=	1059
1965	157	393	+	637	=	1030
HEQ		456		645		1101

WILLIE McCOVEY —
FIRST BASE

	Games	Def.		Off.		HEQ
1963	152	261	+	540	=	801
1965	160	334	+	520	=	854
1966	150	312	+	515	=	827
1967	135	316	+	447	=	763
1968	148	349	+	511	=	860

WILLIE McCOVEY — FIRST BASE (cont.)

	Games	Def.		Off.		HEQ
1969	149	345	+	610	=	955
1970	152	405	+	596	=	1001
1973	130	268	+	390	=	658
1975	122	269	+	331	=	600
1977	141	263	+	418	=	681
HEQ		312		488		800

JOE MEDWICK — LEFT FIELD

	Games	Def.		Off.		HEQ
1933	148	380	+	504	=	884
1934	149	338	+	558	=	896
1935	154	358	+	642	=	1000
1936	155	435	+	640	=	1075
1937	156	361	+	696	=	1057
1938	146	384	+	559	=	943
1939	150	341	+	551	=	892
1940	143	341	+	467	=	808
1941	133	312	+	487	=	799
1944	128	326	+	389	=	715
HEQ		358		549		907

JOHNNY MIZE — FIRST BASE

	Games	Def.		Off.		HEQ
1936	126	257	+	434	=	691
1937	145	305	+	579	=	884
1938	149	352	+	550	=	902
1939	153	353	+	611	=	964
1940	155	337	+	664	=	1001
1941	126	318	+	459	=	777
1942	142	333	+	522	=	855
1946	101	275	+	391	=	666
1947	154	412	+	674	=	1086
1948	152	388	+	602	=	990
HEQ		333		549		882

JOE MORGAN — SECOND BASE

	Games	Def.		Off.		HEQ
1965	157	399	+	460	=	859
1969	147	322	+	440	=	762
1970	144	388	+	464	=	852
1971	160	408	+	454	=	862
1972	149	406	+	551	=	957
1973	157	435	+	605	=	1040

JOE MORGAN — SECOND BASE (cont.)

	Games	Def.		Off.		HEQ
1974	149	366	+	545	=	911
1975	146	393	+	587	=	980
1976	141	339	+	613	=	952
1977	153	368	+	548	=	916
HEQ		382		527		909

STAN MUSIAL — LEFT FIELD

	Games	Def.		Off.		HEQ
1943	157	438	+	531	=	1019
1944	146	415	+	570	=	985
1946	156	404	+	637	=	1041
1948	155	390	+	742	=	1132
1949	157	386	+	690	=	1076
1951	152	424	+	640	=	1064
1952	154	372	+	557	=	929
1953	157	324	+	657	=	981
1954	153	341	+	658	=	999
1955	154	379	+	568	=	947
HEQ		387		630		1017

MEL OTT — RIGHT FIELD

	Games	Def.		Off.		HEQ
1929	150	470	+	698	=	1168
1930	148	414	+	603	=	1017
1931	138	414	+	540	=	954
1932	154	399	+	638	=	1037
1934	153	322	+	641	=	963
1935	152	411	+	604	=	1015
1936	150	334	+	631	=	965
1937	151	336	+	537	=	873
1938	150	361	+	600	=	961
1942	152	335	+	545	=	880
HEQ		379		604		983

PEE WEE REESE — SHORTSTOP

	Games	Def.		Off.		HEQ
1942	151	465	+	383	=	848
1946	152	438	+	398	=	836
1947	142	414	+	416	=	830
1948	151	449	+	457	=	906
1949	155	453	+	542	=	995
1950	141	419	+	414	=	833
1951	154	411	+	481	=	892
1952	149	386	+	429	=	815

PEE WEE REESE — SHORTSTOP (cont.)

	Games	Def.		Off.		HEQ
1953	140	374	+	452	=	826
1954	141	395	+	472	=	867
HEQ		420		445		865

SAM RICE — RIGHT FIELD

1917	155	365	+	422	=	787
1920	153	530	+	513	=	1043
1921	143	434	+	468	=	902
1922	154	449	+	472	=	921
1923	148	403	+	508	=	911
1924	154	395	+	515	=	910
1925	152	423	+	530	=	953
1926	152	432	+	505	=	937
1929	150	354	+	486	=	840
1930	147	341	+	506	=	847
HEQ		413		492		905

PHIL RIZZUTO — SHORTSTOP

1941	133	385	+	344	=	729
1942	144	451	+	398	=	849
1946	126	378	+	268	=	646
1947	153	466	+	378	=	844
1948	128	361	+	303	=	664
1949	153	461	+	449	=	910
1950	155	465	+	420	=	885
1951	144	432	+	364	=	796
1952	152	463	+	380	=	843
1953	134	370	+	293	=	663
HEQ		423		360		783

BROOKS ROBINSON — THIRD BASE

1960	152	452	+	444	=	896
1961	163	433	+	440	=	873
1962	162	455	+	495	=	950
1964	163	437	+	546	=	982
1966	157	434	+	496	=	930
1967	158	503	+	458	=	961
1968	162	462	+	416	=	878
1969	156	483	+	423	=	906
1970	158	421	+	467	=	888
1971	156	433	+	434	=	867
HEQ		451		462		913

FRANK ROBINSON — RIGHT FIELD

	Games	Def.		Off.		HEQ
1956	152	331	+	564	=	895
1957	150	448	+	527	=	975
1958	148	365	+	493	=	858
1959	146	342	+	599	=	941
1960	153	331	+	499	=	830
1961	162	359	+	632	=	982
1962	162	357	+	706	=	1065
1964	156	311	+	573	=	884
1965	156	300	+	584	=	884
1966	155	269	+	663	=	932
HEQ		341		584		925

JACKIE ROBINSON — SECOND BASE

1947	151	367	+	491	=	858
1948	147	393	+	503	=	896
1949	156	415	+	639	=	1054
1950	144	396	+	491	=	887
1951	153	436	+	548	=	984
1952	149	380	+	496	=	876
1953	136	302	+	497	=	799
1954	124	241	+	355	=	596
1955	105	241	+	245	=	486
1956	117	232	+	293	=	525
HEQ		340		456		796

EDD ROUSH — CENTER FIELD

1915	145	403	+	395	=	798
1917	136	367	+	421	=	788
1918	113	352	+	356	=	708
1919	133	435	+	402	=	837
1920	149	506	+	490	=	996
1923	138	383	+	489	=	872
1924	121	314	+	409	=	723
1925	134	399	+	481	=	880
1926	144	330	+	461	=	791
1927	140	401	+	401	=	802
HEQ		389		431		820

BABE RUTH — RIGHT FIELD

1920	142	317	+	771	=	1088
1921	152	414	+	894	=	1308

BABE RUTH — RIGHT FIELD (cont.)

	Games	Def.		Off.		HEQ
1923	152	447	+	783	=	1230
1924	153	400	+	735	=	1135
1926	152	361	+	733	=	1094
1927	151	374	+	815	=	1189
1928	154	324	+	757	=	1081
1929	135	260	+	664	=	924
1930	145	286	+	760	=	1046
1931	145	251	+	755	=	1006
HEQ		343		767		1110

RAY SCHALK — CATCHER

	Games	Def.		Off.		HEQ
1913	129	475	+	230	=	705
1914	136	516	+	232	=	748
1915	135	499	+	281	=	780
1916	129	526	+	253	=	779
1917	140	478	+	272	=	750
1919	131	420	+	254	=	674
1920	151	451	+	338	=	789
1921	128	383	+	239	=	622
1922	142	470	+	327	=	797
1923	123	347	+	219	=	566
HEQ		457		264		721

MIKE SCHMIDT — THIRD BASE

	Games	Def.		Off.		HEQ
1974	162	467	+	610	=	1077
1975	158	443	+	562	=	1005
1976	160	447	+	589	=	1036
1977	154	445	+	594	=	1039
1979	160	413	+	597	=	1010
1980	150	397	+	624	=	1021
1982	148	369	+	544	=	913
1983	154	384	+	564	=	948
1985	158	433	+	519	=	952
1986	160	355	+	574	=	929
HEQ		415		578		993

RED SCHOENDIENST — SECOND BASE

	Games	Def.		Off.		HEQ
1946	142	391	+	367	=	758
1947	151	403	+	388	=	791
1949	151	463	+	418	=	881
1950	153	453	+	423	=	876

RED SCHOENDIENST — SECOND BASE (cont.)

	Games	Def.		Off.		HEQ
1951	135	406	+	384	=	790
1952	152	457	+	451	=	908
1953	146	403	+	502	=	905
1954	148	447	+	469	=	916
1955	145	346	+	361	=	707
1957	150	421	+	469	=	890
HEQ		419		423		842

JOE SEWELL — SHORTSTOP

	Games	Def.		Off.		HEQ
1921	154	427	+	495	=	922
1922	153	430	+	424	=	854
1923	153	409	+	530	=	939
1924	153	475	+	497	=	972
1925	155	481	+	473	=	954
1926	154	439	+	476	=	915
1927	153	469	+	445	=	914
1928	155	496	+	431	=	927
1929	152	445	+	440	=	885
1932	125	302	+	388	=	690
HEQ		437		460		897

AL SIMMONS — LEFT FIELD

	Games	Def.		Off.		HEQ
1925	153	455	+	668	=	1123
1926	147	379	+	562	=	941
1927	126	287	+	482	=	769
1929	143	425	+	664	=	1089
1930	138	313	+	738	=	1051
1931	128	319	+	589	=	908
1932	154	330	+	690	=	1020
1933	146	428	+	520	=	948
1934	138	346	+	532	=	878
1936	143	378	+	514	=	892
HEQ		366		596		962

GEORGE SISLER — FIRST BASE

	Games	Def.		Off.		HEQ
1917	135	358	+	408	=	766
1919	132	361	+	492	=	853
1920	154	431	+	723	=	1154
1921	138	360	+	607	=	967
1922	142	398	+	663	=	1061
1924	151	376	+	471	=	847

GEORGE SISLER —
FIRST BASE (cont.)

	Games	Def.		Off.		HEQ
1925	150	406	+	541	=	947
1926	150	371	+	420	=	791
1927	149	422	+	487	=	909
1929	154	383	+	436	=	819
HEQ		387		525		912

ENOS SLAUGHTER —
RIGHT FIELD

1939	149	416	+	496	=	912
1940	140	313	+	462	=	775
1942	152	347	+	543	=	890
1946	156	388	+	557	=	945
1947	147	374	+	469	=	843
1948	146	350	+	484	=	834
1949	151	362	+	521	=	883
1950	148	288	+	450	=	738
1952	140	300	+	442	=	742
1953	143	241	+	410	=	651
HEQ		338		483		821

DUKE SNIDER —
CENTER FIELD

1949	146	399	+	504	=	903
1950	152	428	+	604	=	1032
1951	150	424	+	535	=	959
1952	144	399	+	471	=	870
1953	153	400	+	685	=	1085
1954	149	382	+	676	=	1058
1955	148	366	+	661	=	1027
1956	151	394	+	590	=	984
1957	139	326	+	523	=	849
1959	126	161	+	375	=	536
HEQ		368		562		930

TRIS SPEAKER —
CENTER FIELD

1909	143	487	+	445	=	932
1912	153	512	+	648	=	1160
1913	141	472	+	521	=	993
1914	158	557	+	559	=	1116
1915	150	474	+	472	=	946
1916	151	459	+	531	=	990
1917	142	461	+	468	=	929

TRIS SPEAKER —
CENTER FIELD (cont.)

	Games	Def.		Off.		HEQ
1920	150	473	+	613	=	1086
1923	150	475	+	670	=	1145
1926	150	472	+	488	=	960
HEQ		484		542		1026

WILLIE STARGELL —
RIGHT FIELD

1965	144	265	+	463	=	728
1966	140	224	+	494	=	718
1969	145	215	+	503	=	718
1970	136	245	+	419	=	664
1971	141	277	+	592	=	869
1972	138	257	+	497	=	754
1973	148	307	+	602	=	909
1974	140	271	+	503	=	774
1975	124	272	+	428	=	700
1979	126	242	+	400	=	642
HEQ		258		490		748

BILL TERRY — FIRST BASE

1925	133	308	+	402	=	710
1927	150	424	+	553	=	977
1928	149	385	+	534	=	919
1929	150	434	+	571	=	1005
1930	154	440	+	697	=	1137
1931	153	379	+	588	=	967
1932	154	449	+	634	=	1083
1933	123	316	+	350	=	666
1934	153	420	+	501	=	921
1935	145	375	+	452	=	827
HEQ		393		528		921

JOE TINKER — SHORTSTOP

1902	131	348	+	313	=	661
1903	124	315	+	358	=	673
1904	141	393	+	307	=	700
1905	149	453	+	359	=	812
1906	148	397	+	342	=	739
1908	157	468	+	395	=	863
1909	143	405	+	337	=	742
1910	134	361	+	337	=	698
1911	144	419	+	389	=	808
1912	142	437	+	392	=	829
HEQ		400		353		753

PIE TRAYNOR —
THIRD BASE

	Games	Def.		Off.		HEQ
1923	153	423	+	555	=	978
1924	142	398	+	438	=	836
1925	150	467	+	535	=	1002
1926	152	414	+	452	=	866
1927	149	432	+	482	=	914
1928	144	384	+	504	=	888
1929	130	328	+	485	=	813
1930	130	325	+	493	=	818
1931	155	358	+	473	=	831
1933	154	389	+	422	=	811
HEQ		392		484		876

ARKY VAUGHAN —
SHORTSTOP

	Games	Def.		Off.		HEQ
1932	129	346	+	367	=	713
1933	152	438	+	491	=	929
1934	149	441	+	561	=	1002
1935	137	359	+	573	=	932
1936	156	436	+	534	=	970
1937	126	337	+	394	=	731
1938	148	468	+	462	=	930
1939	152	491	+	455	=	946
1940	156	464	+	533	=	997
1943	149	391	+	480	=	871
HEQ		417		485		902

HONUS WAGNER —
SHORTSTOP

	Games	Def.		Off.		HEQ
1899	147	399	+	550	=	949
1901	140	346	+	574	=	920
1903	129	387	+	531	=	918
1905	147	456	+	576	=	1032
1906	142	422	+	493	=	915
1907	142	374	+	528	=	902
1908	151	422	+	597	=	1019
1909	137	402	+	502	=	904
1910	150	428	+	465	=	893
1912	145	446	+	526	=	972
HEQ		408		534		942

BOBBY WALLACE —
SHORTSTOP

	Games	Def.		Off.		HEQ
1897	130	341	+	509	=	850
1898	154	461	+	427	=	888

BOBBY WALLACE —
SHORTSTOP (cont.)

	Games	Def.		Off.		HEQ
1899	151	491	+	505	=	996
1900	126	384	+	352	=	736
1901	134	440	+	433	=	873
1902	133	415	+	369	=	784
1904	139	402	+	359	=	761
1905	156	442	+	367	=	809
1906	139	403	+	348	=	751
1907	147	438	+	341	=	779
HEQ		422		401		823

LLOYD WANER —
CENTER FIELD

	Games	Def.		Off.		HEQ
1927	150	413	+	451	=	864
1928	152	476	+	496	=	972
1929	151	550	+	550	=	1100
1931	154	564	+	451	=	1015
1932	134	450	+	393	=	843
1933	121	301	+	261	=	562
1934	140	423	+	383	=	806
1935	122	366	+	357	=	723
1937	129	336	+	356	=	692
1938	147	411	+	403	=	814
HEQ		429		410		839

PAUL WANER —
RIGHT FIELD

	Games	Def.		Off.		HEQ
1926	144	387	+	507	=	894
1927	155	423	+	622	=	1045
1928	152	371	+	602	=	973
1929	151	408	+	609	=	1017
1930	145	366	+	550	=	916
1931	150	489	+	454	=	943
1932	154	411	+	551	=	962
1933	154	404	+	486	=	890
1934	146	377	+	577	=	954
1936	148	383	+	549	=	932
HEQ		402		551		953

ZACK WHEAT —
LEFT FIELD

	Games	Def.		Off.		HEQ
1910	156	432	+	417	=	849
1913	138	402	+	384	=	786
1914	145	407	+	440	=	847

ZACK WHEAT —
LEFT FIELD (cont.)

	Games	Def.		Off.		HEQ
1915	146	397	+	367	=	764
1916	149	371	+	452	=	823
1920	148	329	+	464	=	793
1921	148	317	+	484	=	801
1922	152	371	+	538	=	909
1924	141	326	+	528	=	854
1925	150	354	+	587	=	941
HEQ		371		466		837

BILLY WILLIAMS —
LEFT FIELD

1963	161	350	+	527	=	877
1964	162	263	+	581	=	844
1965	164	324	+	622	=	946
1966	162	351	+	531	=	882
1967	162	281	+	521	=	802
1968	163	259	+	538	=	797
1969	163	294	+	535	=	829
1970	161	309	+	682	=	991
1971	157	314	+	525	=	839
1972	150	261	+	599	=	860
HEQ		301		566		867

TED WILLIAMS —
LEFT FIELD

1939	149	336	+	676	=	1012
1940	144	336	+	632	=	968
1941	143	300	+	665	=	965
1942	150	380	+	692	=	1072
1946	150	341	+	686	=	1027
1947	156	377	+	655	=	1032
1948	137	323	+	631	=	954
1949	155	385	+	759	=	1144
1951	148	379	+	603	=	982
1957	132	221	+	550	=	771
HEQ		338		655		993

HACK WILSON —
CENTER FIELD

	Games	Def.		Off.		HEQ
1924	107	254	+	331	=	585
1926	142	392	+	536	=	928
1927	146	436	+	616	=	1052
1928	145	345	+	558	=	903
1929	150	428	+	691	=	1119
1930	155	363	+	815	=	1178
1931	112	240	+	332	=	572
1932	135	270	+	487	=	757
1933	117	191	+	268	=	459
1934	74	102	+	146	=	400
HEQ		302		478		780

CARL YASTRZEMSKI —
LEFT FIELD

1962	160	379	+	536	=	915
1963	151	355	+	486	=	841
1964	151	443	+	444	=	887
1966	160	368	+	467	=	835
1967	161	339	+	649	=	988
1968	157	359	+	504	=	863
1969	162	361	+	579	=	940
1970	161	326	+	649	=	975
1973	152	338	+	489	=	827
1977	150	373	+	531	=	904
HEQ		364		533		897

ROSS YOUNGS —
RIGHT FIELD

1917	7	28	+	25	=	53
1918	121	250	+	305	=	555
1919	130	323	+	369	=	692
1920	153	376	+	503	=	879
1921	141	319	+	479	=	798
1922	149	378	+	496	=	874
1923	152	372	+	524	=	896
1924	133	293	+	510	=	803
1925	130	298	+	371	=	669
1926	95	160	+	293	=	453
HEQ		280	+	387		667

Appendix E:
The HOF Candidates —
Their Ten Best Seasons

DICK ALLEN — FIRST BASE

	Games	Def.		Off.		HEQ
1964	162	379	+	605	=	984
1965	161	365	+	536	=	901
1966	141	292	+	597	=	889
1967	122	264	+	486	=	750
1968	152	228	+	492	=	720
1969	118	248	+	460	=	708
1970	122	251	+	487	=	738
1971	155	346	+	484	=	830
1972	148	301	+	577	=	871
1974	128	244	+	468	=	712
HEQ		292		519		811

WADE BOGGS — THIRD BASE

	Games	Def.		Off.		HEQ
1983	153	419	+	506	=	925
1984	158	409	+	472	=	881
1985	161	413	+	547	=	960
1986	149	337	+	513	=	850
1987	147	352	+	575	=	927
1988	155	326	+	537	=	863
1989	156	339	+	502	=	841
1990	155	290	+	455	=	745
1991	144	333	+	441	=	774
1993	143	347	+	382	=	729
HEQ		357		493		850

BARRY BONDS — LEFT FIELD

	Games	Def.		Off.		HEQ
1987	150	392	+	488	=	880
1989	159	413	+	480	=	893
1990	151	390	+	610	=	1000
1991	153	371	+	570	=	941
1992	140	320	+	610	=	930
1993	159	328	+	709	=	1037
1995	144	323	+	596	=	919
1996	158	318	+	685	=	1003
1997	159	324	+	645	=	969
1998	156	295	+	671	=	966
HEQ		348		606		954

BOB BOONE — CATCHER

	Games	Def.		Off.		HEQ
1973	145	480	+	317	=	797
1974	146	445	+	271	=	716
1977	132	402	+	339	=	741
1978	132	344	+	320	=	664
1980	141	437	+	278	=	715
1982	143	405	+	279	=	684
1983	142	379	+	279	=	658
1985	150	397	+	258	=	655
1986	144	478	+	255	=	733
1989	131	419	+	235	=	654
HEQ		419		283		702

KEN BOYER —
THIRD BASE

	Games	Def.		Off.		HEQ
1955	147	322	+	406	=	728
1956	150	391	+	510	=	901
1957	142	387	+	400	=	787
1958	150	461	+	510	=	971
1959	149	387	+	512	=	899
1960	151	390	+	538	=	928
1961	153	389	+	558	=	947
1962	160	414	+	527	=	941
1963	159	335	+	513	=	848
1964	162	400	+	564	=	964
HEQ		387		504	=	891

GEORGE BRETT —
THIRD BASE

1975	159	411	+	498	=	909
1976	159	407	+	505	=	912
1977	139	385	+	535	=	920
1978	128	343	+	422	=	765
1979	154	435	+	632	=	1067
1980	117	313	+	547	=	860
1982	144	376	+	504	=	880
1985	155	399	+	603	=	1002
1988	157	290	+	548	=	838
1990	142	283	+	486	=	769
HEQ		364		528		892

GARY CARTER — CATCHER

1977	154	497	+	478	=	975
1978	157	457	+	414	=	871
1979	141	454	+	417	=	871
1980	154	501	+	476	=	977
1982	154	491	+	513	=	1004
1983	145	507	+	409	=	918
1984	159	485	+	505	=	990
1985	149	458	+	490	=	948
1986	132	436	+	433	=	869
1987	139	455	+	364	=	819
HEQ		474		450		924

ORLANDO CEPEDA —
FIRST BASE

1958	148	367	+	515	=	882
1959	151	309	+	553	=	862

ORLANDO CEPEDA —
FIRST BASE (cont.)

	Games	Def.		Off.		HEQ
1960	151	325	+	492	=	817
1961	152	317	+	635	=	952
1962	162	358	+	572	=	930
1963	156	313	+	550	=	863
1964	142	304	+	488	=	792
1967	151	346	+	539	=	885
1969	154	360	+	447	=	807
1970	148	374	+	536	=	910
HEQ		337		533		870

JACK CLARK — LEFT FIELD

1977	136	266	+	320	=	586
1978	156	392	+	546	=	938
1979	143	331	+	464	=	795
1980	127	245	+	424	=	669
1982	157	317	+	515	=	832
1983	135	321	+	407	=	728
1985	126	293	+	423	=	716
1987	131	309	+	518	=	827
1989	142	316	+	451	=	767
1990	115	245	+	355	=	600
HEQ		304		442		746

DAVE CONCEPCION —
SHORTSTOP

1974	160	446	+	451	=	877
1975	140	417	+	343	=	760
1976	152	465	+	420	=	885
1977	156	465	+	386	=	851
1978	153	406	+	420	=	826
1979	149	453	+	471	=	924
1980	156	429	+	404	=	833
1982	147	428	+	349	=	777
1984	154	323	+	322	=	645
1985	155	349	+	333	=	682
HEQ		418		390		808

ANDRE DAWSON —
LEFT FIELD

1977	139	384	+	416	=	800
1978	157	477	+	468	=	945
1979	155	416	+	530	=	946
1980	151	466	+	523	=	989

ANDRE DAWSON —
LEFT FIELD (cont.)

	Games	Def.		Off.		HEQ
1982	148	443	+	549	=	992
1983	159	449	+	602	=	1051
1984	138	333	+	411	=	744
1987	153	311	+	607	=	918
1988	157	293	+	486	=	779
1990	147	296	+	492	=	788
HEQ		387		508		895

DWIGHT EVANS —
RIGHT FIELD

	Games	Def.		Off.		HEQ
1976	146	396	+	374	=	770
1978	147	357	+	402	=	759
1979	152	379	+	391	=	770
1980	148	330	+	391	=	721
1982	162	374	+	604	=	978
1984	162	343	+	611	=	954
1985	159	325	+	532	=	857
1986	152	322	+	487	=	809
1987	154	320	+	597	=	917
1988	149	273	+	522	=	795
HEQ		342		491		833

CARLTON FISK — CATCHER

	Games	Def.		Off.		HEQ
1972	131	448	+	412	=	860
1973	135	390	+	386	=	776
1976	134	383	+	376	=	759
1977	152	435	+	532	=	967
1978	157	443	+	496	=	939
1982	135	370	+	363	=	733
1983	138	375	+	456	=	831
1985	153	439	+	500	=	939
1987	135	362	+	369	=	731
1990	137	387	+	372	=	759
HEQ		403		426		829

CURT FLOOD —
CENTER FIELD

	Games	Def.		Off.		HEQ
1958	121	414	+	270	=	684
1960	140	314	+	233	=	547
1962	151	447	+	462	=	909
1963	158	447	+	480	=	927
1964	162	429	+	430	=	859
1965	156	379	+	468	=	847
1966	160	415	+	397	=	812

CURT FLOOD —
CENTER FIELD (cont.)

	Games	Def.		Off.		HEQ
1967	134	326	+	352	=	678
1968	150	432	+	385	=	817
1969	153	418	+	392	=	810
HEQ		402		387		789

STEVE GARVEY—
FIRST BASE

	Games	Def.		Off.		HEQ
1974	156	338	+	528	=	866
1975	160	350	+	522	=	872
1976	162	372	+	493	=	865
1977	162	351	+	556	=	907
1978	162	363	+	551	=	914
1979	162	365	+	546	=	911
1980	163	425	+	515	=	940
1982	162	410	+	428	=	838
1984	161	350	+	401	=	751
1985	162	390	+	460	=	850
HEQ		371		500		871

KIRK GIBSON —
LEFT FIELD

	Games	Def.		Off.		HEQ
1981	83	138	+	246	=	384
1982	69	193	+	209	=	402
1983	128	118	+	318	=	436
1984	149	245	+	518	=	763
1985	154	286	+	560	=	846
1986	119	198	+	455	=	653
1987	128	263	+	474	=	737
1988	150	323	+	512	=	835
1990	89	209	+	269	=	478
1991	132	166	+	375	=	541
HEQ		214		394		608

BOBBY GRICH —
SECOND BASE

	Games	Def.		Off.		HEQ
1973	162	488	+	428	=	916
1974	160	473	+	487	=	960
1975	150	454	+	415	=	869
1976	144	394	+	420	=	814
1978	144	366	+	312	=	678
1979	153	397	+	497	=	894
1980	150	407	+	370	=	777
1982	145	404	+	410	=	814

BOBBY GRICH —
SECOND BASE (cont.)

	Games	Def.		Off.		HEQ
1983	120	338	+	345	=	683
1985	144	388	+	349	=	737
HEQ		411		403		814

PEDRO GUERRERO —
FIRST BASE

1981	98	203	+	277	=	480
1982	150	366	+	550	=	916
1983	160	351	+	559	=	910
1984	144	285	+	438	=	723
1985	137	300	+	521	=	821
1987	152	284	+	518	=	802
1988	103	187	+	284	=	471
1989	162	330	+	481	=	821
1990	136	274	+	357	=	631
1991	115	243	+	288	=	531
HEQ		283		428		711

JOE JACKSON —
RIGHT FIELD

1910	20	50	+	78	=	128
1911	147	378	+	615	=	993
1912	154	369	+	604	=	973
1913	148	267	+	537	=	804
1914	122	225	+	367	=	592
1915	128	188	+	391	=	579
1916	155	362	+	509	=	871
1917	146	417	+	439	=	856
1919	139	310	+	475	=	785
1920	146	354	+	599	=	953
HEQ		292		461		753

TONY GWYNN —
RIGHT FIELD

1984	158	397	+	491	=	888
1985	154	393	+	427	=	820
1986	160	417	+	529	=	946
1987	157	342	+	571	=	913
1988	133	290	+	402	=	692
1989	158	397	+	468	=	865
1990	141	369	+	428	=	797
1991	134	325	+	385	=	710

TONY GWYNN —
RIGHT FIELD (cont.)

	Games	Def.		Off.		HEQ
1995	135	277	+	466	=	743
1997	149	258	+	574	=	832
HEQ		347		474		821

RICKEY HENDERSON —
LEFT FIELD

1980	158	457	+	558	=	1015
1982	149	369	+	563	=	932
1983	145	383	+	529	=	912
1984	142	351	+	510	=	861
1985	143	461	+	630	=	1091
1986	153	430	+	621	=	1051
1988	140	344	+	523	=	867
1989	150	355	+	526	=	881
1990	136	299	+	576	=	875
1998	152	341	+	471	=	812
HEQ		379		551		930

KEITH HERNANDEZ —
FIRST BASE

1977	161	410	+	485	=	895
1978	159	383	+	419	=	802
1979	161	479	+	585	=	1064
1980	159	442	+	561	=	1003
1982	160	474	+	481	=	955
1983	150	468	+	426	=	894
1984	154	429	+	475	=	904
1985	158	434	+	475	=	909
1986	149	435	+	472	=	907
1987	154	439	+	473	=	912
HEQ		440		485		925

GIL HODGES —
FIRST BASE

1949	156	358	+	522	=	880
1950	153	388	+	539	=	927
1951	158	442	+	584	=	1026
1952	153	412	+	499	=	911
1953	141	328	+	548	=	876
1954	154	437	+	611	=	1048
1955	151	375	+	492	=	868
1956	153	353	+	493	=	846

GIL HODGES — FIRST BASE (cont.)

	Games	Def.		Off.		HEQ
1957	150	388	+	525	=	913
1958	141	281	+	372	=	653
HEQ		376		519		895

CARNEY LANSFORD — THIRD BASE

1979	157	367	+	518	=	885
1980	151	348	+	441	=	789
1982	128	265	+	374	=	639
1984	151	352	+	435	=	787
1986	151	277	+	437	=	714
1987	151	339	+	474	=	813
1988	150	302	+	384	=	686
1989	148	267	+	419	=	686
1990	134	270	+	309	=	579
1992	135	238	+	352	=	590
HEQ		303		414		717

DON MATTINGLY — FIRST BASE

1984	153	441	+	547	=	988
1985	159	367	+	652	=	1019
1986	162	390	+	645	=	1035
1987	141	354	+	553	=	907
1988	144	368	+	481	=	849
1989	158	361	+	522	=	883
1991	152	324	+	388	=	712
1992	157	393	+	464	=	857
1993	134	349	+	461	=	780
1995	128	290	+	317	=	607
HEQ		364		500		864

BILL MAZEROSKI — SECOND BASE

1957	148	374	+	344	=	718
1958	152	425	+	400	=	825
1960	151	446	+	357	=	803
1961	152	466	+	356	=	822
1962	159	480	+	397	=	877
1963	142	437	+	294	=	731
1964	162	444	+	375	=	819
1966	162	503	+	404	=	907

BILL MAZEROSKI — SECOND BASE (cont.)

	Games	Def.		Off.		HEQ
1967	163	465	+	381	=	846
1968	143	397	+	259	=	656
HEQ		444		356		800

MINNIE MINOSO — LEFT FIELD

1951	146	318	+	520	=	838
1952	147	375	+	456	=	831
1953	151	343	+	529	=	872
1954	153	407	+	596	=	1003
1955	139	361	+	425	=	786
1956	151	316	+	535	=	851
1957	153	327	+	515	=	842
1958	149	341	+	487	=	828
1959	148	364	+	486	=	850
1960	154	338	+	521	=	859
HEQ		349		507		856

PAUL MOLITOR — THIRD BASE

1979	140	372	+	481	=	853
1982	160	413	+	583	=	996
1983	152	402	+	464	=	864
1987	118	123	+	532	=	655
1988	154	227	+	527	=	754
1989	155	307	+	469	=	776
1991	158	119	+	591	=	710
1992	158	119	+	527	=	646
1993	160	49	+	617	=	666
1996	161	43	+	567	=	610
HEQ		217		536		753

DALE MURPHY — CENTER FIELD

1978	151	360	+	386	=	746
1980	156	434	+	516	=	950
1982	162	421	+	595	=	1016
1983	162	401	+	645	=	1046
1984	162	403	+	585	=	988
1985	162	368	+	616	=	984
1986	160	319	+	510	=	829
1987	159	369	+	622	=	991

DALE MURPHY—
CENTER FIELD (cont.)

	Games	Def.		Off.		HEQ
1988	156	410	+	443	=	853
1990	154	343	+	418	=	761
HEQ		382		534		916

EDDIE MURRAY—
FIRST BASE

	Games	Def.		Off.		HEQ
1978	161	422	+	514	=	936
1979	159	408	+	523	=	931
1980	158	364	+	572	=	936
1982	151	360	+	541	=	901
1983	156	411	+	587	=	998
1984	162	479	+	570	=	1049
1985	156	462	+	587	=	1049
1987	160	461	+	513	=	974
1989	160	434	+	443	=	877
1990	155	358	+	530	=	888
HEQ		416		538		954

GRAIG NETTLES —
THIRD BASE

	Games	Def.		Off.		HEQ
1970	157	442	+	409	=	851
1971	158	527	+	472	=	999
1972	150	388	+	386	=	774
1973	160	456	+	398	=	854
1974	155	454	+	408	=	862
1975	157	450	+	439	=	889
1976	158	455	+	500	=	955
1977	158	408	+	534	=	942
1978	159	393	+	475	=	868
1979	145	397	+	384	=	781
HEQ		437		441		878

TONY OLIVA — LEFT FIELD

	Games	Def.		Off.		HEQ
1964	161	321	+	606	=	927
1965	149	314	+	535	=	849
1966	159	363	+	532	=	895
1967	146	318	+	450	=	768
1968	128	251	+	379	=	630
1969	153	367	+	547	=	914
1970	157	391	+	550	=	941
1971	126	238	+	437	=	675
1973	146	—	+	414	=	414
1974	127	—	+	304	=	304
HEQ		256		476		732

AL OLIVER —
CENTER FIELD

	Games	Def.		Off.		HEQ
1971	143	366	+	387	=	753
1972	140	346	+	444	=	790
1973	158	363	+	509	=	872
1974	147	392	+	501	=	893
1975	155	408	+	476	=	884
1977	154	321	+	463	=	784
1979	136	290	+	397	=	687
1980	163	340	+	553	=	893
1982	160	334	+	552	=	886
1983	157	367	+	429	=	796
HEQ		353		471		824

RAFAEL PALMEIRO—
FIRST BASE

	Games	Def.		Off.		HEQ
1988	152	317	+	412	=	729
1989	156	371	+	385	=	756
1990	154	350	+	464	=	814
1991	159	357	+	577	=	934
1992	159	436	+	471	=	907
1993	160	460	+	619	=	1079
1995	143	396	+	550	=	946
1996	162	426	+	650	=	1076
1997	158	393	+	542	=	935
1998	162	430	+	620	=	1050
HEQ		394		529		923

DAVE PARKER —
RIGHT FIELD

	Games	Def.		Off.		HEQ
1975	148	329	+	505	=	834
1976	138	314	+	461	=	775
1977	159	499	+	579	=	1078
1978	148	336	+	608	=	944
1979	158	375	+	584	=	959
1980	139	273	+	410	=	683
1984	156	308	+	448	=	756
1985	160	361	+	594	=	955
1986	162	304	+	538	=	842
1987	153	339	+	458	=	797
HEQ		344		518		862

TONY PEREZ — FIRST BASE

	Games	Def.		Off.		HEQ
1967	156	316	+	491	=	807
1968	160	424	+	483	=	907

TONY PEREZ — FIRST BASE (cont.)

	Games	Def.		Off.		HEQ
1969	160	399	+	592	=	991
1970	158	354	+	632	=	986
1971	158	395	+	460	=	855
1973	151	352	+	511	=	863
1974	158	330	+	488	=	818
1975	137	311	+	449	=	760
1977	154	369	+	457	=	826
1980	151	365	+	473	=	838
HEQ		361		504		865

VADA PINSON — CENTER FIELD

	Games	Def.		Off.		HEQ
1959	154	469	+	594	=	1063
1960	154	433	+	532	=	965
1961	154	463	+	537	=	1000
1962	155	392	+	551	=	943
1963	162	377	+	582	=	959
1964	156	341	+	492	=	833
1965	159	388	+	558	=	946
1966	156	358	+	454	=	812
1967	158	351	+	490	=	841
1970	148	299	+	453	=	752
HEQ		387		524		911

KIRBY PUCKETT — CENTER FIELD

	Games	Def.		Off.		HEQ
1984	128	512	+	303	=	815
1985	161	545	+	462	=	1007
1986	161	461	+	617	=	1078
1987	157	371	+	556	=	927
1988	158	508	+	606	=	1114
1989	159	498	+	487	=	985
1990	146	394	+	442	=	836
1991	152	433	+	489	=	922
1992	160	436	+	566	=	1002
1993	156	368	+	505	=	873
HEQ		453		503		956

WILLIE RANDOLPH — SECOND BASE

	Games	Def.		Off.		HEQ
1976	125	355	+	306	=	661
1977	147	405	+	389	=	794
1978	134	342	+	384	=	726

WILLIE RANDOLPH — SECOND BASE (cont.)

	Games	Def.		Off.		HEQ
1979	153	430	+	451	=	881
1980	138	378	+	444	=	822
1982	144	370	+	368	=	738
1984	142	386	+	366	=	752
1985	143	373	+	351	=	724
1986	141	344	+	358	=	702
1987	120	317	+	401	=	718
HEQ		370		382		752

JIM RICE — LEFT FIELD

	Games	Def.		Off.		HEQ
1975	144	186	+	499	=	685
1976	153	217	+	462	=	679
1977	160	95	+	632	=	727
1978	163	295	+	702	=	997
1979	158	269	+	654	=	923
1982	145	307	+	494	=	801
1983	155	431	+	586	=	1017
1984	159	388	+	553	=	941
1985	140	254	+	482	=	736
1986	157	378	+	542	=	920
HEQ		282		561		843

CAL RIPKEN JR. — SHORTSTOP

	Games	Def.		Off.		HEQ
1982	160	452	+	493	=	945
1983	162	476	+	595	=	1071
1984	162	521	+	554	=	1075
1985	161	455	+	563	=	1018
1986	162	439	+	505	=	944
1987	162	429	+	511	=	940
1988	161	461	+	469	=	930
1989	162	499	+	464	=	963
1991	162	486	+	614	=	1100
1996	163	427	+	525	=	952
HEQ		465		529		994

PETE ROSE — LEFT FIELD

	Games	Def.		Off.		HEQ
1965	162	385	+	540	=	925
1966	156	403	+	491	=	894
1969	156	360	+	574	=	934
1970	159	347	+	526	=	873

PETE ROSE —
LEFT FIELD (cont.)

	Games	Def.		Off.		HEQ
1972	154	394	+	481	=	875
1973	160	397	+	519	=	916
1974	163	400	+	469	=	869
1976	162	414	+	544	=	958
1979	163	375	+	487	=	862
1980	162	423	+	436	=	859
HEQ		390		507		897

RYNE SANDBERG —
SECOND BASE

	Games	Def.		Off.		HEQ
1982	156	387	+	413	=	800
1983	158	460	+	427	=	887
1984	156	439	+	587	=	1026
1985	153	427	+	586	=	1013
1986	154	403	+	459	=	862
1988	155	400	+	457	=	857
1989	157	381	+	526	=	907
1990	155	374	+	610	=	984
1991	158	386	+	554	=	940
1992	158	414	+	550	=	964
HEQ		407		517		924

RON SANTO —
THIRD BASE

	Games	Def.		Off.		HEQ
1961	154	393	+	483	=	876
1963	162	429	+	508	=	937
1964	161	456	+	588	=	1044
1965	164	450	+	546	=	996
1966	155	483	+	541	=	1024
1967	161	498	+	554	=	1052
1968	162	454	+	478	=	932
1969	160	397	+	548	=	945
1970	154	396	+	509	=	905
1971	154	356	+	444	=	800
HEQ		431		520		951

STEVE SAX —
SECOND BASE

	Games	Def.		Off.		HEQ
1982	150	388	+	438	=	826
1983	155	342	+	438	=	780
1984	145	380	+	336	=	716
1986	157	385	+	493	=	878
1987	157	380	+	414	=	794

STEVE SAX —
SECOND BASE (cont.)

	Games	Def.		Off.		HEQ
1988	160	343	+	409	=	752
1989	158	400	+	472	=	872
1990	155	382	+	380	=	762
1991	158	373	+	463	=	836
1992	143	336	+	353	=	689
HEQ		371		420		791

OZZIE SMITH —
SHORTSTOP

	Games	Def.		Off.		HEQ
1978	159	471	+	363	=	834
1979	156	470	+	305	=	775
1980	158	534	+	363	=	897
1982	140	487	+	313	=	800
1983	159	483	+	370	=	853
1985	158	491	+	382	=	873
1987	158	467	+	497	=	964
1988	153	432	+	418	=	850
1989	155	401	+	403	=	804
1993	141	418	+	365	=	783
HEQ		465		378		843

JOE TORRE —
CATCHER

	Games	Def.		Off.		HEQ
1963	142	431	+	366	=	797
1964	154	459	+	515	=	974
1965	148	437	+	435	=	872
1966	148	434	+	520	=	954
1967	135	410	+	374	=	784
1969	159	392	+	475	=	867
1970	161	459	+	537	=	996
1971	161	344	+	622	=	966
1973	141	328	+	380	=	708
1974	147	386	+	377	=	763
HEQ		408		460		868

ALAN TRAMMELL —
SHORTSTOP

	Games	Def.		Off.		HEQ
1979	142	373	+	321	=	694
1980	146	384	+	445	=	829
1982	157	429	+	361	=	790
1983	142	355	+	446	=	801
1984	139	299	+	463	=	762
1985	149	375	+	405	=	780

ALAN TRAMMELL —
SHORTSTOP (cont.)

	Games	Def.		Off.		HEQ
1986	151	404	+	506	=	910
1987	151	383	+	594	=	977
1988	128	326	+	388	=	714
1990	146	392	+	457	=	849
HEQ		372		439		811

LOU WHITAKER —
SECOND BASE

	Games	Def.		Off.		HEQ
1978	139	377	+	340	=	717
1982	152	414	+	419	=	833
1983	161	374	+	511	=	885
1984	143	344	+	410	=	754
1985	152	371	+	499	=	870
1986	144	356	+	468	=	824
1987	149	348	+	476	=	824
1989	148	367	+	448	=	815
1990	132	342	+	372	=	714
1991	138	322	+	451	=	773
HEQ		362		469		801

WILLIE WILSON —
CENTER FIELD

	Games	Def.		Off.		HEQ
1979	154	420	+	506	=	926
1980	161	510	+	572	=	1082
1981	102	359	+	289	=	648
1982	136	382	+	435	=	817
1983	137	348	+	402	=	750
1984	128	407	+	403	=	810
1985	141	394	+	435	=	829
1986	156	426	+	402	=	828

WILLIE WILSON —
CENTER FIELD (cont.)

	Games	Def.		Off.		HEQ
1987	146	356	+	432	=	788
1988	147	361	+	361	=	722
HEQ		396		424		820

DAVE WINFIELD —
RIGHT FIELD

	Games	Def.		Off.		HEQ
1977	157	418	+	528	=	946
1978	158	339	+	527	=	866
1979	159	402	+	606	=	1008
1980	162	361	+	490	=	851
1982	140	339	+	520	=	859
1983	152	327	+	566	=	893
1984	141	318	+	531	=	849
1985	155	374	+	562	=	936
1986	154	338	+	500	=	838
1988	149	286	+	543	=	829
HEQ		350		538		888

ROBIN YOUNT —
SHORTSTOP

	Games	Def.		Off.		HEQ
1979	149	455	+	366	=	821
1980	143	398	+	558	=	956
1982	156	432	+	651	=	1083
1983	149	397	+	521	=	918
1984	160	353	+	508	=	861
1986	140	402	+	408	=	810
1987	158	408	+	563	=	971
1988	162	496	+	526	=	1022
1989	160	387	+	569	=	956
1990	158	426	+	452	=	878
HEQ		416		512		928

Index